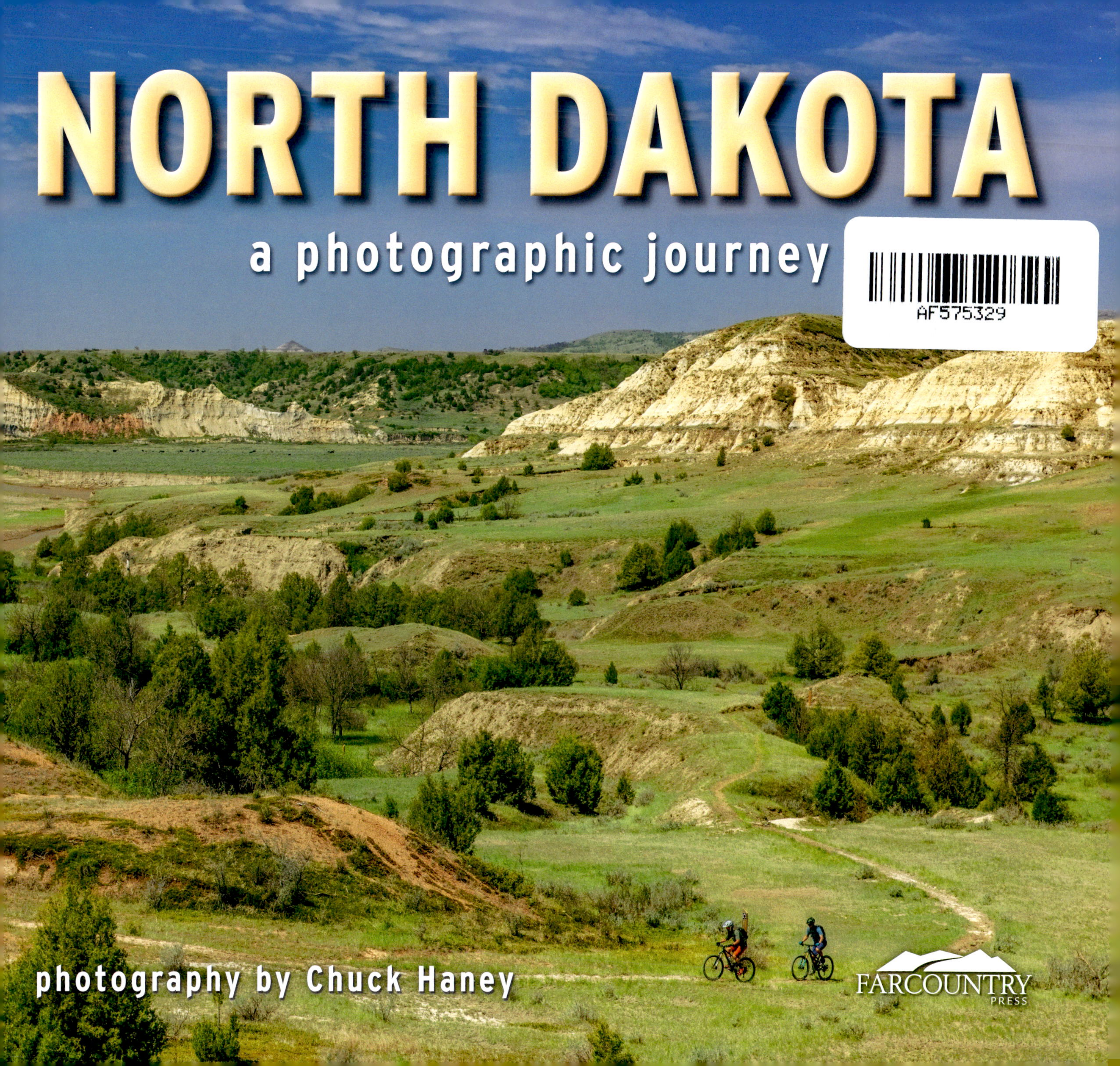

NORTH DAKOTA

a photographic journey

photography by Chuck Haney

FARCOUNTRY PRESS

I would like to dedicate this book to all of my family members, both past and present, whose patience with my lengthy time on the road has allowed me to pursue my craft. My wife, Jarmila, has been a source of inspiration as I continue this journey. Also, there are just too many publishers, fans, and workshop students to single out as they have all supported my 30+ year career as a professional photographer. Thank you!

I've had much local support during my many years traveling across North Dakota. Many assignment photo shoots for North Dakota Tourism buoyed my early career. I have treasured my adventures in Medora along the Maah Daah Hey Trail with good friends Jennifer and Loren Morlock at Dakota Cyclery, where I was able to write and create photographs freely while the trail was in its infancy. Numerous articles later, our beloved trail has become a national destination.

I survived a bout of Rocky Mountain spotted fever from tick bites, apparently the first such case in North Dakota. I almost succumbed to heat stroke during an epic mountain bike ride in abnormally hot June weather, and had the hair stand up on the back of my neck with lightning that came in frighteningly too close. But, in contrast, I've witnessed the vast raw beauty and peacefulness that reveals in the badlands and short grass prairie in the waning warm light of dawn or dusk too many times to count. After several decades of exploring with my camera, I keep coming back to North Dakota. The allure is intoxicating.

— Chuck Haney

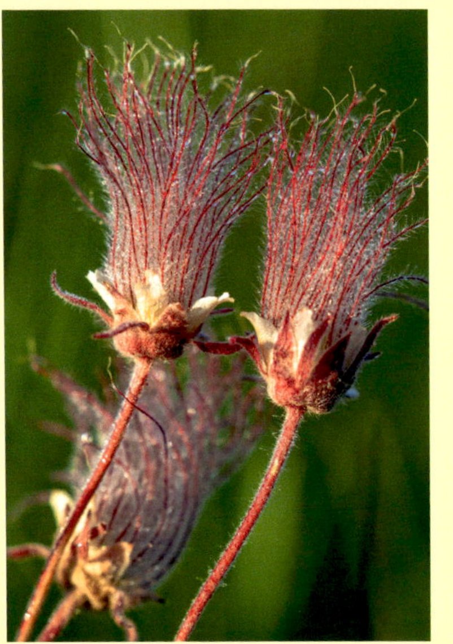

Right: Prairie smoke wildflowers bloom in Theodore Roosevelt National Park.

Far right: A storm-bruised sky lowers over Wind Canyon in Theodore Roosevelt National Park.

Title page: Mountain bikers enjoy the rolling Maah Daah Hey Trail in Little Missouri National Grassland.

Front cover: Sunshine burnishes cliffs over the Little Missouri River in Little Missouri National Grassland.

Back cover: Exploring near Tom's Wash in Little Missouri National Grassland makes for a great day in the saddle.

ISBN: 978-1-56037-844-0

Design by Steph Lehmann

For more information about our books, write Farcountry Press, P.O. Box 5630, Helena, MT 59604; call (800) 821-3874; or visit www.farcountrypress.com.

LCCN: 2024938181

Produced in the United States of America. Printed in China.

28 27 26 25 24 1 2 3 4 5

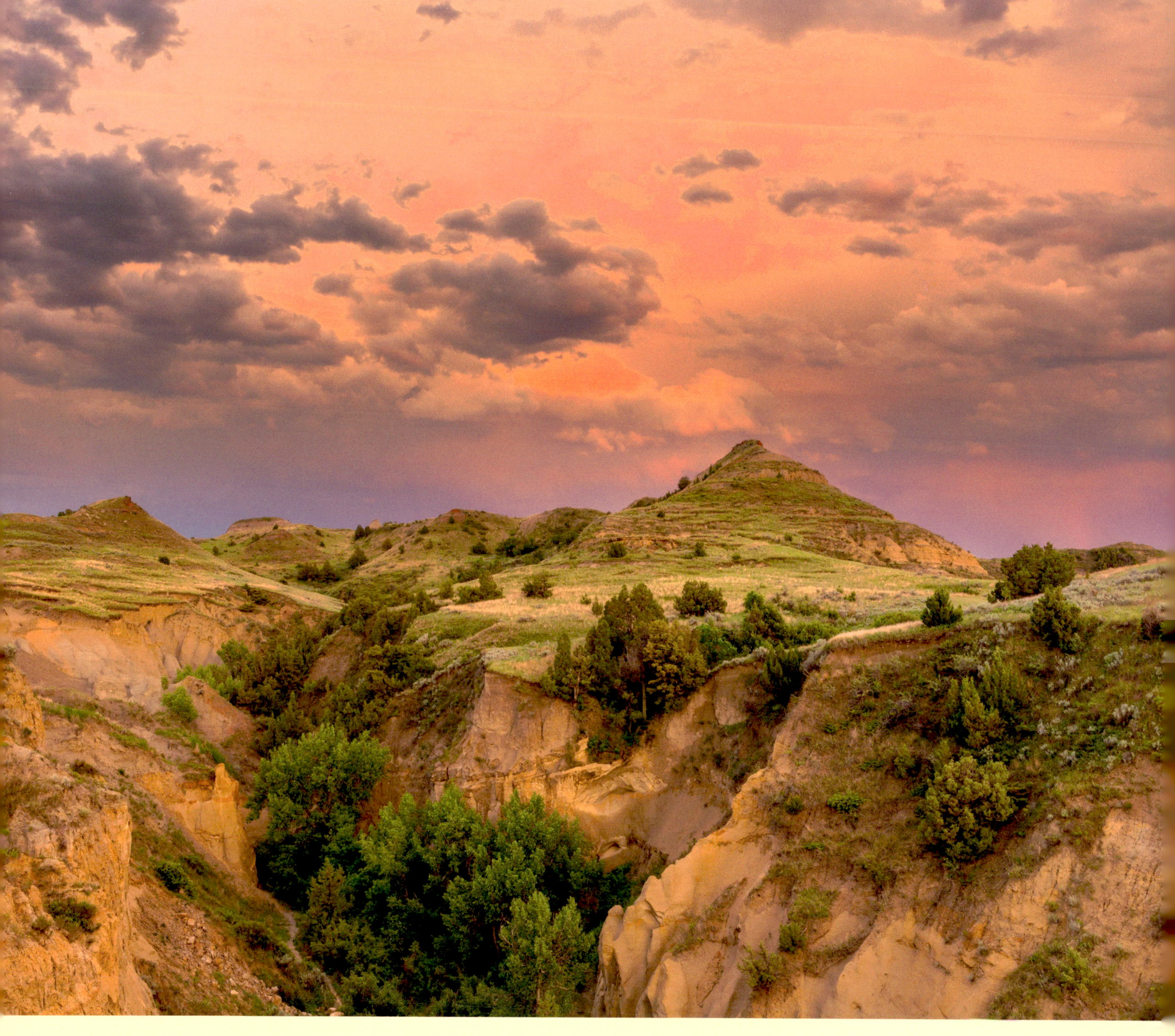

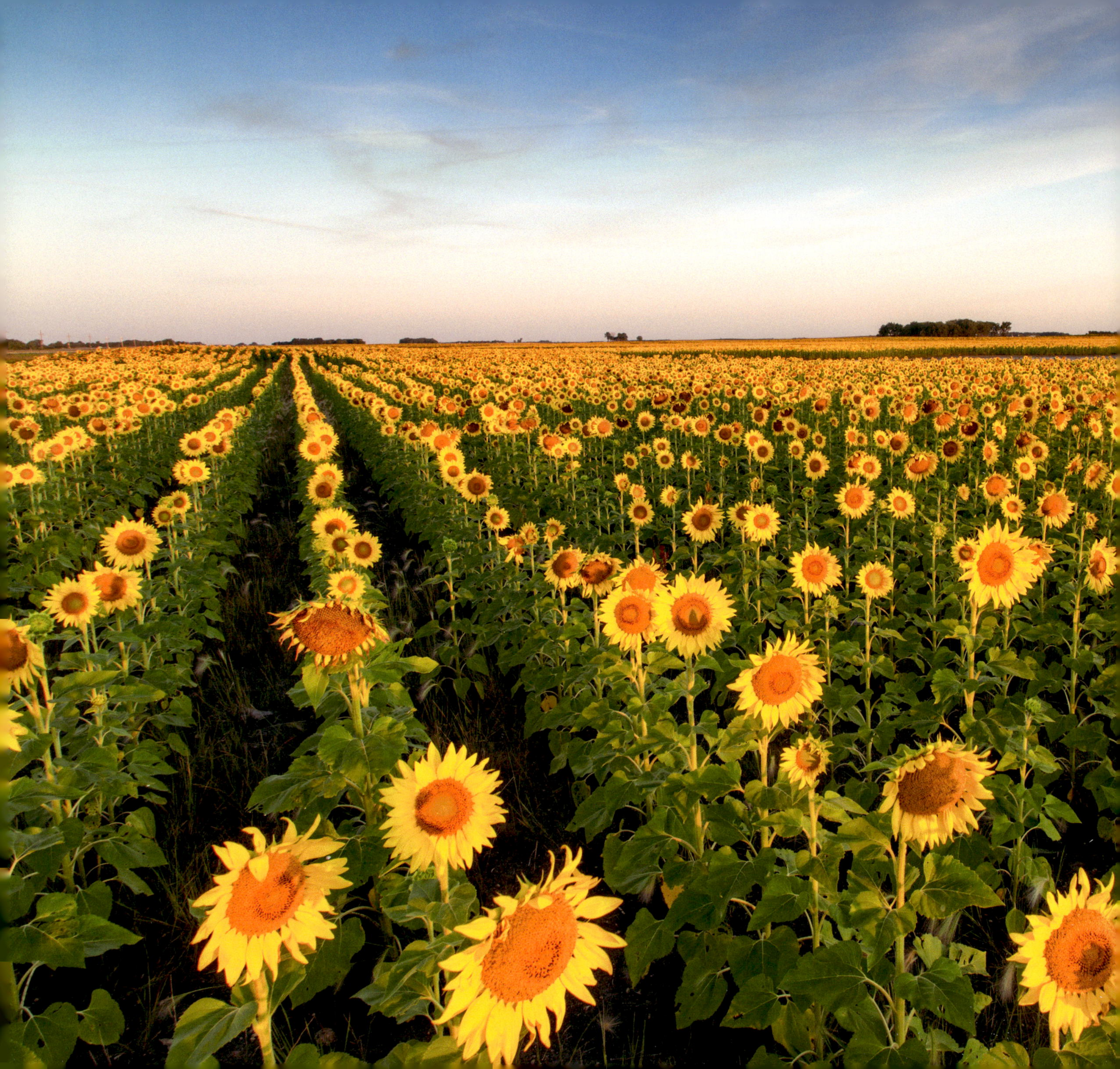

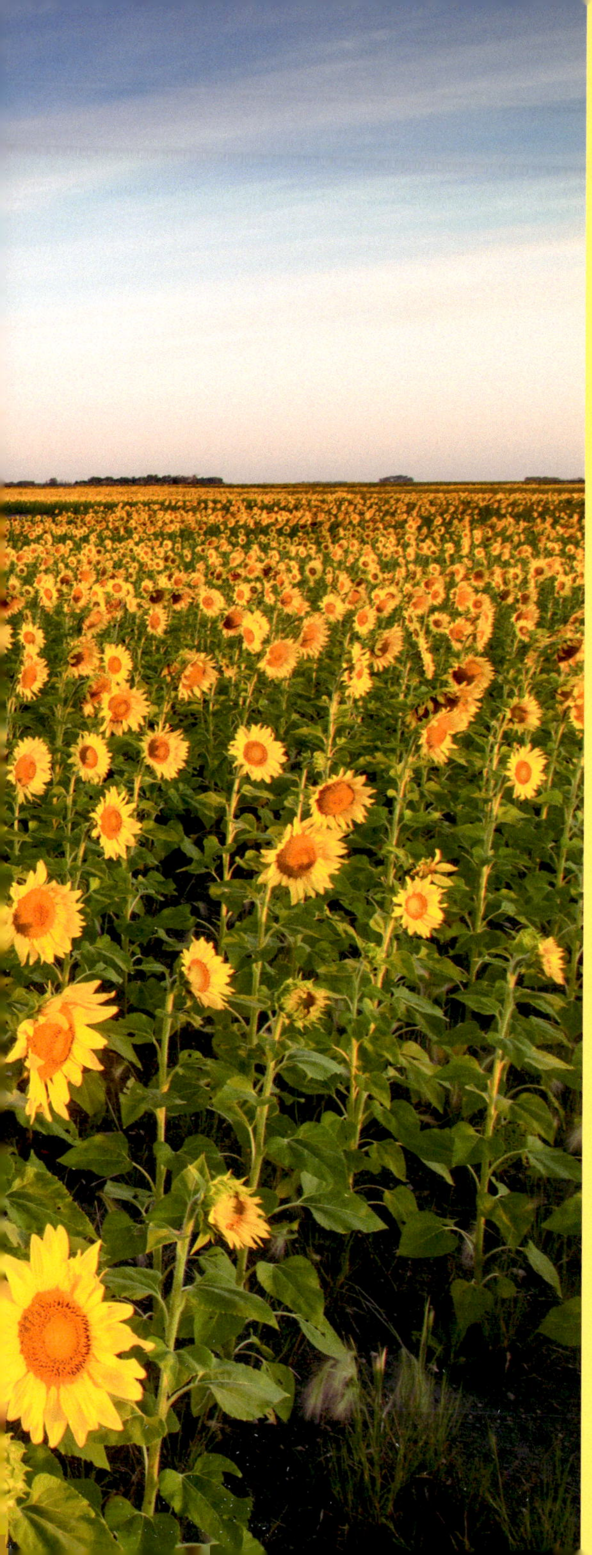

Left: Sunflowers greet the new day near the small town of Michigan.

Below: North Dakota regularly leads the nation in canola production. A member of the mustard family, the bright golden flowers are favored by a wide range of pollinators.

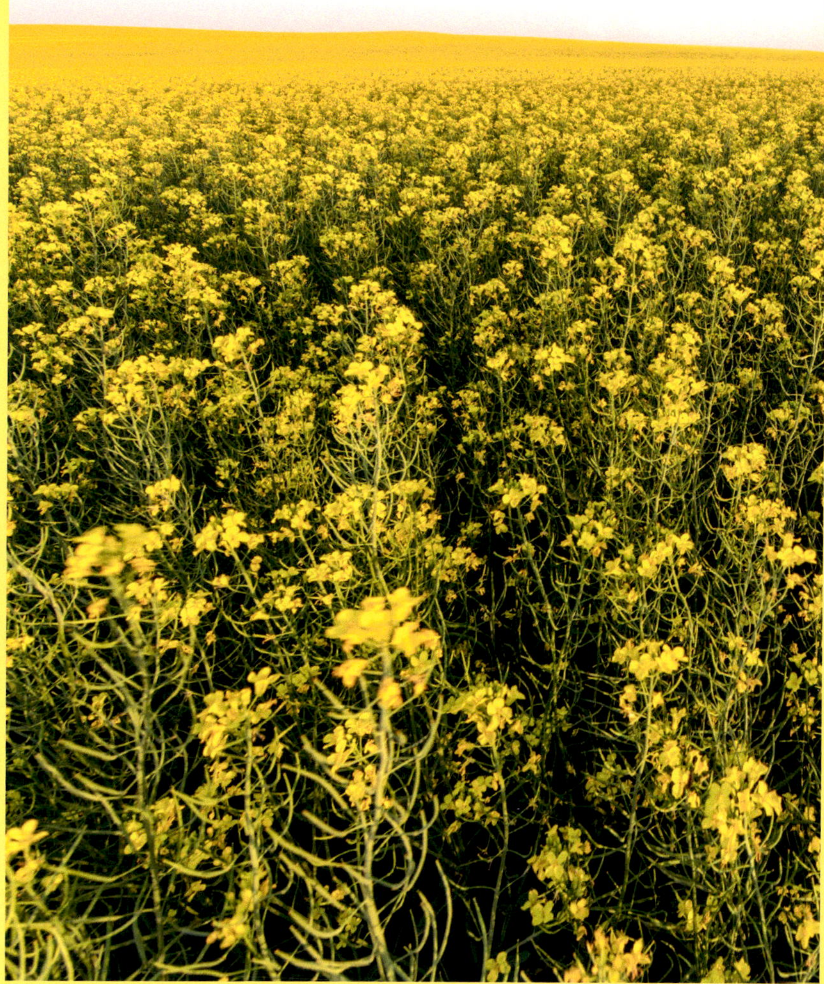

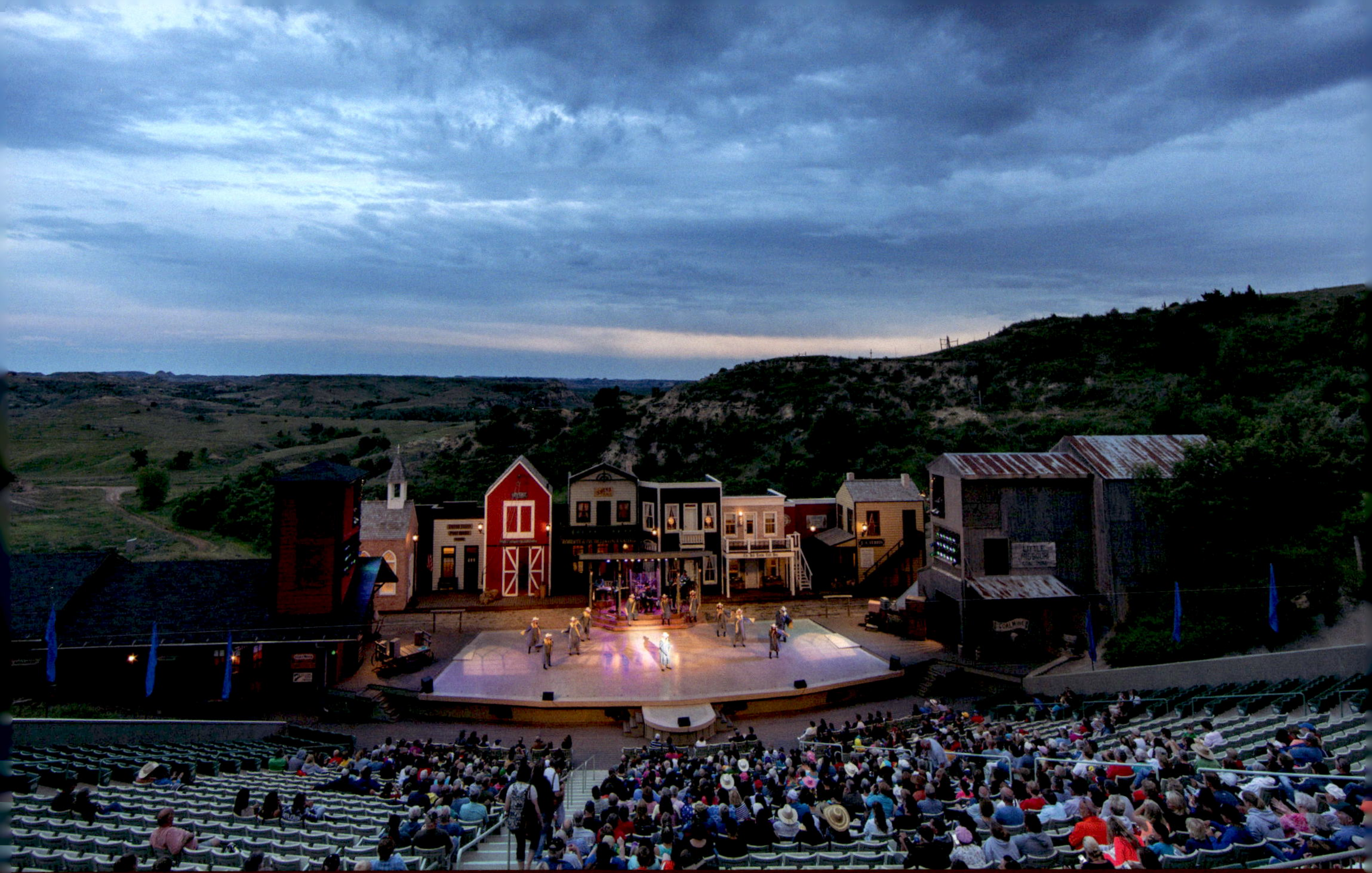

Above: During summer, the Medora Musical draws audiences of all ages to the open-air Burning Hills Amphitheater for a Wild West revue of singing, dancing, and comedy.

Right: More than 40 exhibits at the North Dakota Cowboy Hall of Fame in Medora showcase ranch and rodeo life, bucking bulls, Native American cultures, a Hall of Honorees, and more.

Facing page: Downtown Medora retains much of its Old West charm and history.

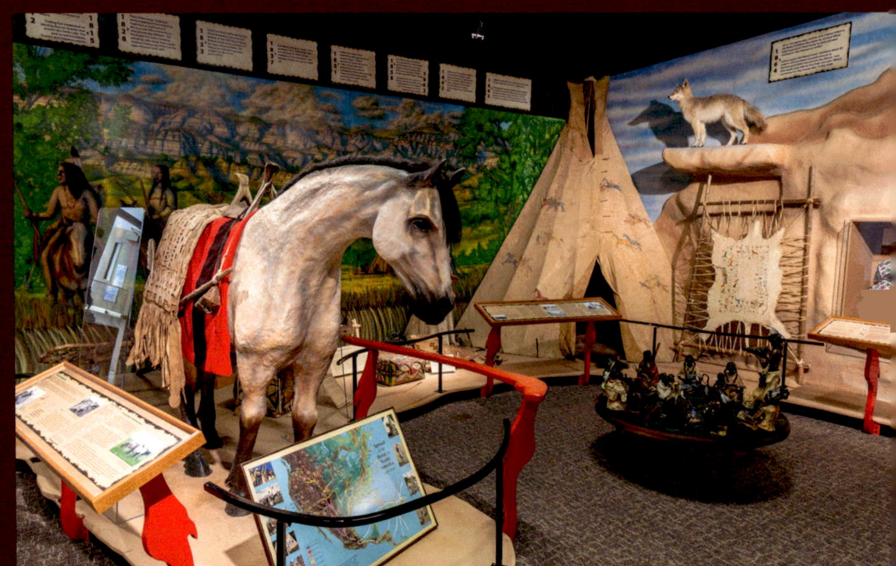

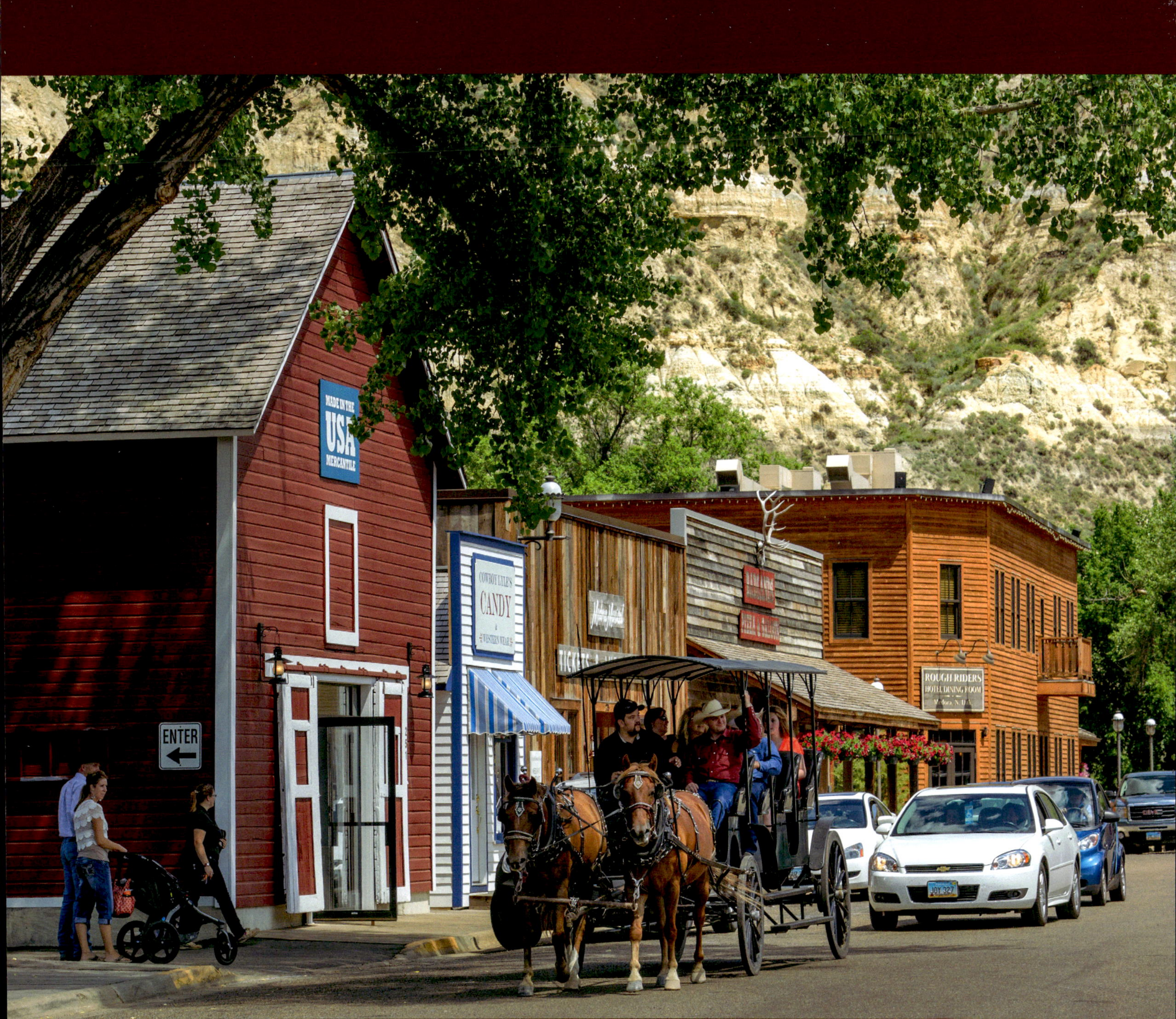
MADE IN THE
USA
MERCANTILE
ENTER
COWBOY LYLE'S
CANDY
&
WESTERN WEAR
ROUGH RIDERS
HOTEL DINING ROOM

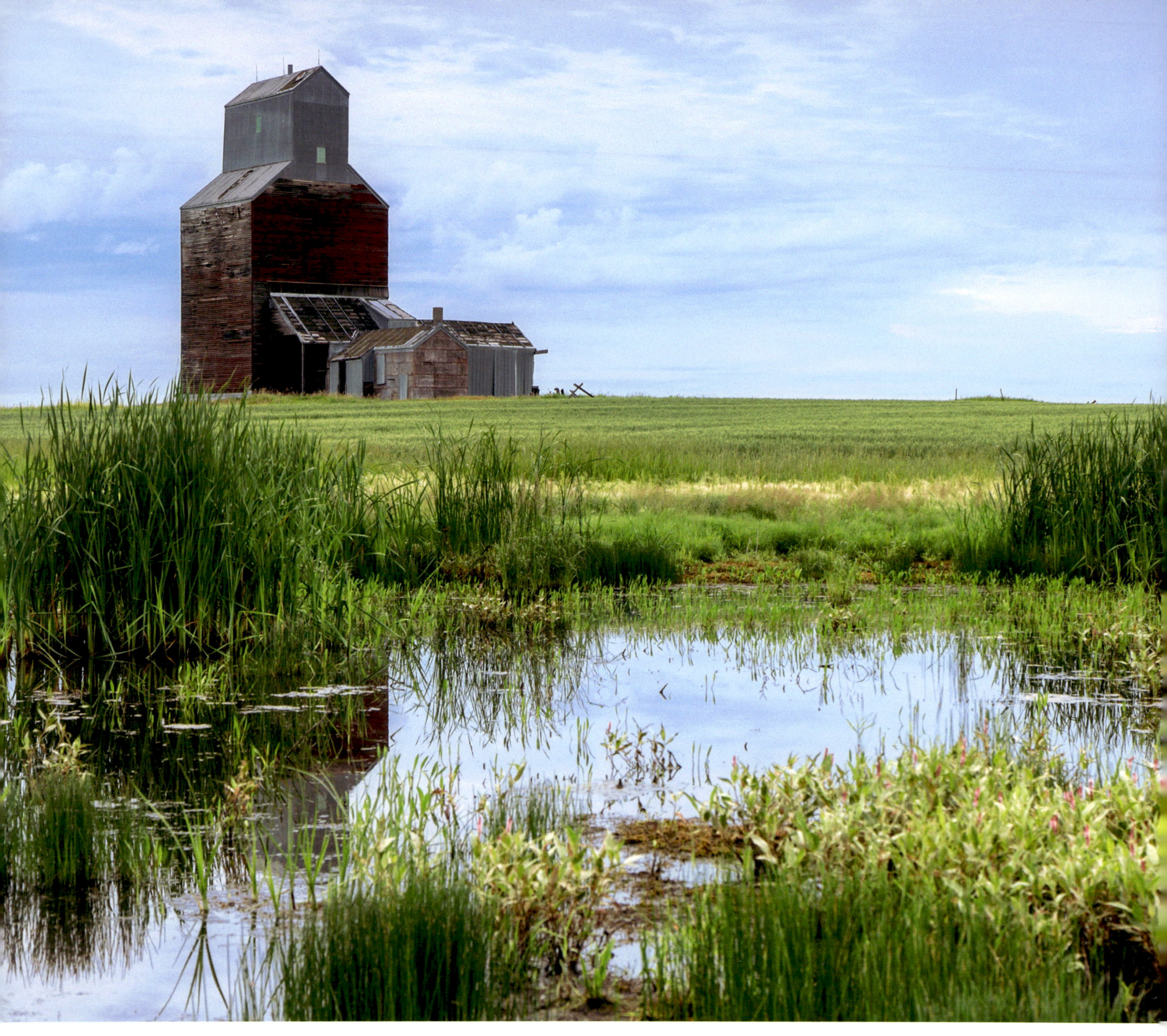

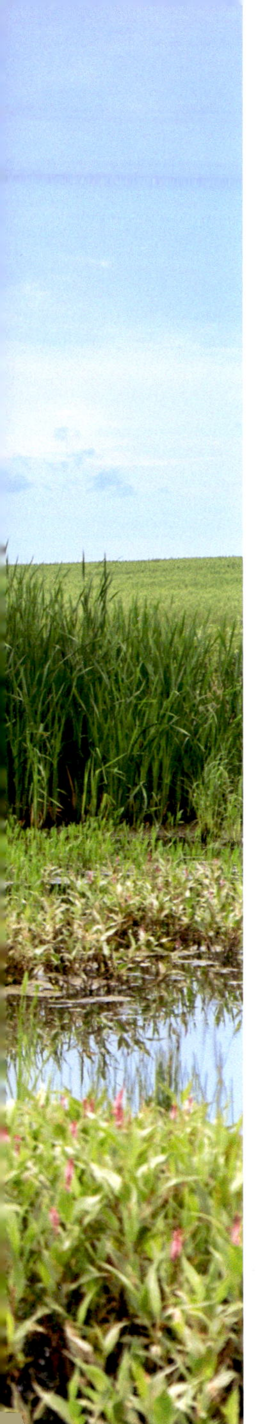

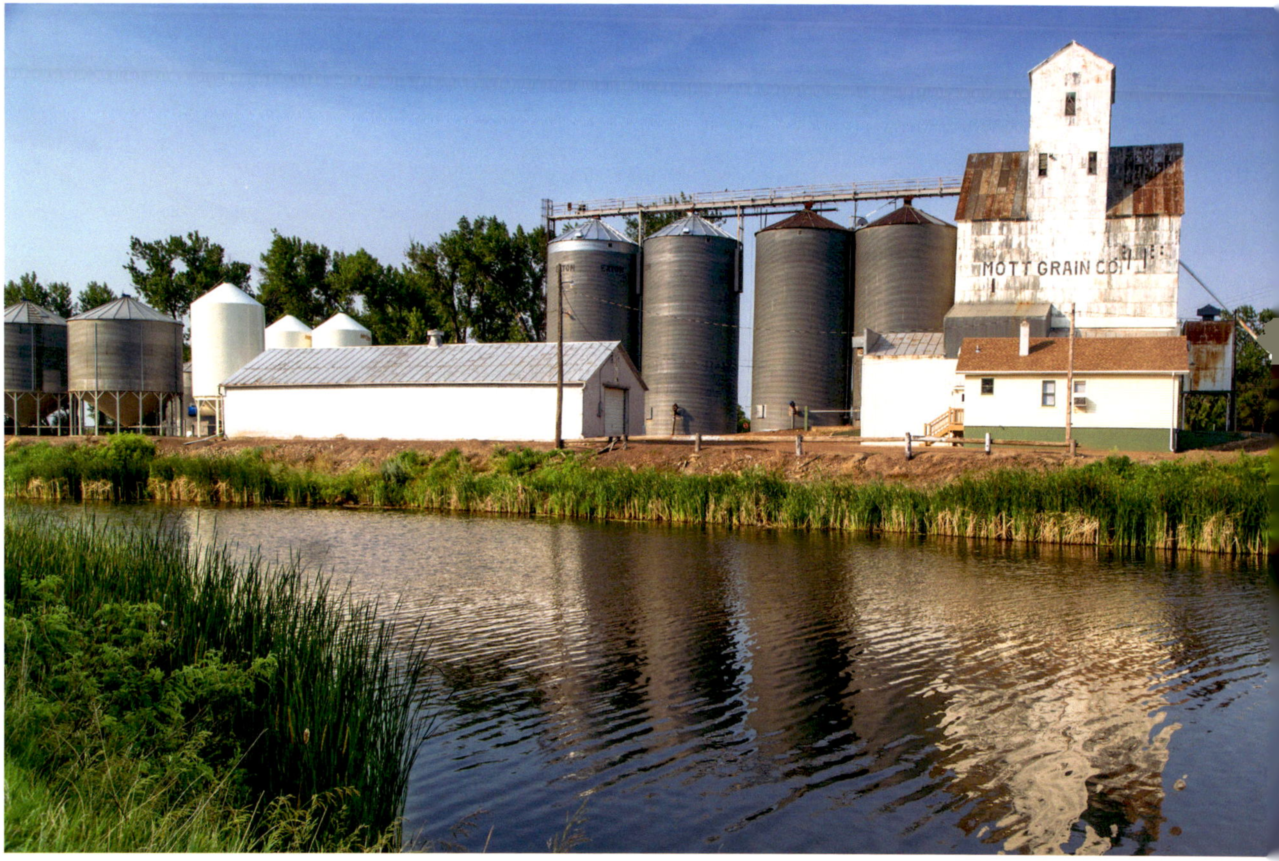

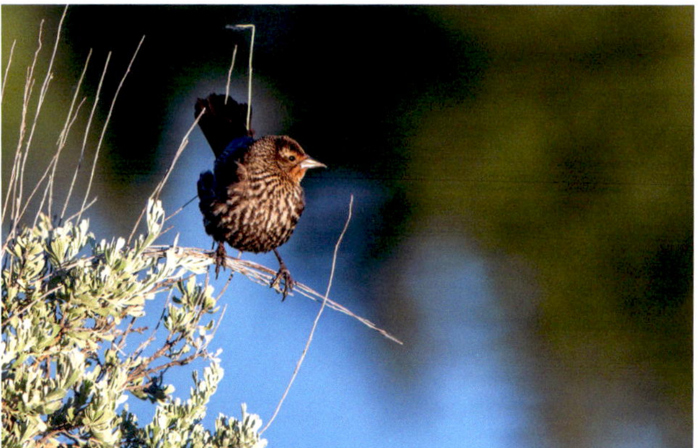

Above: The Cannonball River mirrors the Mott Grain Elevator just south of downtown Mott.

Left: Lincoln's sparrows like this one migrate through North Dakota on their way to nesting sites in northern Canada to Alaska.

Far left: On the northern prairie near the town of Lignite, this old granary has weathered blizzards, thunderstorms, and the summer sun.

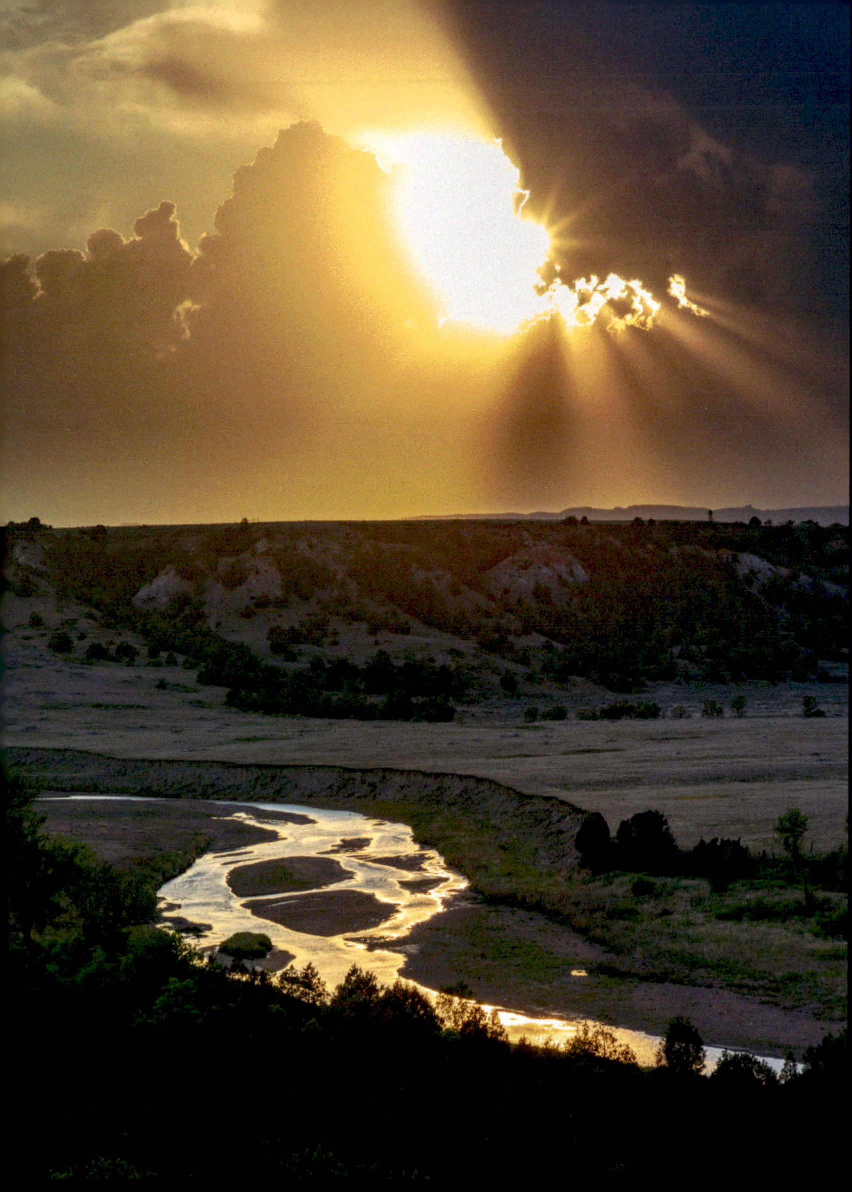

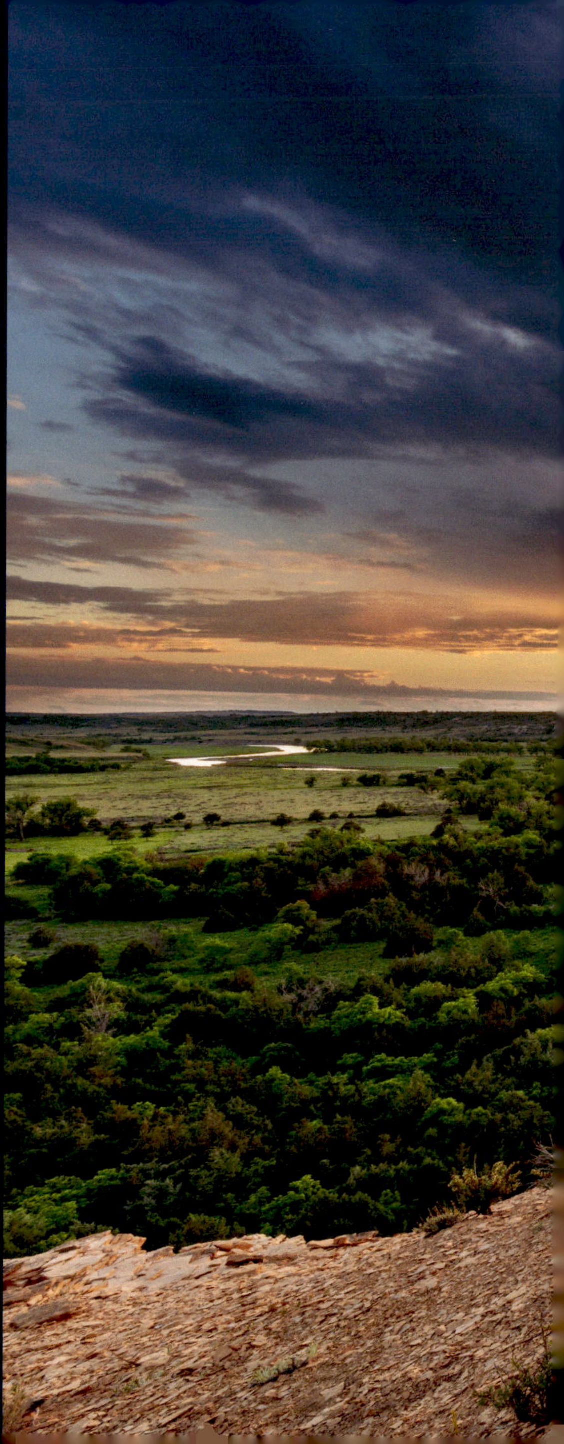

Above: Rays from the setting sun pierce thunderstorm clouds above the Little Missouri River in Little Missouri National Grassland.

Right: A starburst at sunset marks day's end at Little Missouri National Grassland.

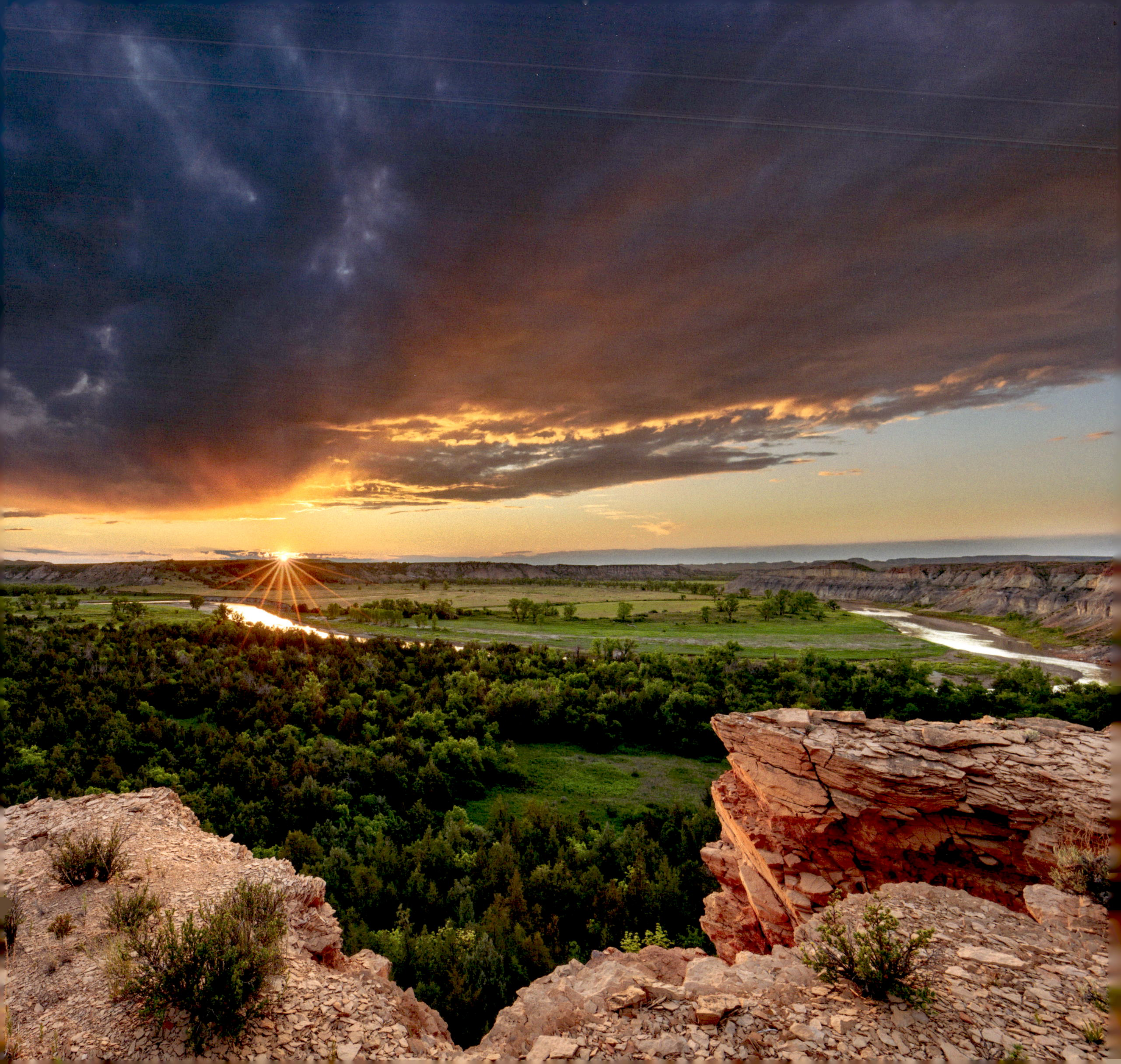

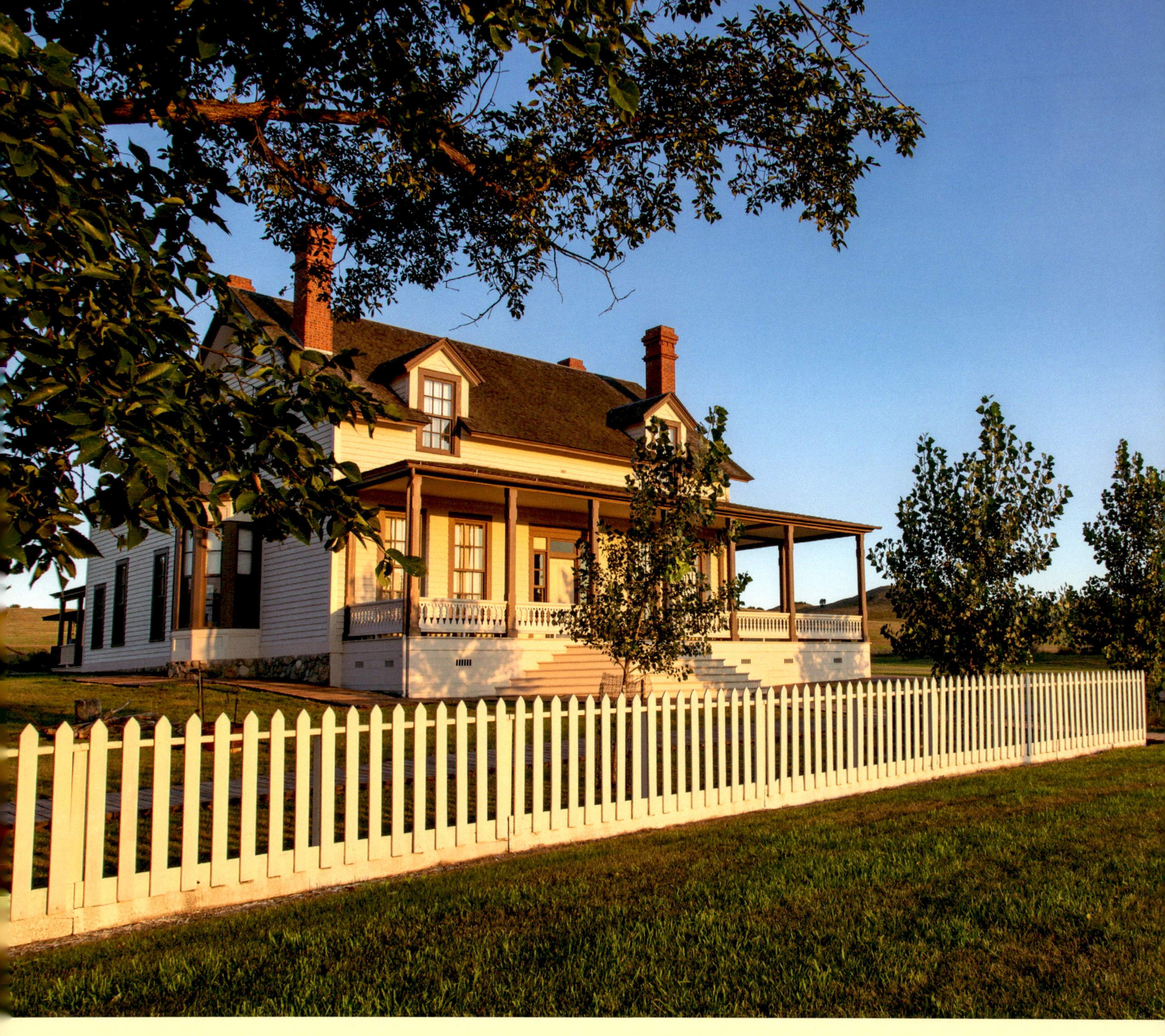

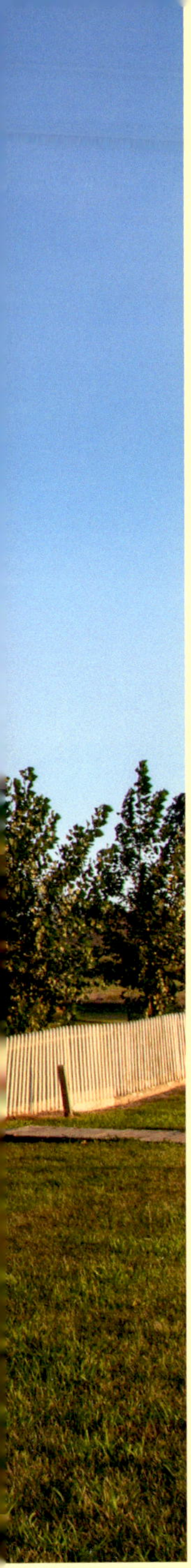

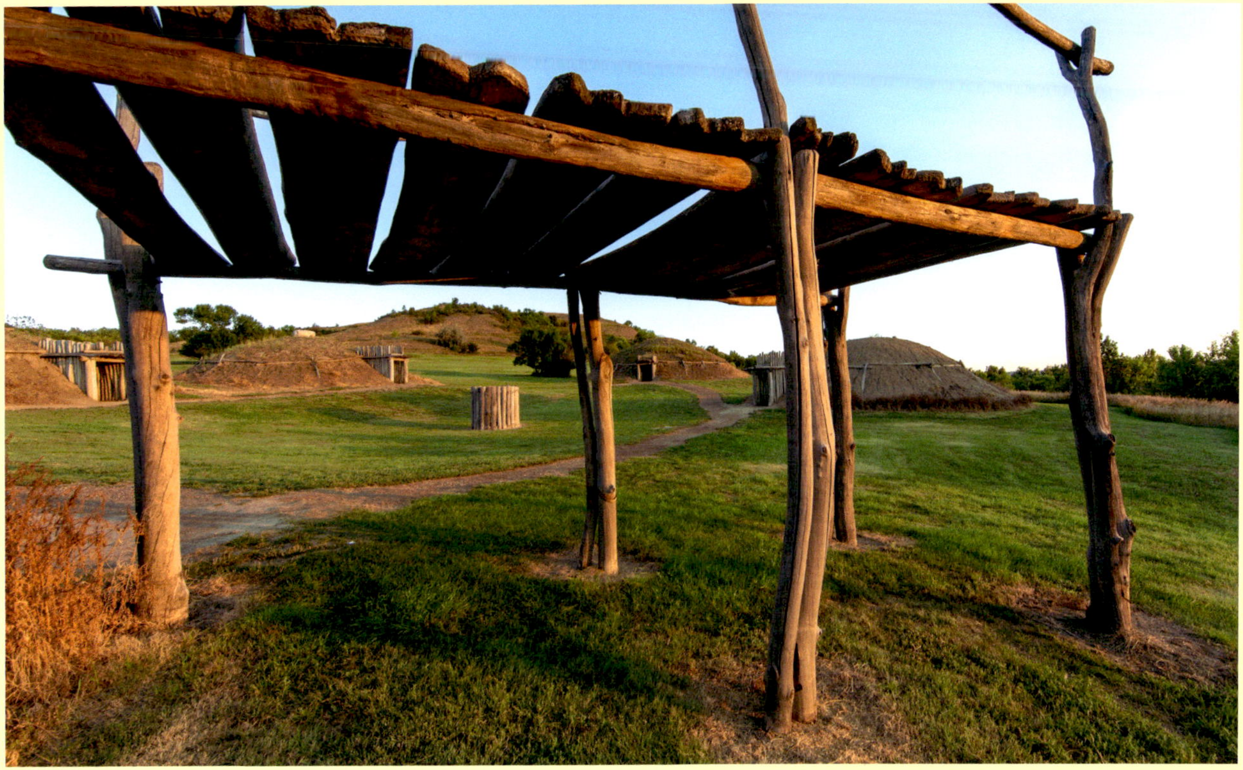

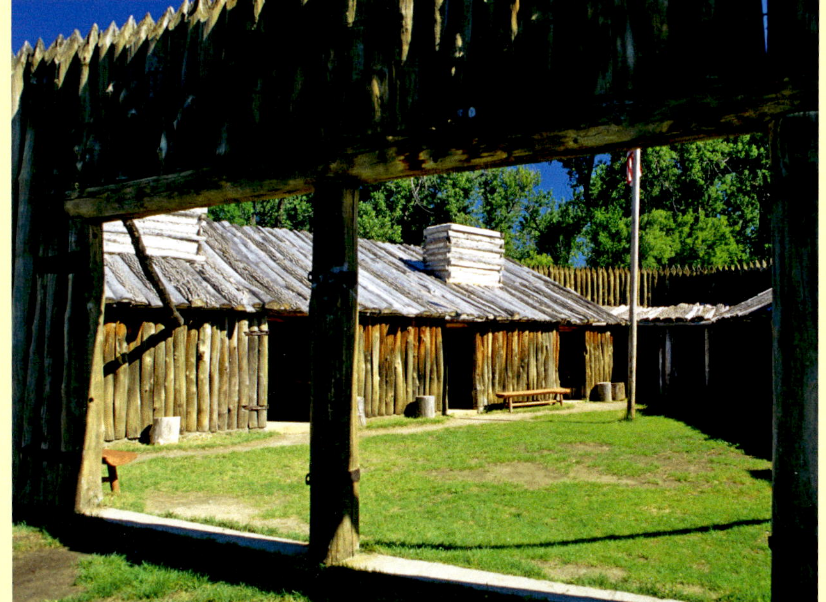

Above: Fort Abraham Lincoln State Park near Mandan includes *Miti O-pa-e-resh* or On-a-Slant village, with reconstructed Mandan earthen lodges on the west bank of the Missouri River.

Left: The Lewis and Clark Expedition built Fort Mandan to winter over before heading west in the spring of 1805. Today, visitors enjoy interpretive tours at the reconstructed fort west of Washburn.

Far left: George Armstrong Custer served as post commander at Fort Abraham Lincoln from 1873 until his demise in 1876. Today, as part of Fort Abraham Lincoln State Park, the Custer House offers guided tours of the home where Custer and his wife, Libbie, lived and entertained.

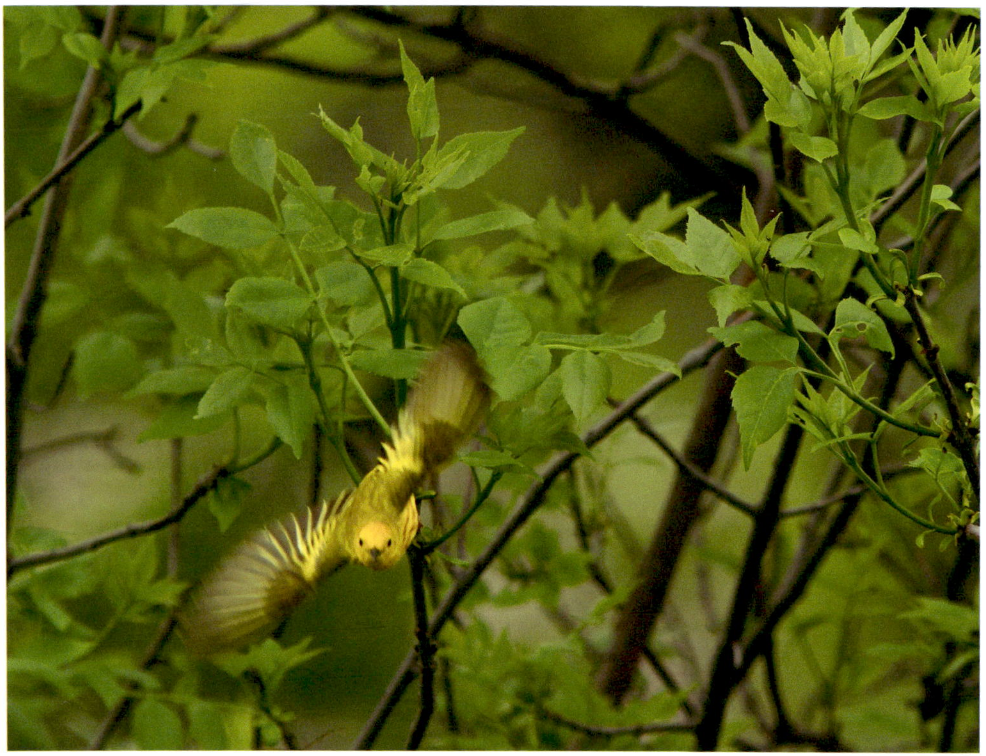

Above: Riparian plants offer rich habitat for a variety of birdlife, including this yellow warbler.

Right: Originally introduced from Asia in the 1880s, ring-necked pheasants are one of the most popular upland game birds across the Great Plains.

Far right: Morning light graces the banks of the Sheyenne River near the hamlet of Fort Ransom.

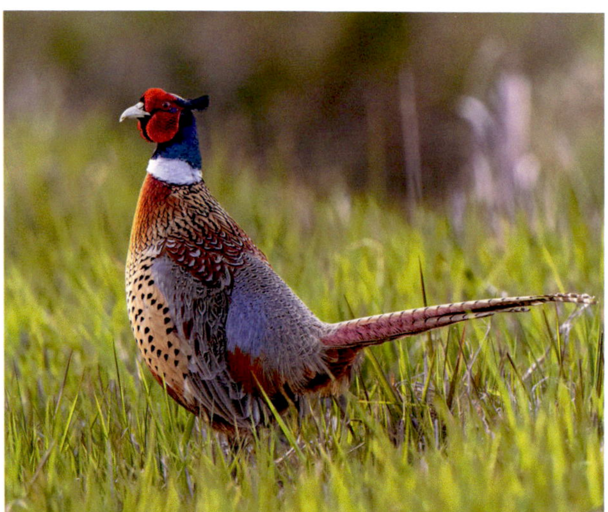

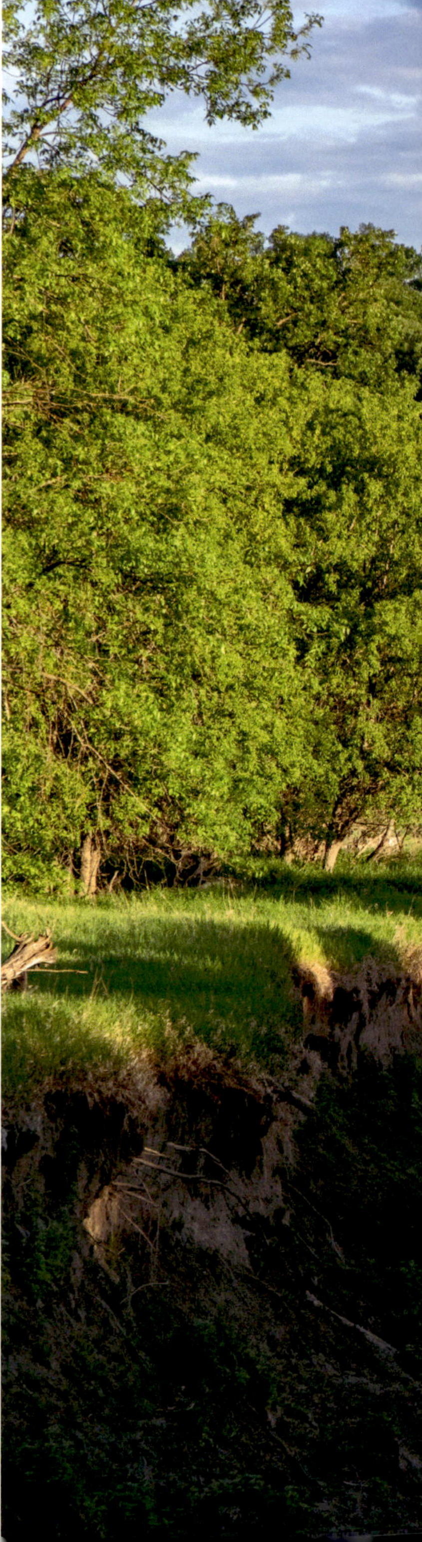

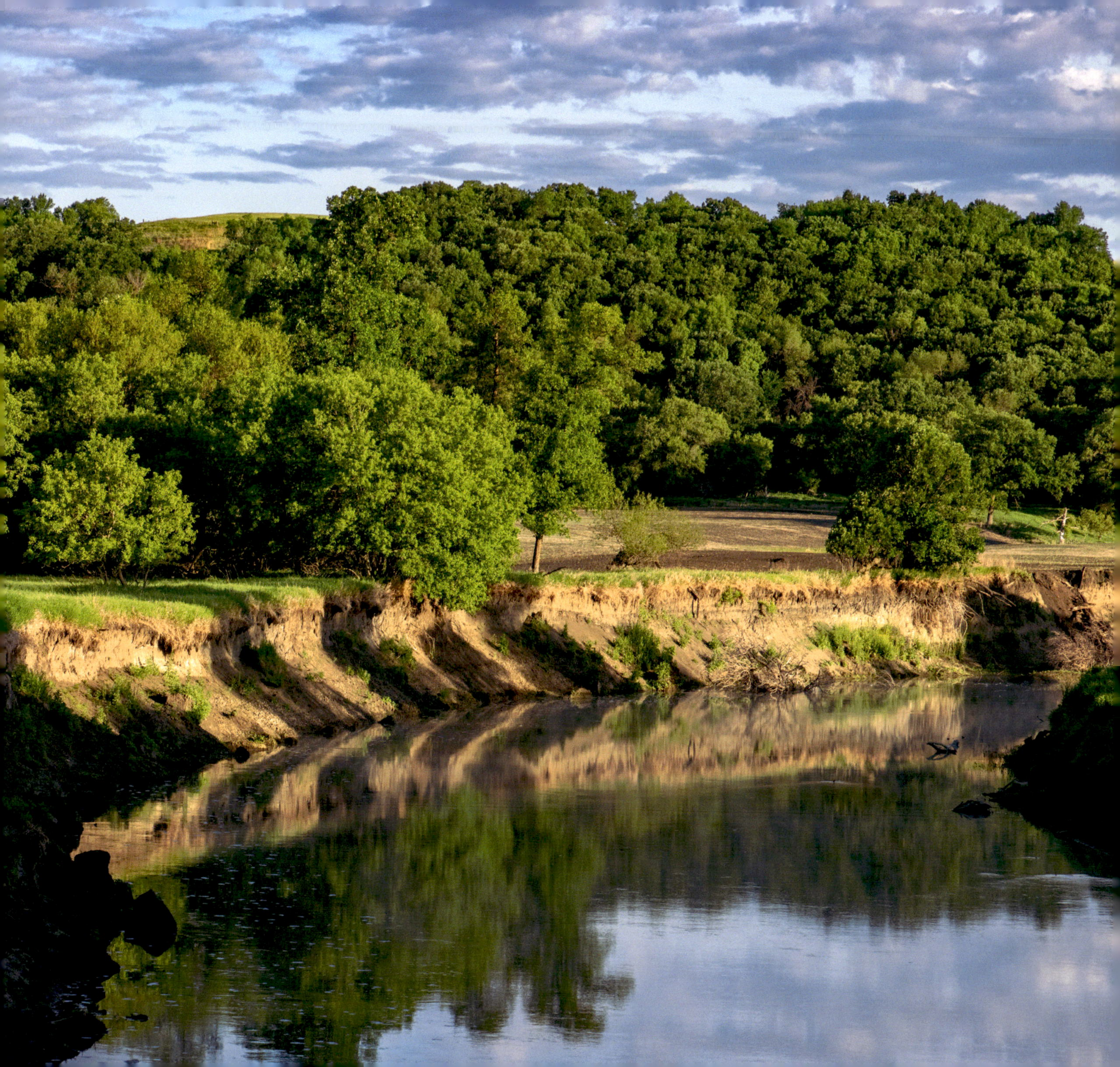

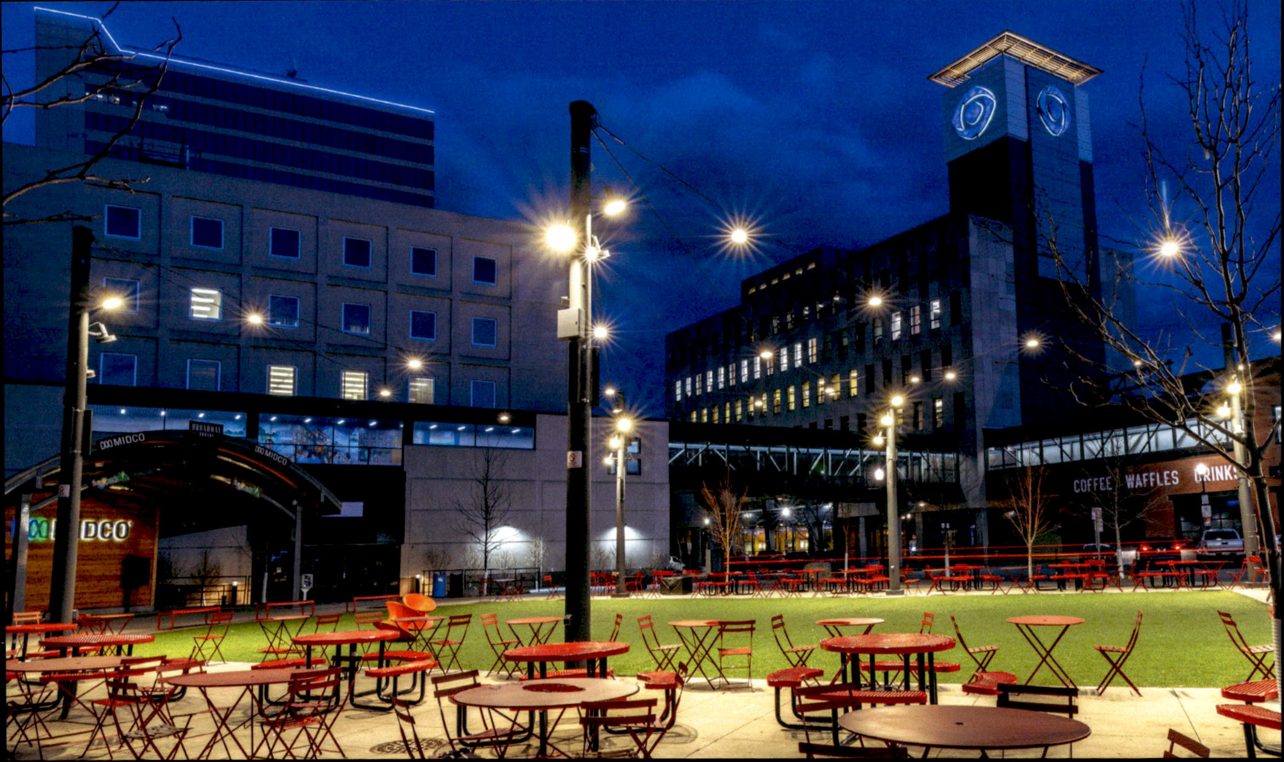

Above: At the corner of Broadway and 2nd Avenue North in downtown Fargo, Broadway Square is a popular lunch and yoga spot, as well as a venue for concerts, films, holiday events, and—in the winter—ice skating.

Right: The historic Art Deco Fargo Theater, restored in 1999, shows current movies and serves as the hub for the annual Fargo Film Festival.

Far right: Founded in 1871, Fargo remains a vibrant center for shopping, health care, education, and arts and culture.

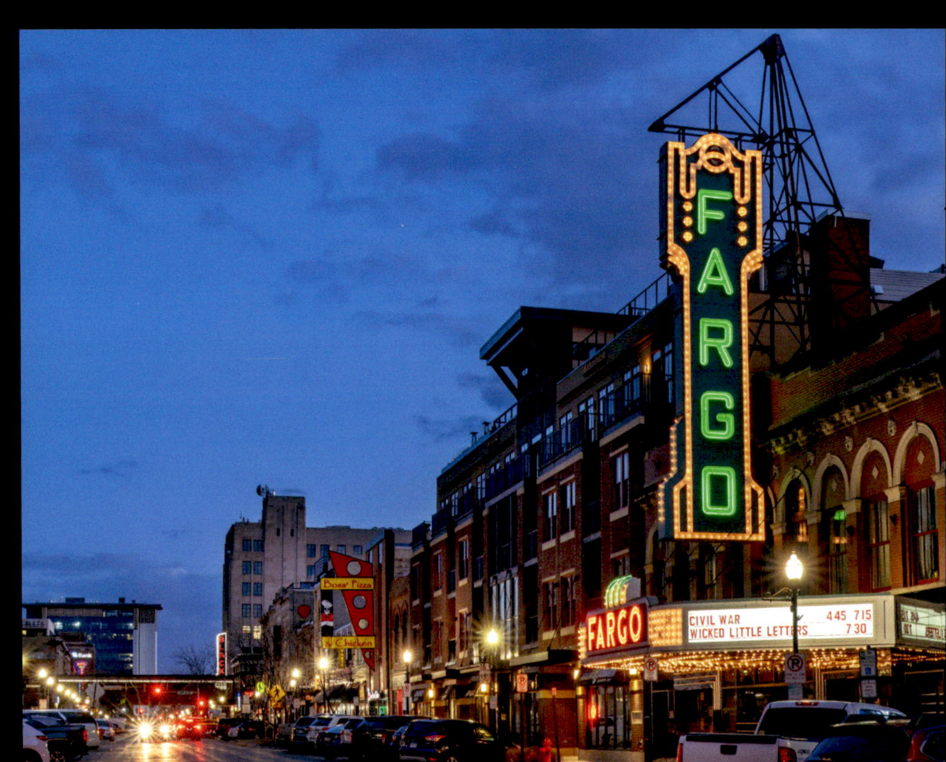

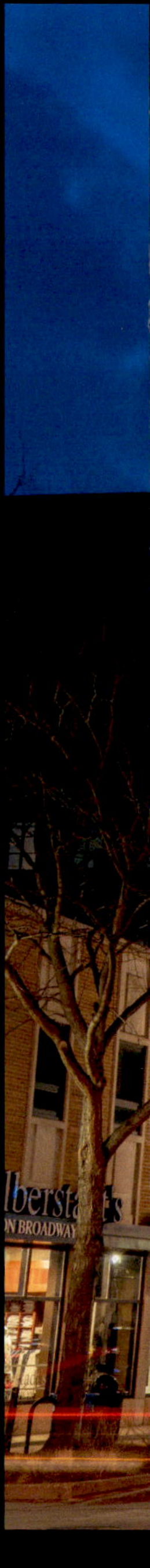

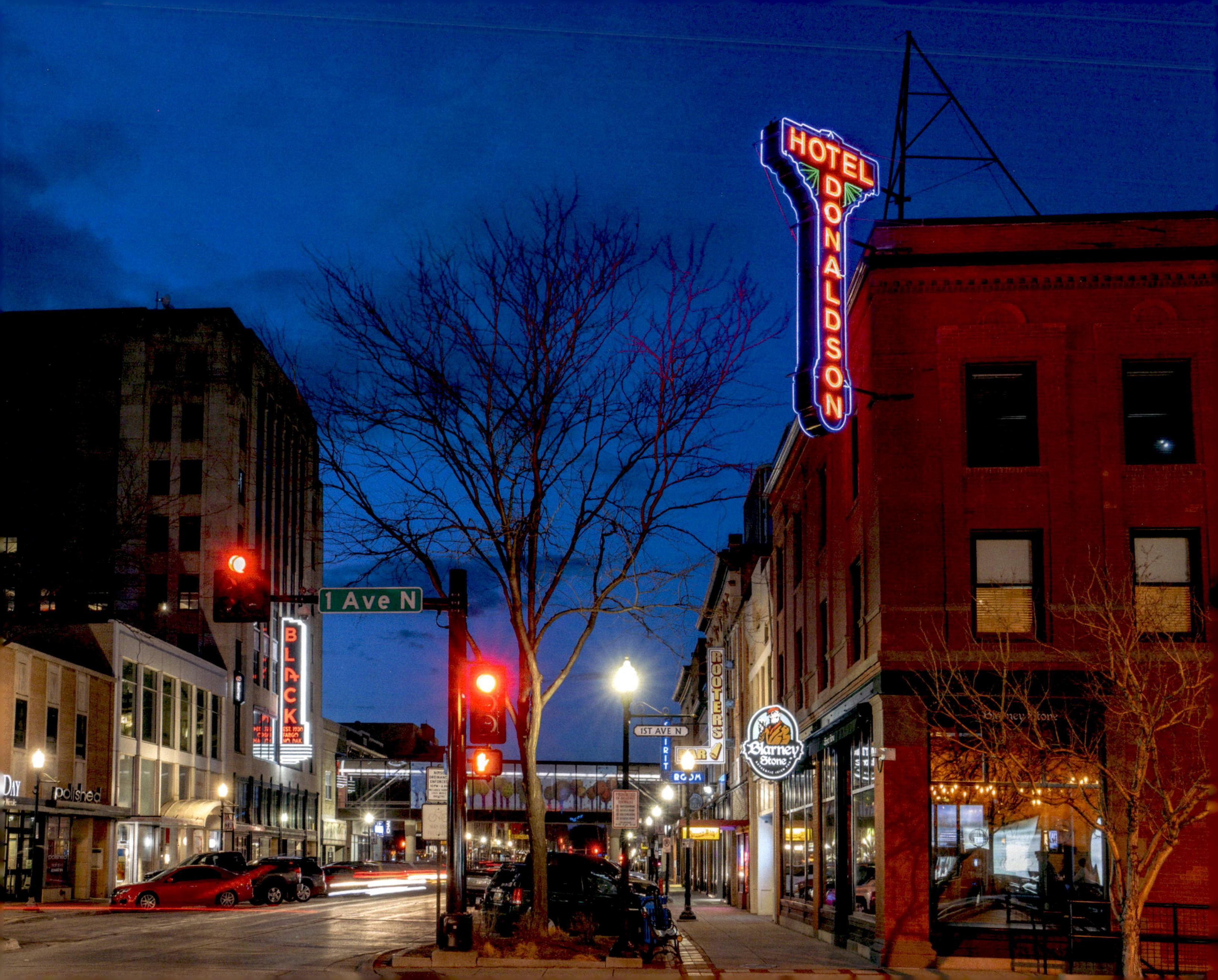
HOTEL
DONALDSON
1 Ave N
BLACK
1ST AVE N
HOOTERS
BAR
Blarney Stone
polished

Right: Mule deer thrive in the grasslands of Theodore Roosevelt National Park.

Far right: Theodore Roosevelt is one of the few national parks where visitors can see free-roaming horses.

Below: The Jones Creek Trail runs through the wild heart of Theodore Roosevelt National Park's South Unit near Medora.

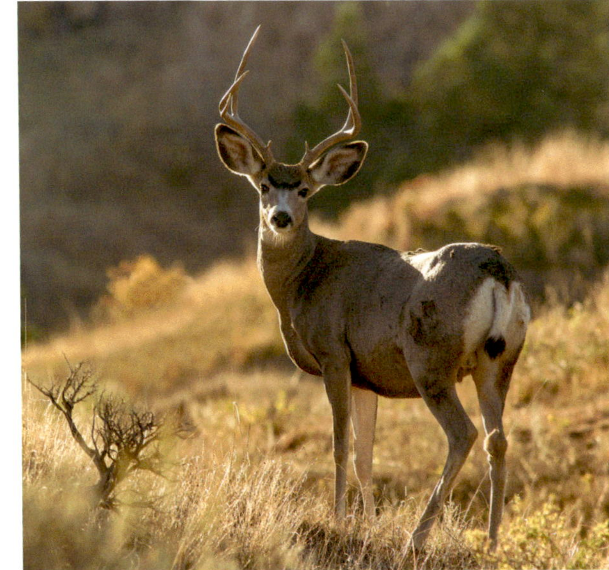

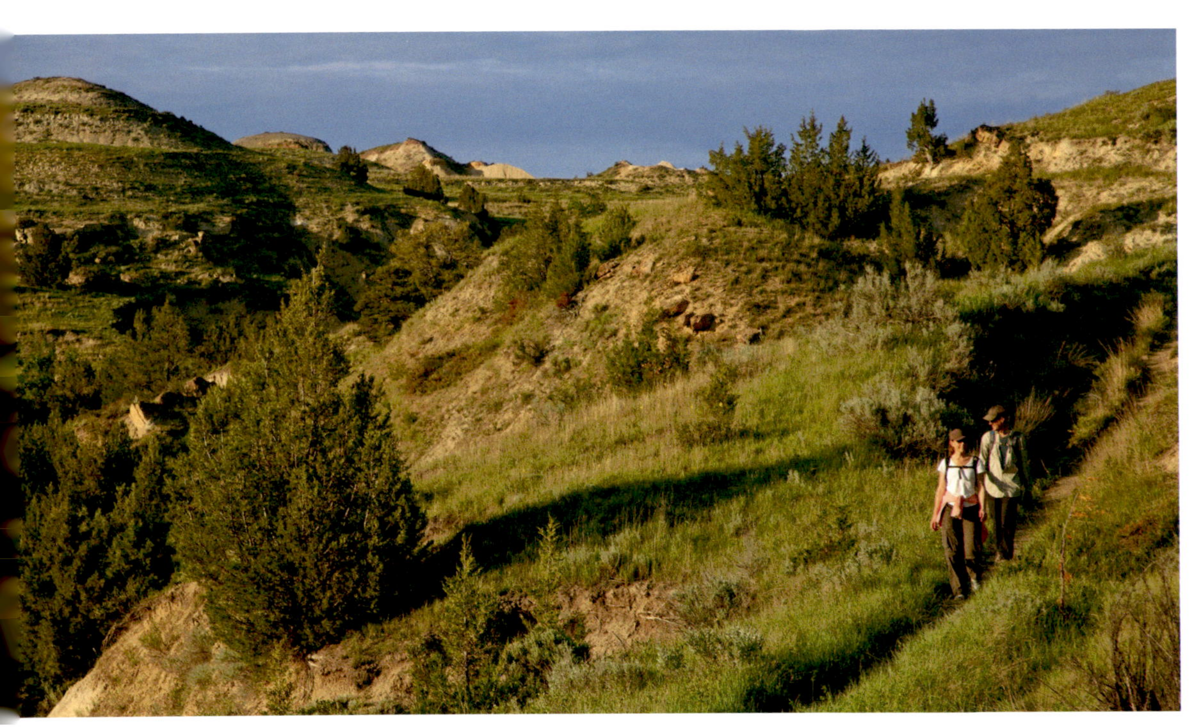

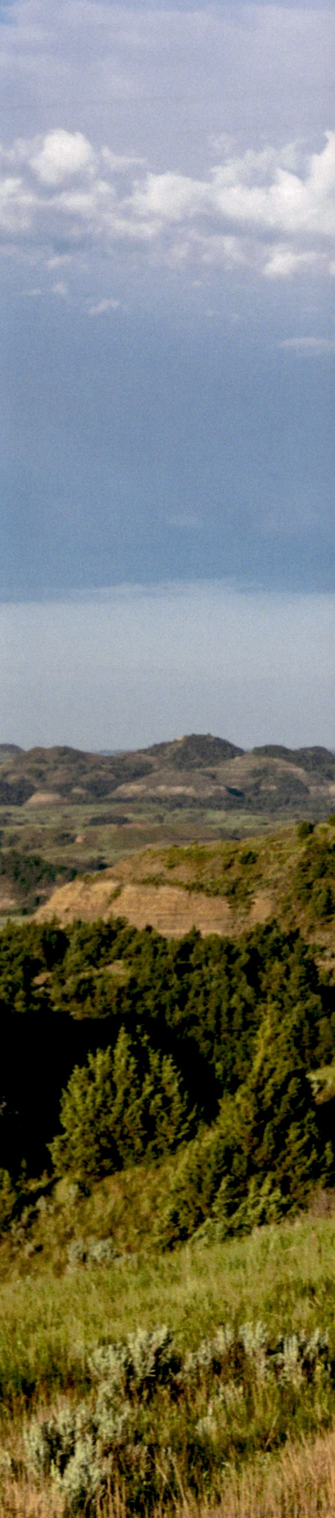

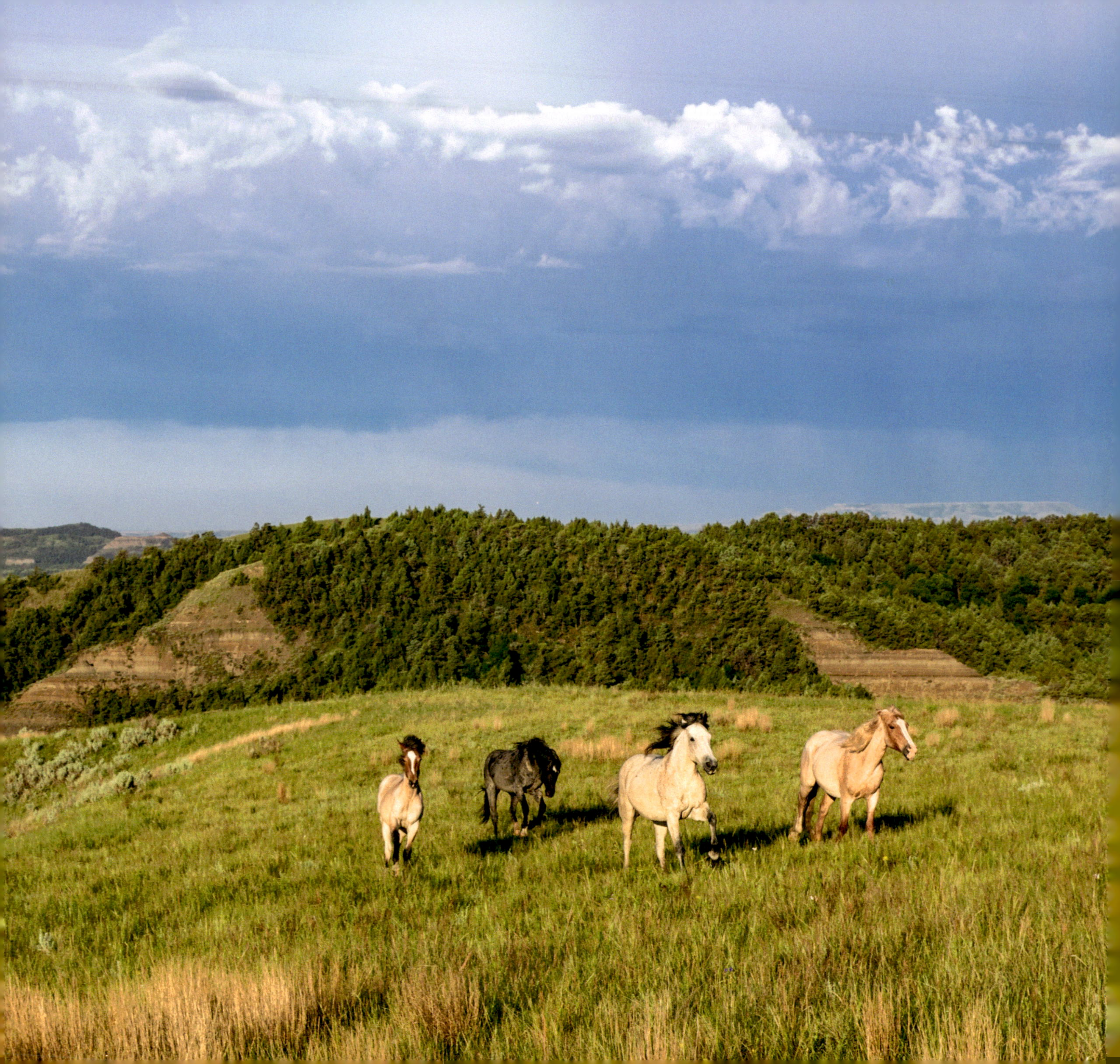

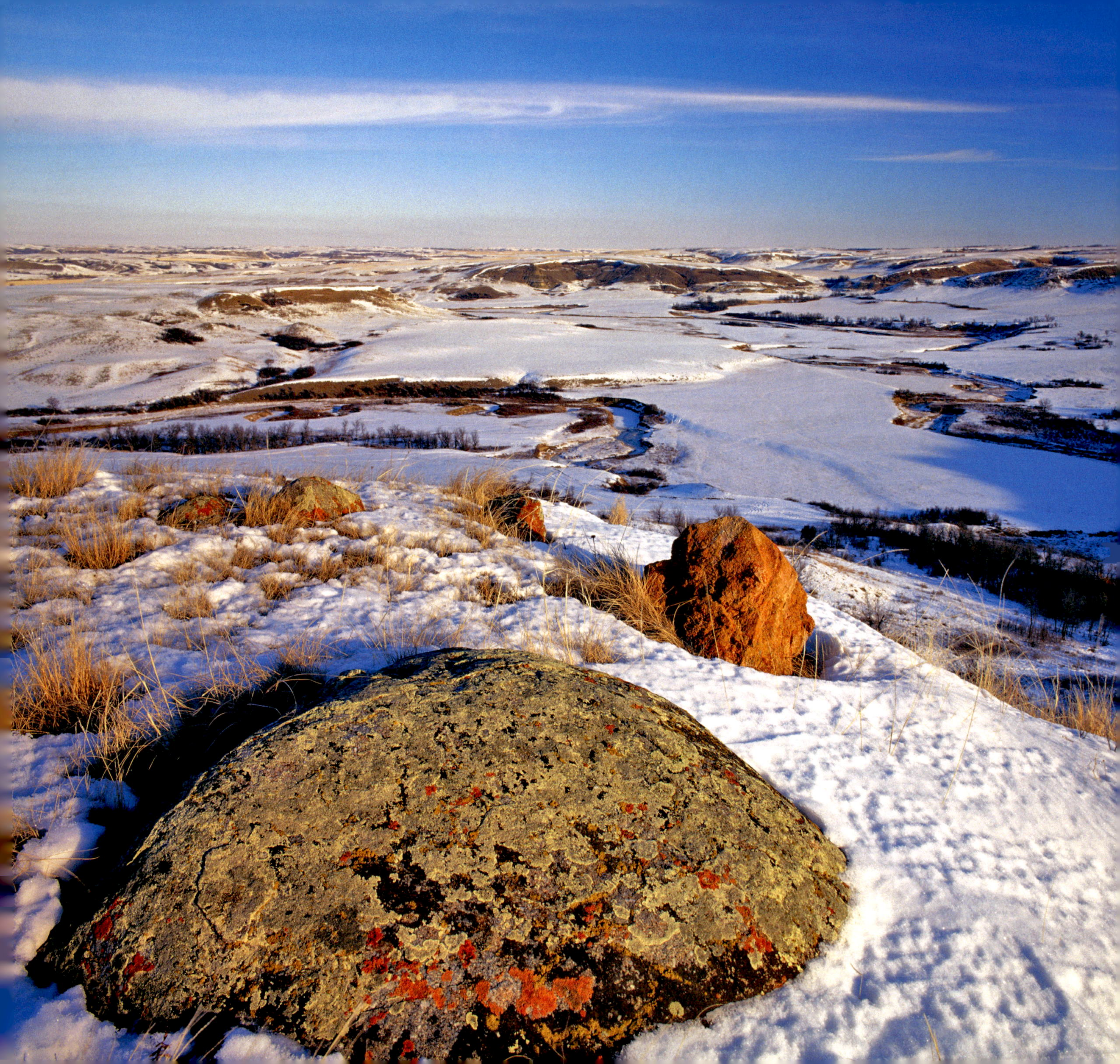

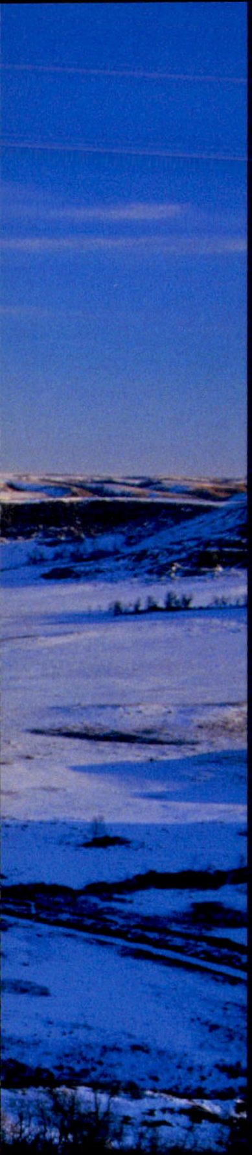

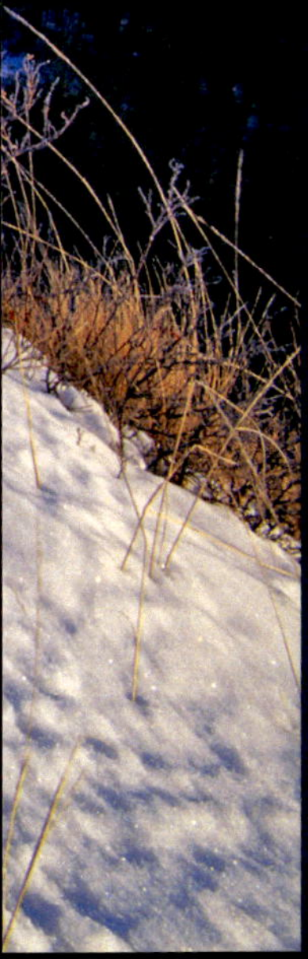

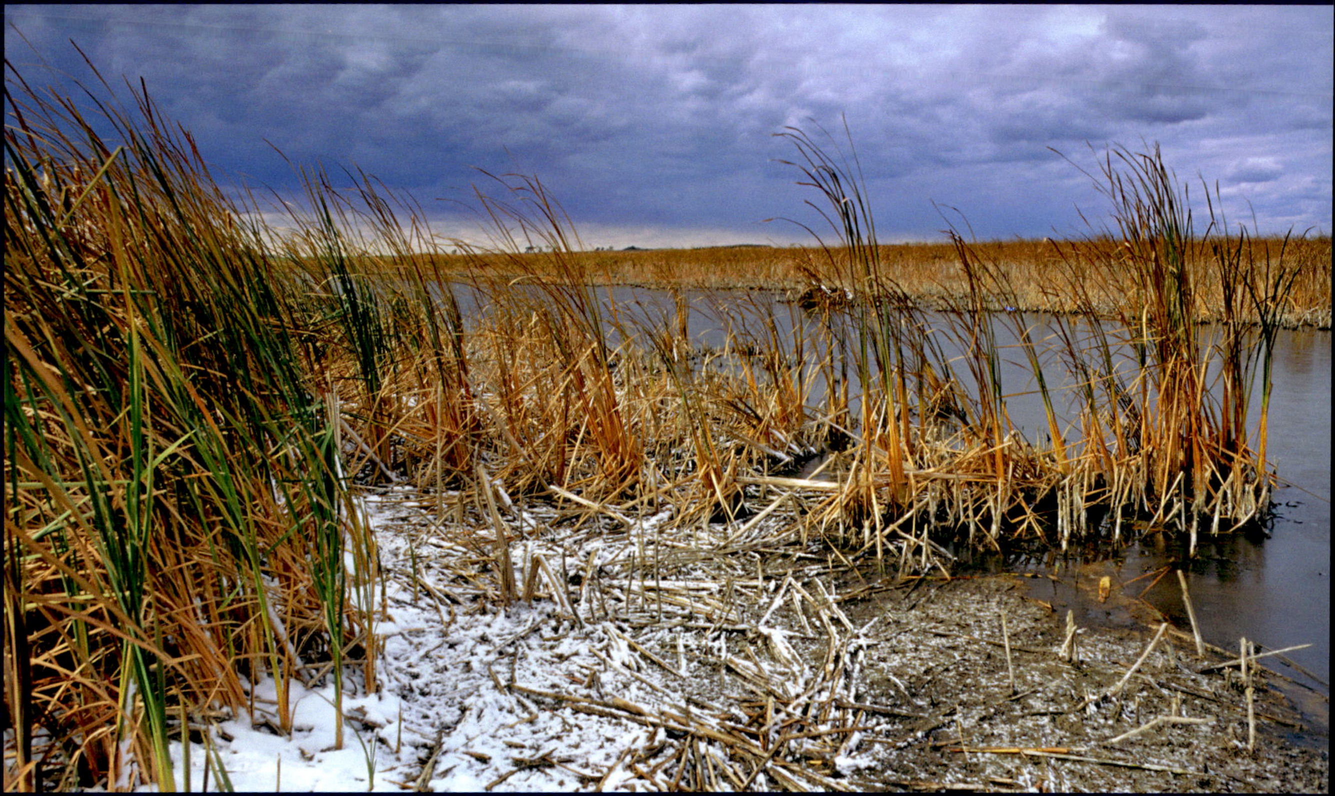

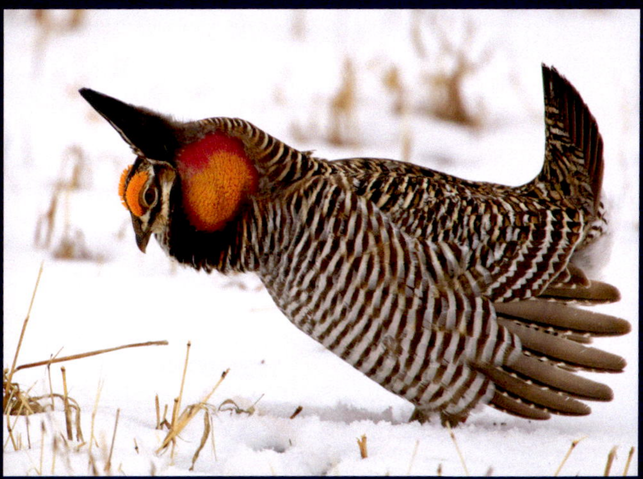

Above: Prairie, woodlands, sandhills, bottomlands, and marshes along the Souris River provide varied habitat for abundant wildlife at the J. Clark Salyer National Wildlife Refuge near Upham.

Left: Greater prairie chickens, like this male, are hardy birds that thrive year-round in North Dakota's fields and prairies.

Far left: Winter white blankets the White Earth River near Stanley.

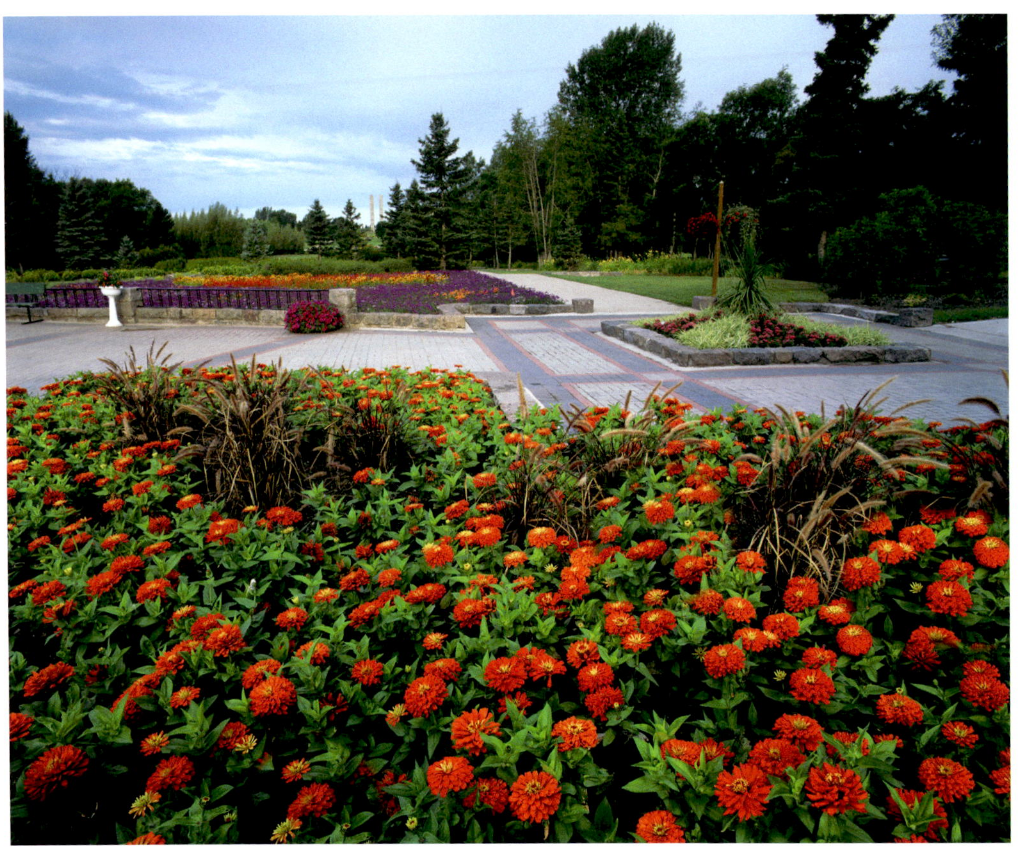

Above: The 2,339-acre International Peace Garden spans the North Dakota-Manitoba border near Dunseith on U.S. Highway 281.

Right: The Peace Garden houses an amazing array of flowers, shrubs, and trees, including these wood lilies.

Far right: Botanical displays are the main feature, but the International Peace Garden also offers kayaking and canoeing, hiking and biking trails, a visitor center and café, and guided tours.

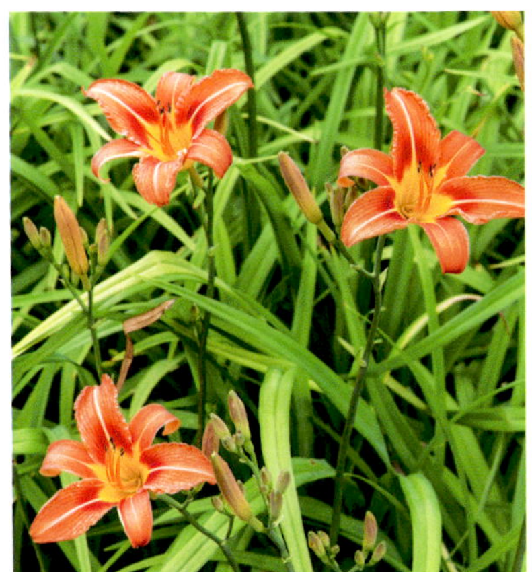

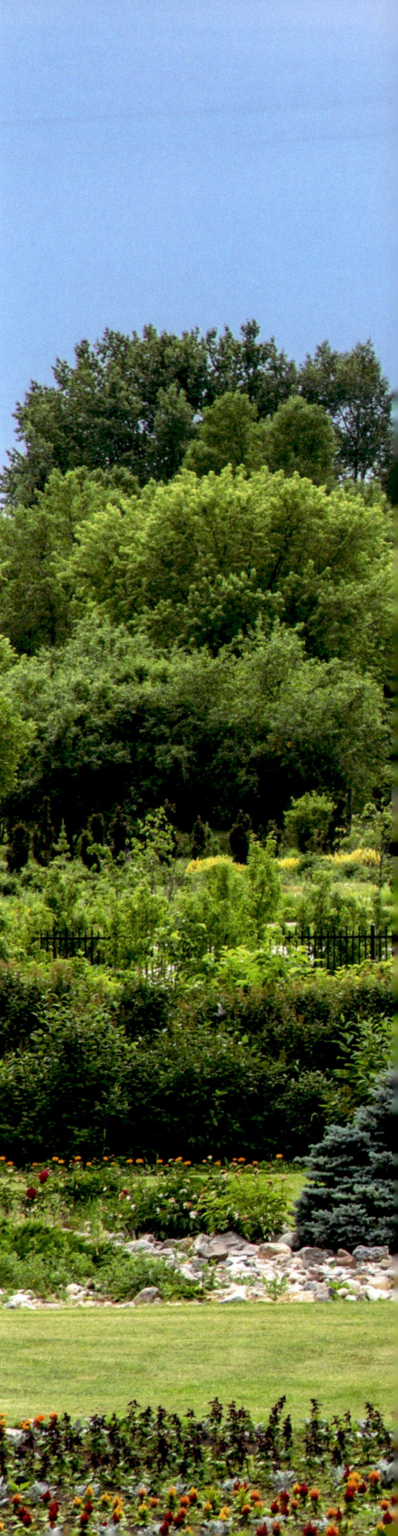

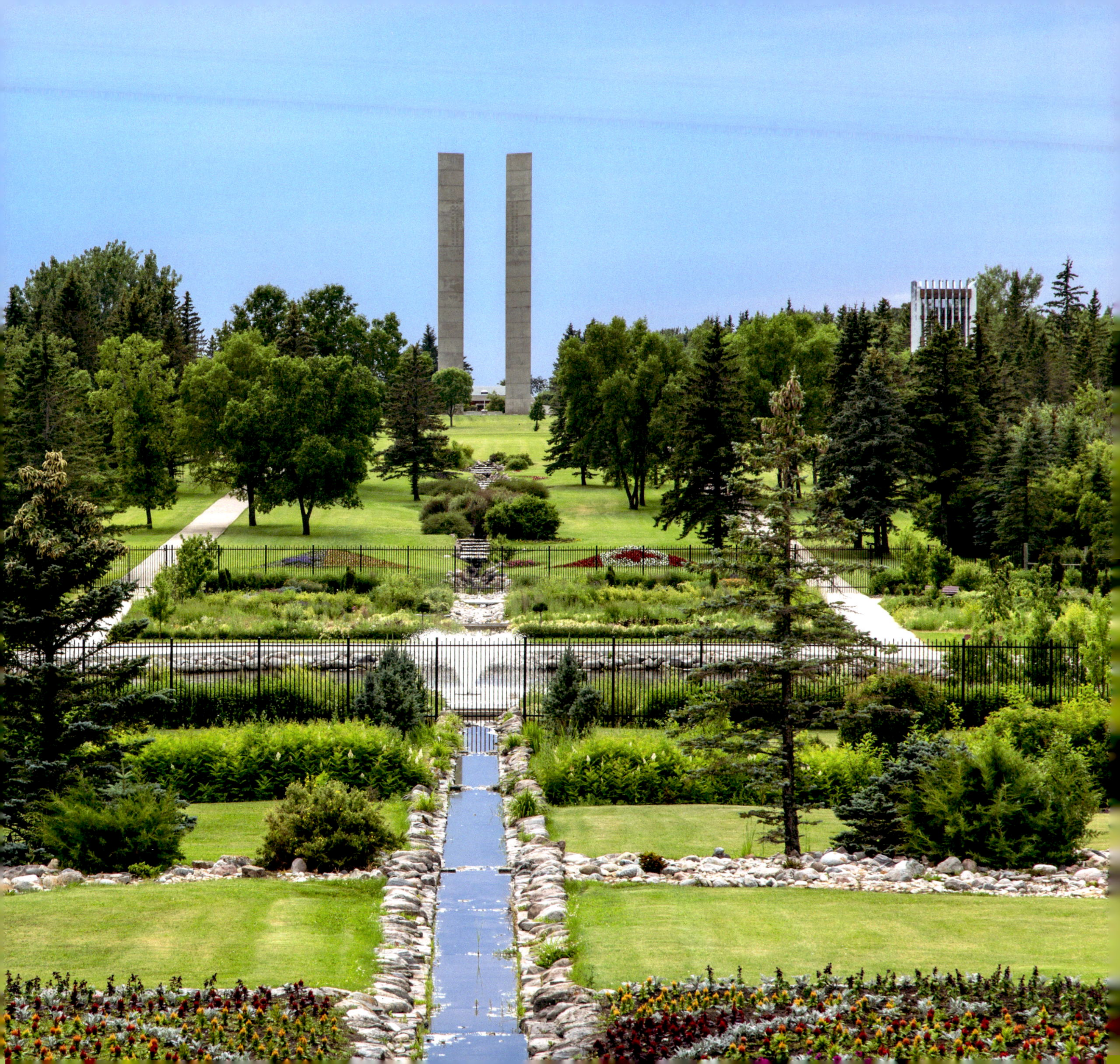

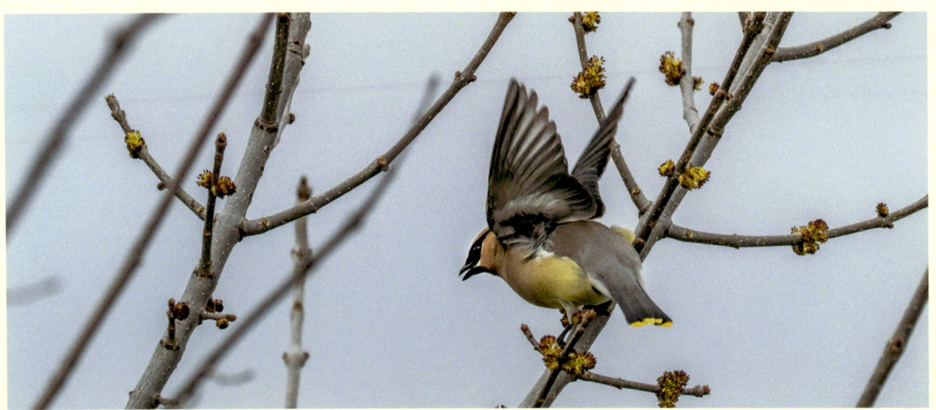

Above: Fruit and insects make up most of a cedar waxwing's diet. These acrobatic flyers thrive in woodlands where berries are abundant.

Right and far right: Theodore Roosevelt National Park is home to two bison herds that roam freely on the North and South Units.

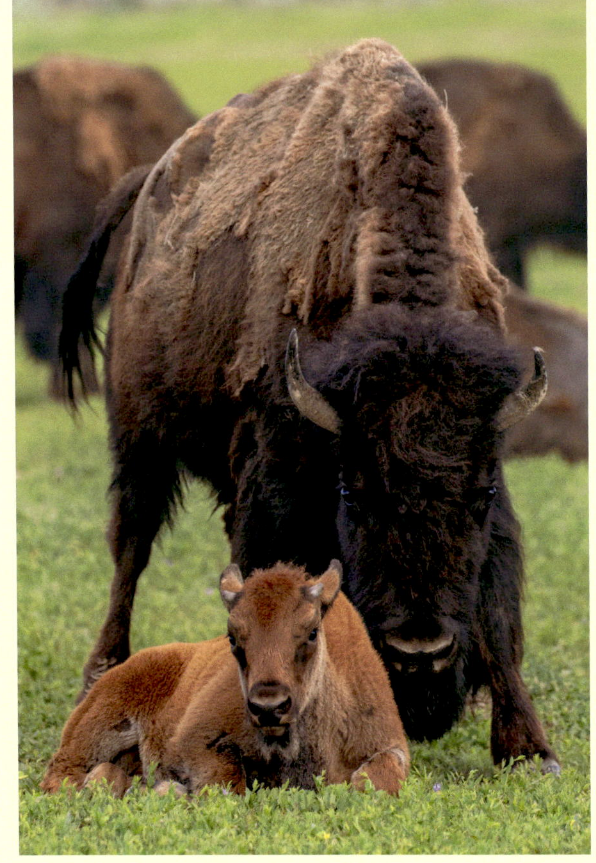

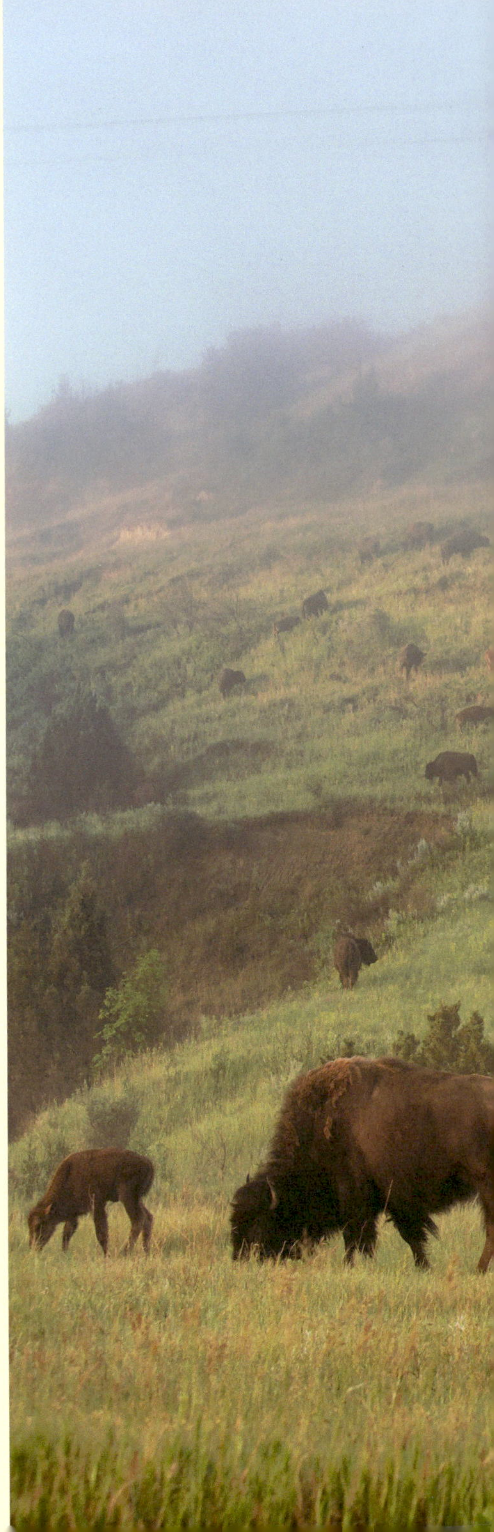

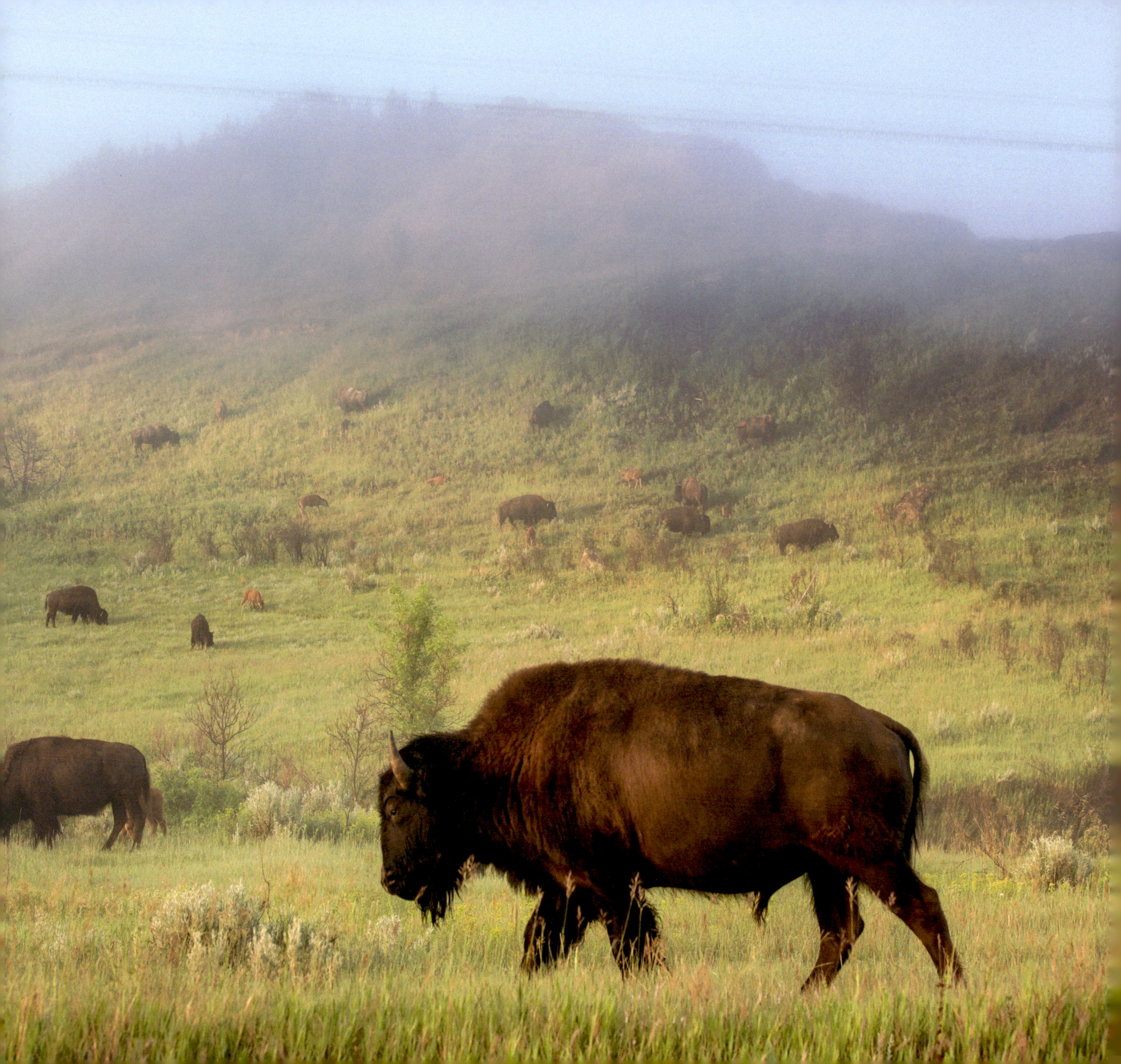

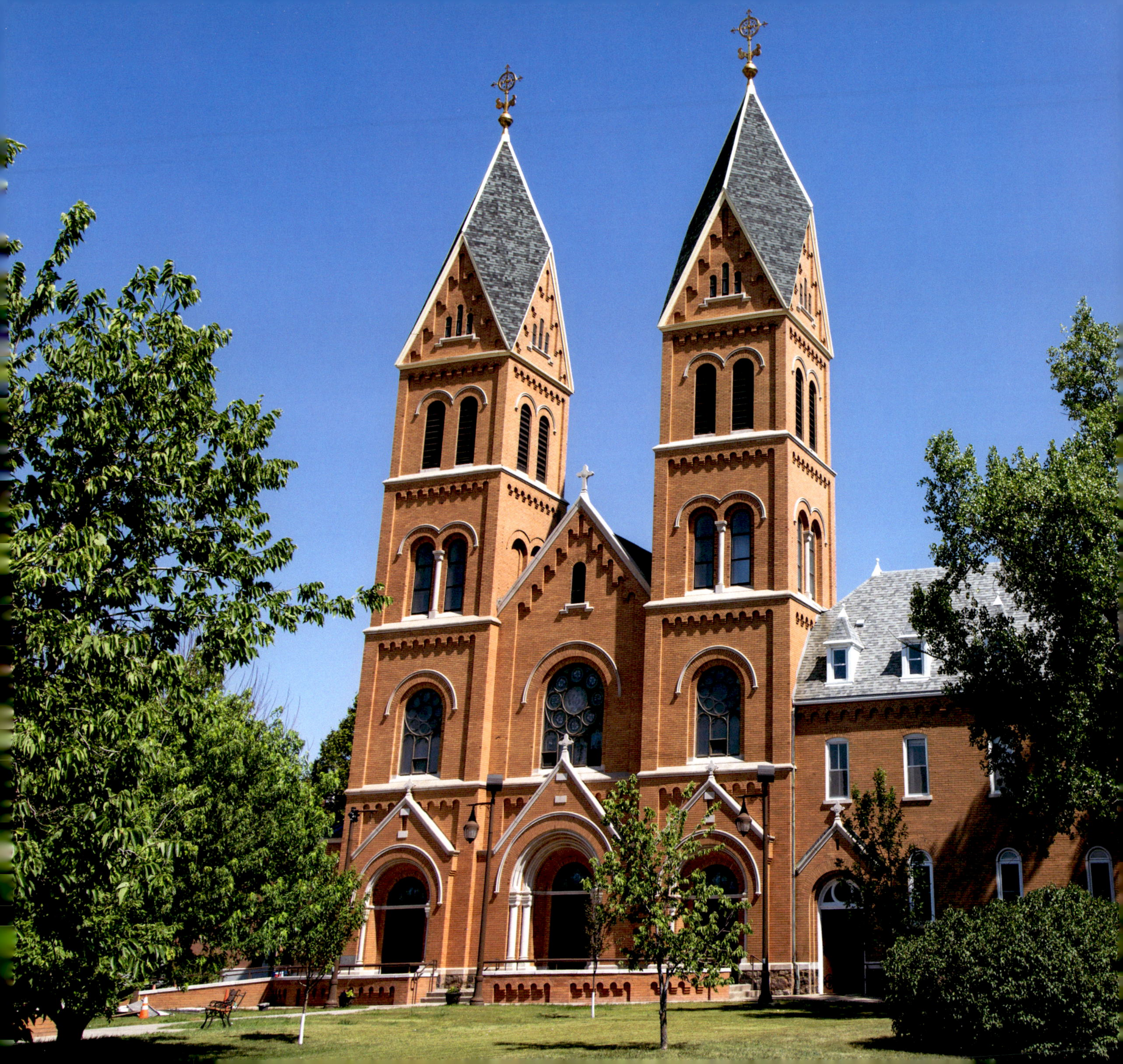

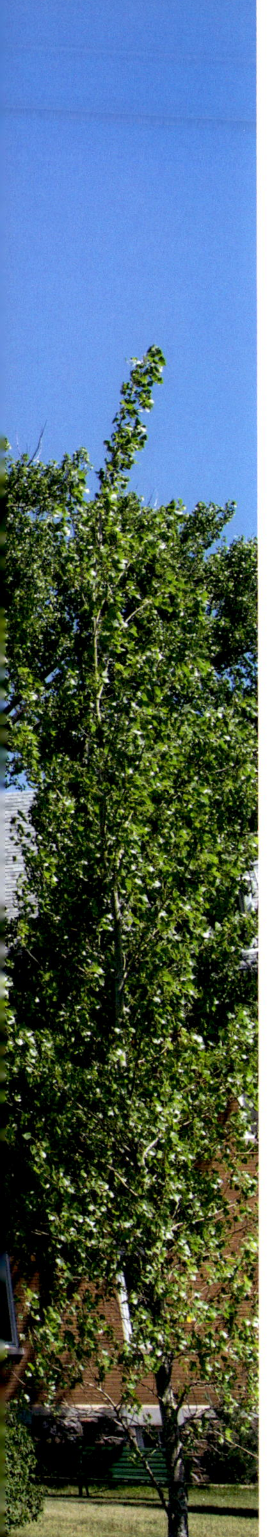

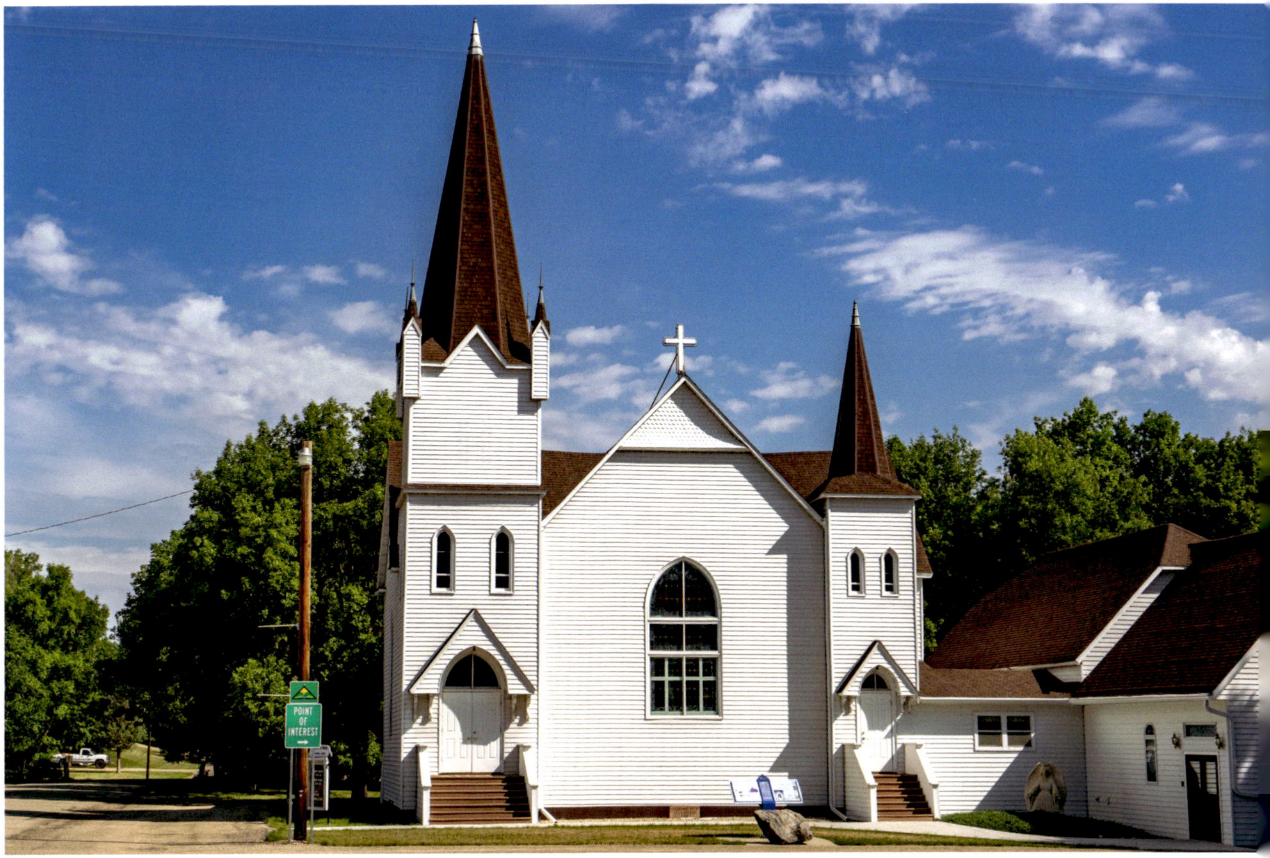

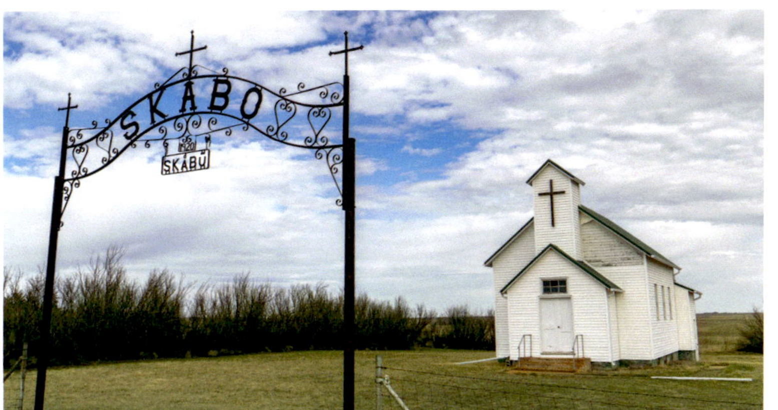

Above: Founded in 1882, Standing Rock Lutheran Church actively serves the local community of Fort Ransom.

Left: The Skabo Lutheran Church in Daneville Township, north of Grenora, was founded in 1920.

Far left: Completed in 1910, the Bavarian Romanesque-style Assumption Abbey in Richardton is a Benedictine Monastery. A visitor center offers information on monastic life and the abbey's history.

Right: A male, or tom, wild turkey displays his breeding plumage.

Far right: Sunrise warms the rock shelter, built by the Civilian Conservation Corps in 1937, at River Bend Overlook in the North Unit of Theodore Roosevelt National Park.

Below: Spring is a time of lush forage and antlers in velvet.

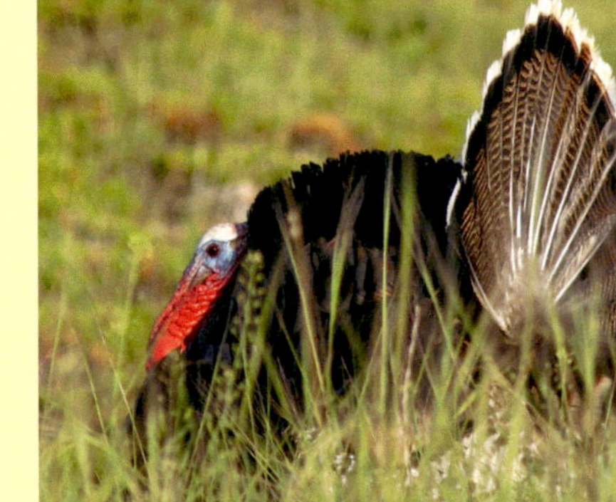

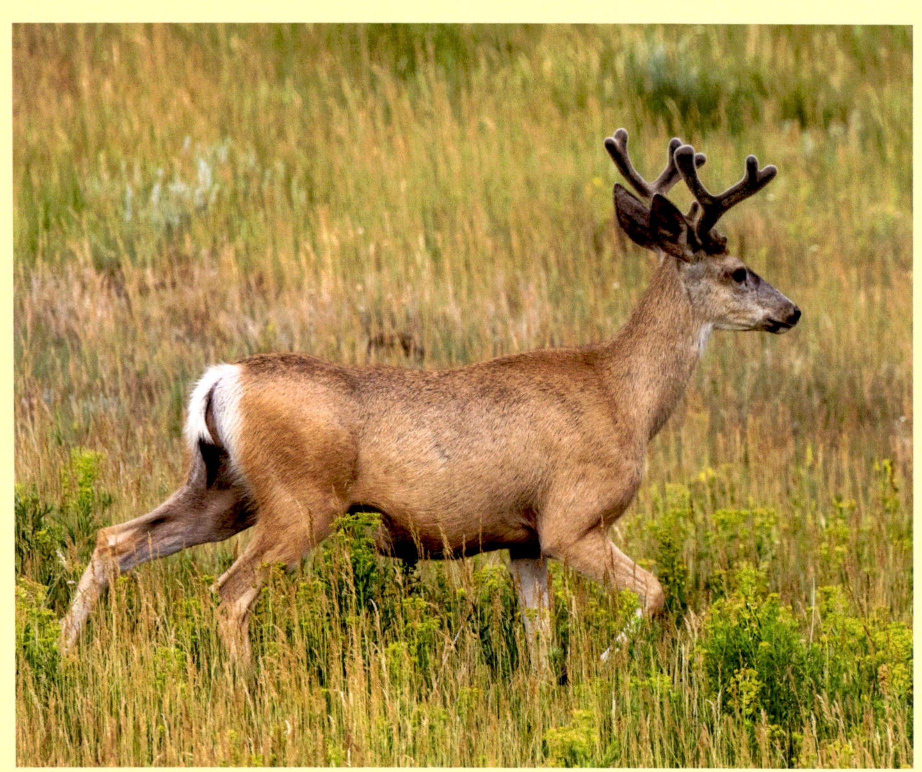

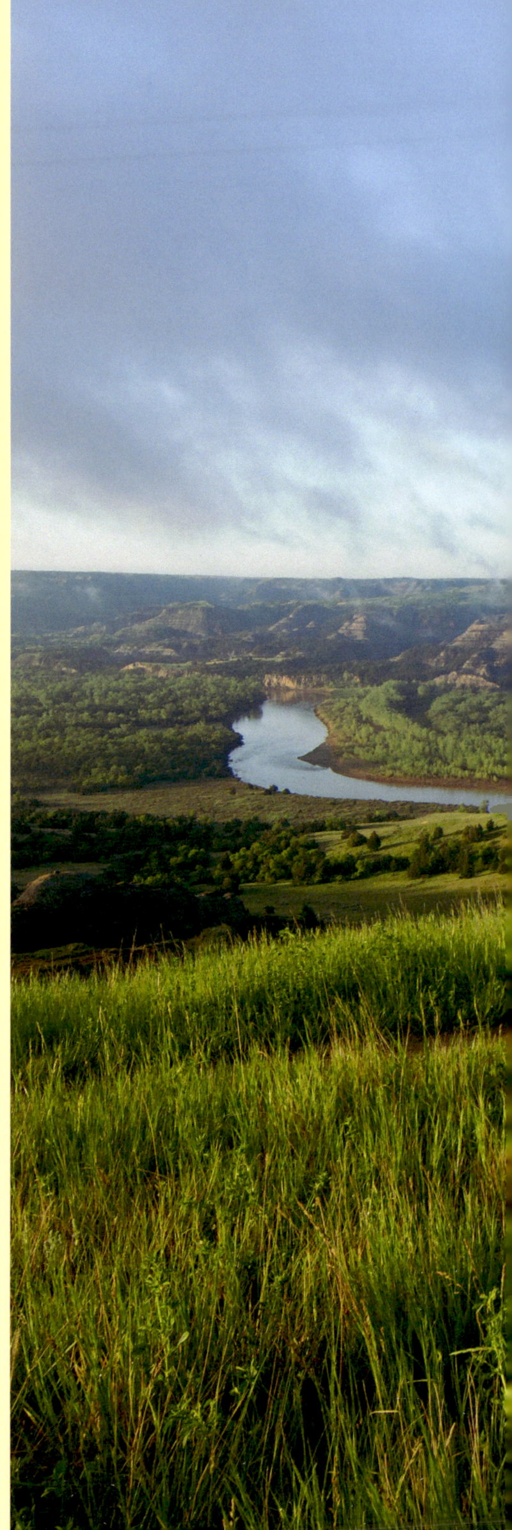

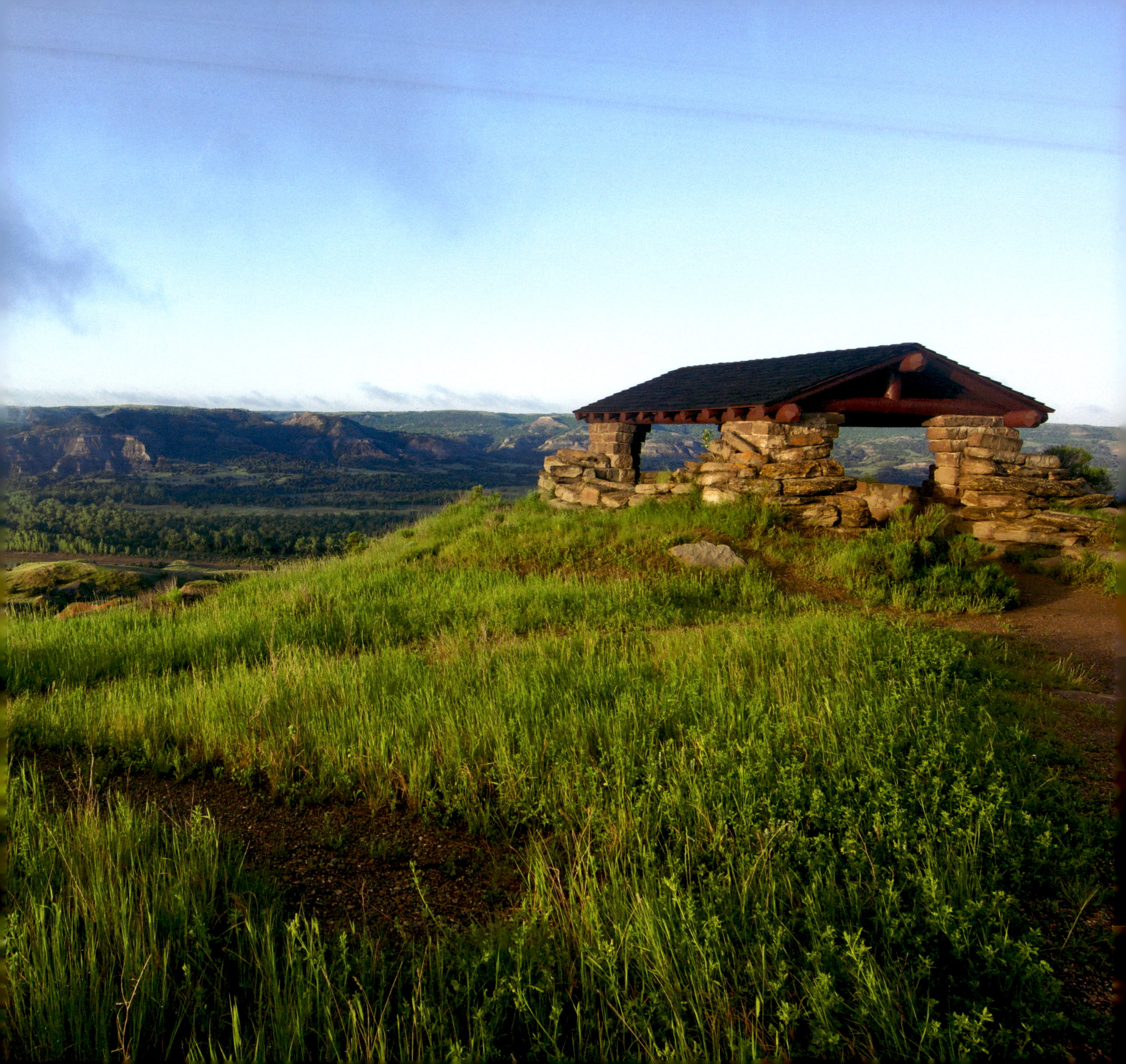

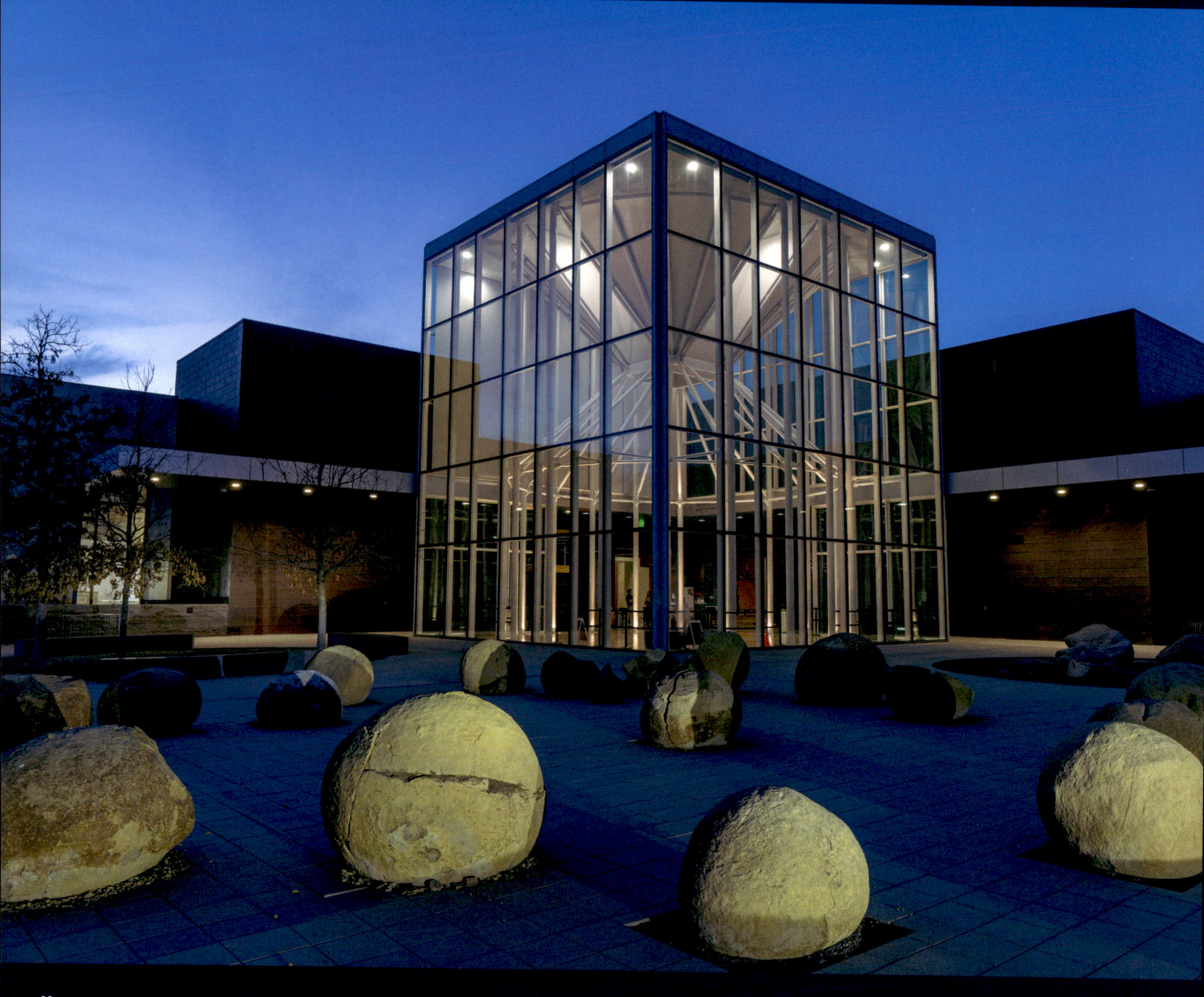

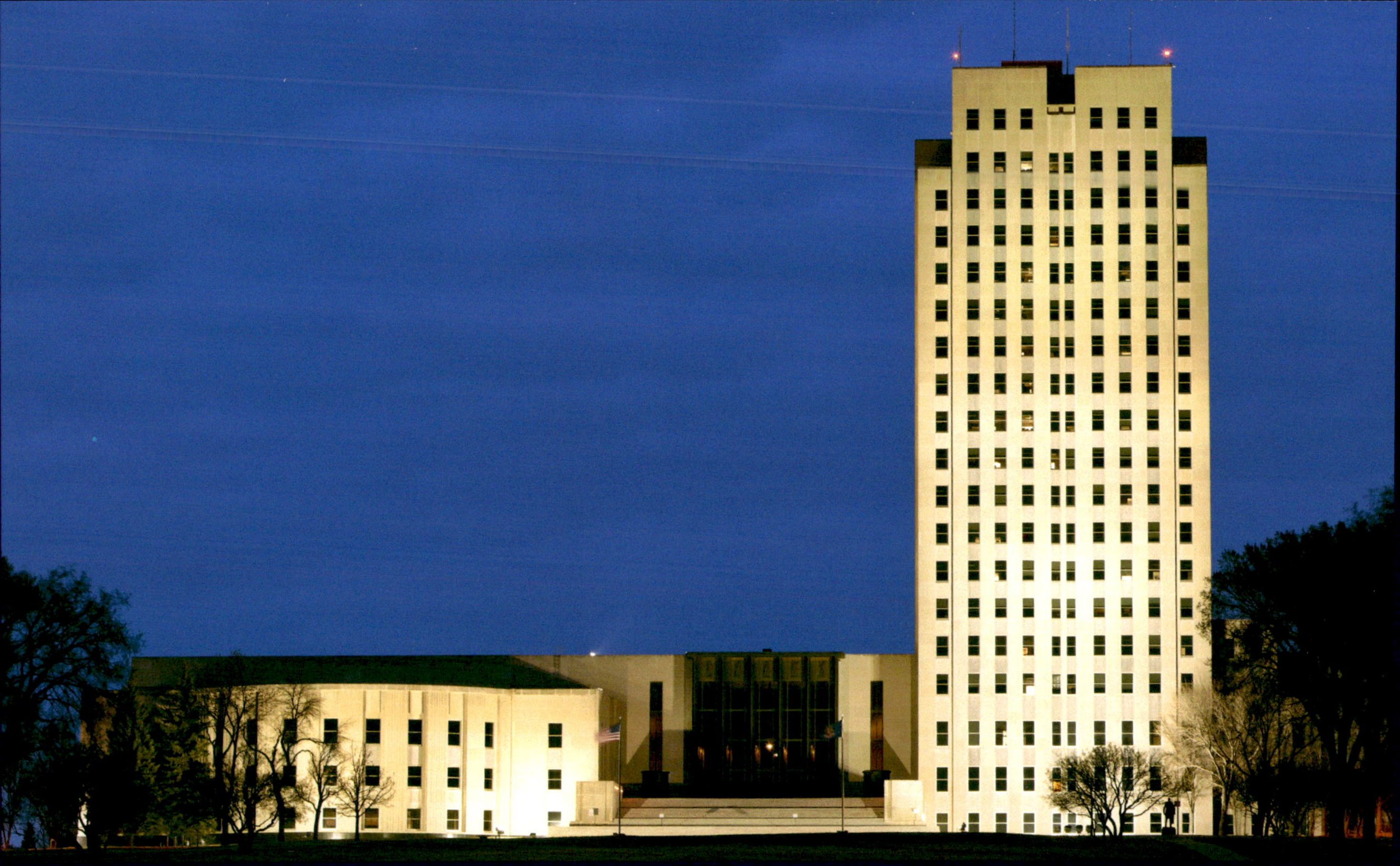

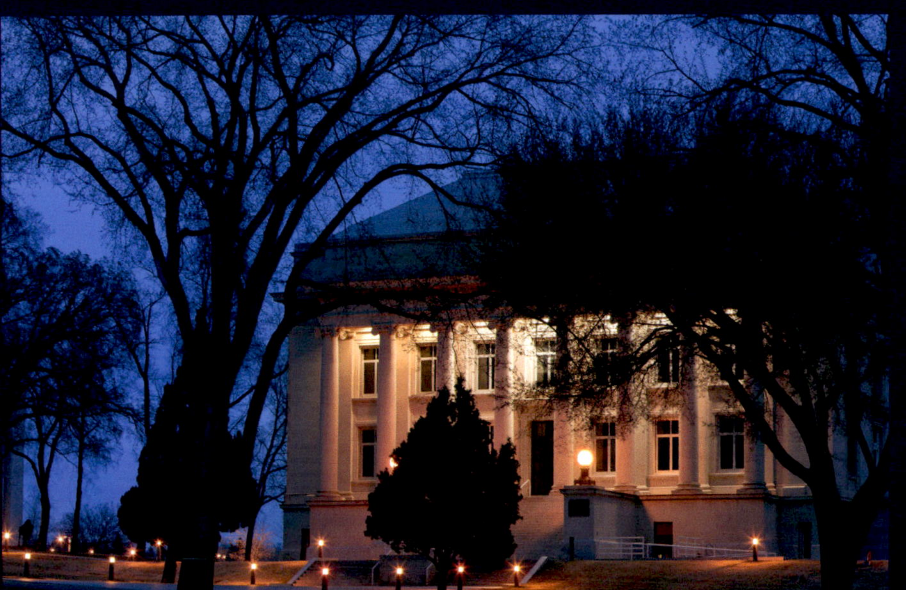

Above: Known as "the Skyscraper on the Prairie," the Art Deco-style North Dakota Capitol in Bismarck is the tallest habitable building in the state.

Left: Sharing the state capitol grounds in Bismarck, the Liberty Memorial Building houses the State Library and offices of the North Dakota Parks & Recreation Department.

Facing page: In Bismarck, the North Dakota Heritage Center & State Museum houses exhibits on geology, dinosaurs, early peoples and Native American cultures, agricultural life, birds of North Dakota, and more. Outside the entrance are seventeen "cannonball" concretions, 56-million-year-old sandstone orbs, that inspired the name of the Cannonball River.

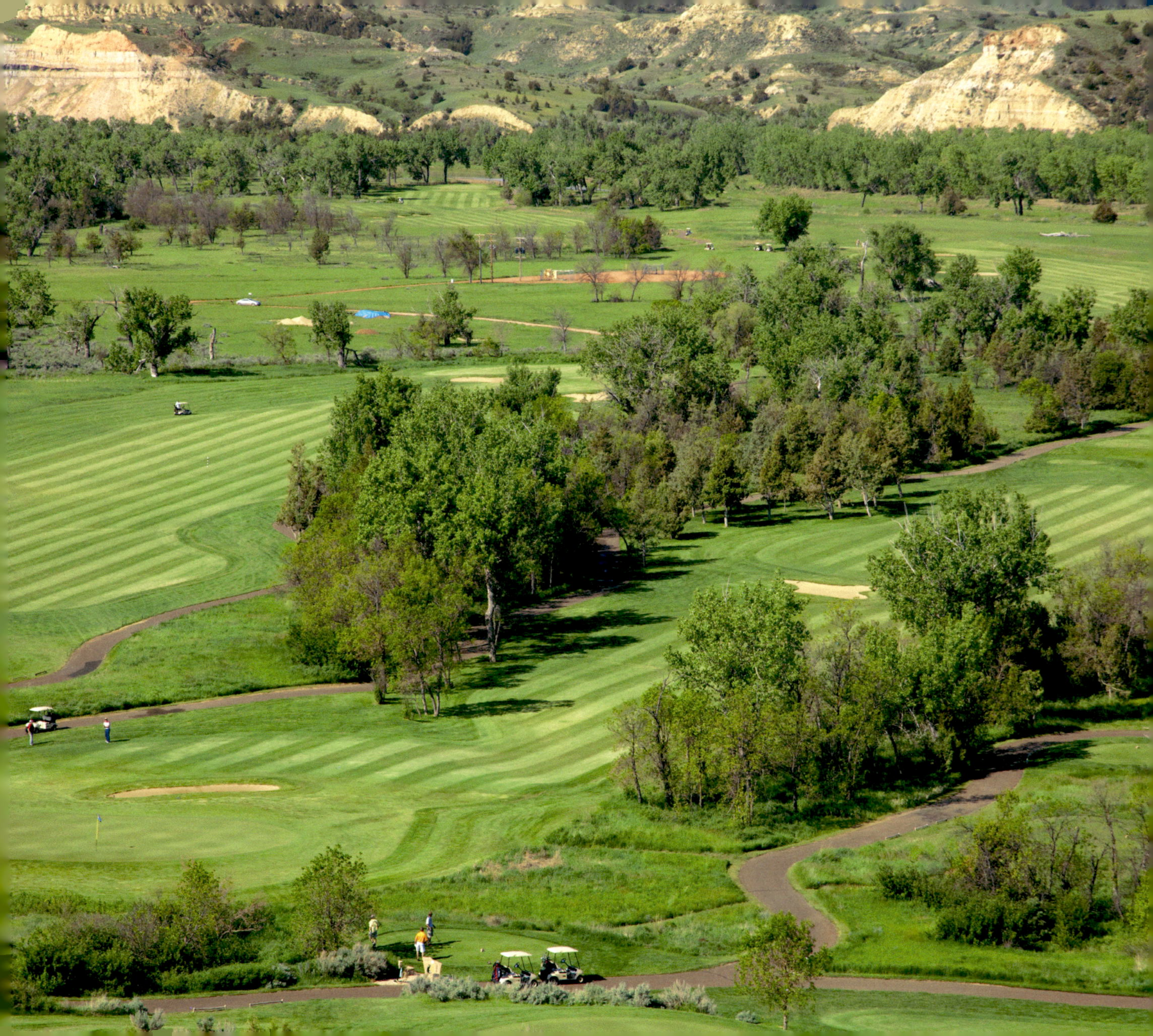

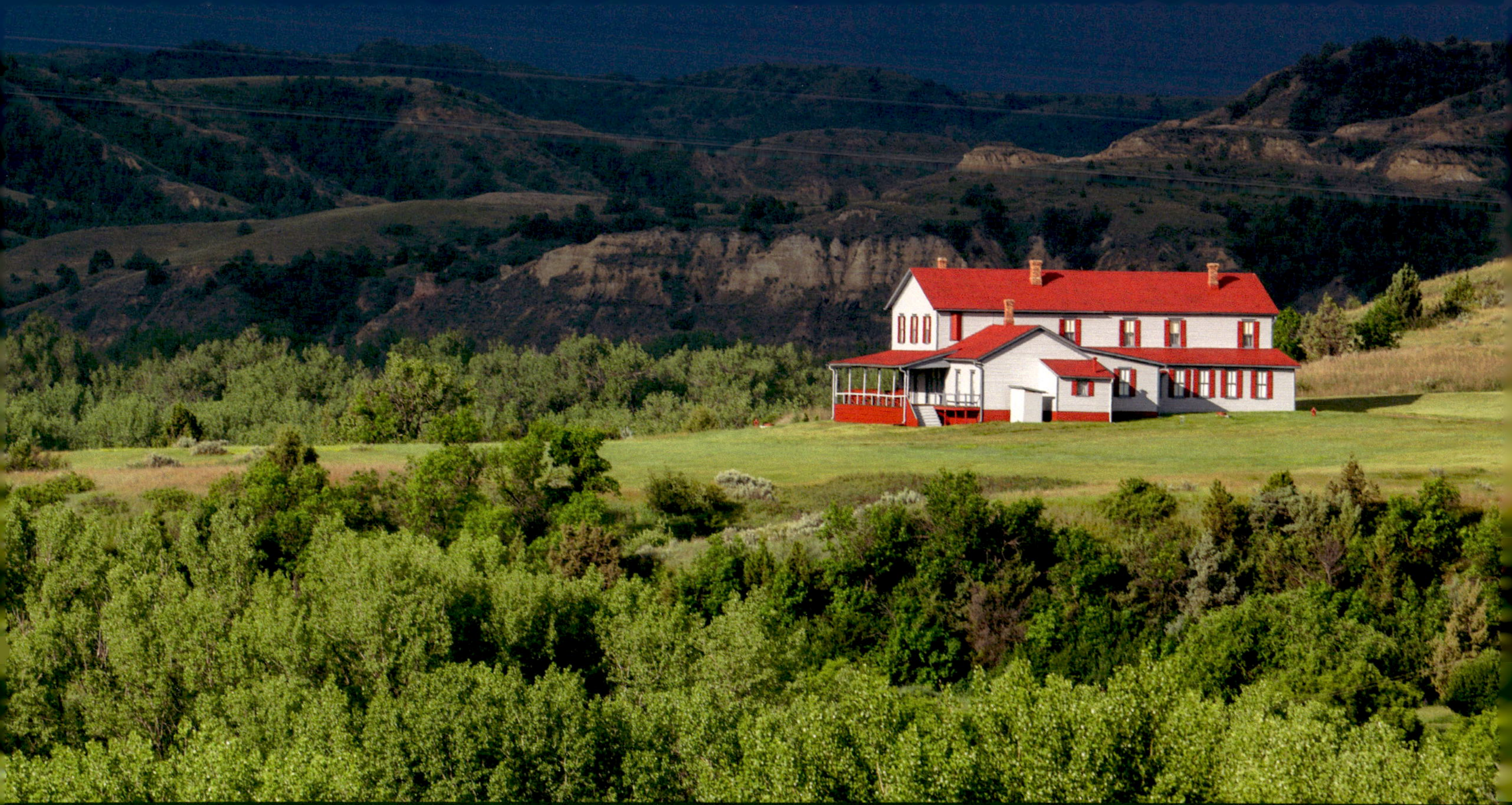

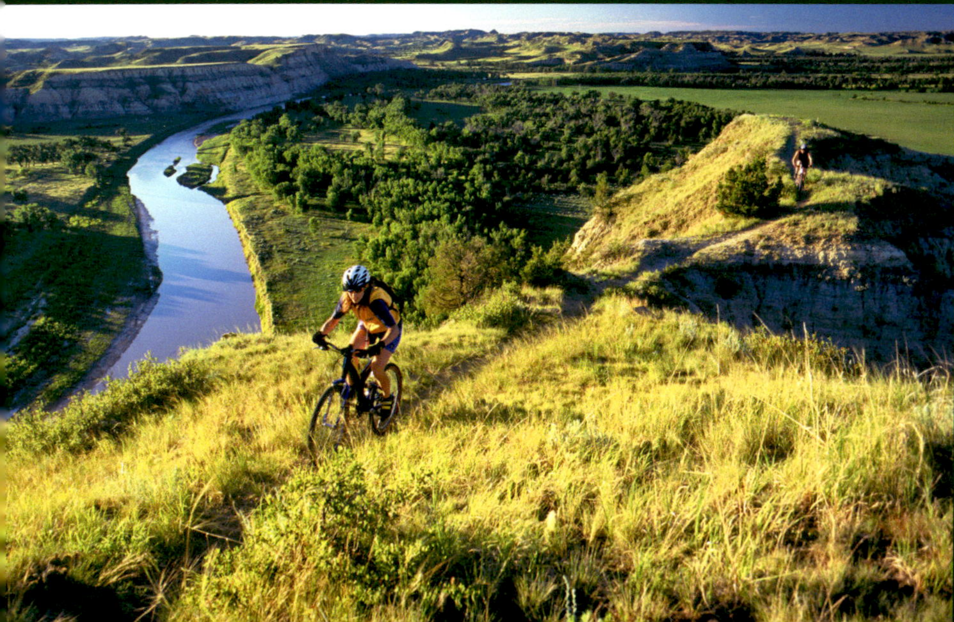

Above: Arriving from France, the Marquis de Mores built Chateau de Mores in 1883 as a hunting lodge and ranch home for his family. Today the home is the centerpiece of a state historic site just west of Medora, which is named for the Marquis' wife, Medora Marie von Hoffman.

Left: Linking the North and South Units of Theodore Roosevelt National Park, the 144-mile Maah Daah Hey Trail draws mountain bikers, hikers, and horseback riders from all over.

Facing page: Nestled between badland buttes and the Little Missouri River just south of Medora, the 18-hole Bully Pulpit Golf Course offers a top-ranked links experience in a uniquely North Dakotan landscape.

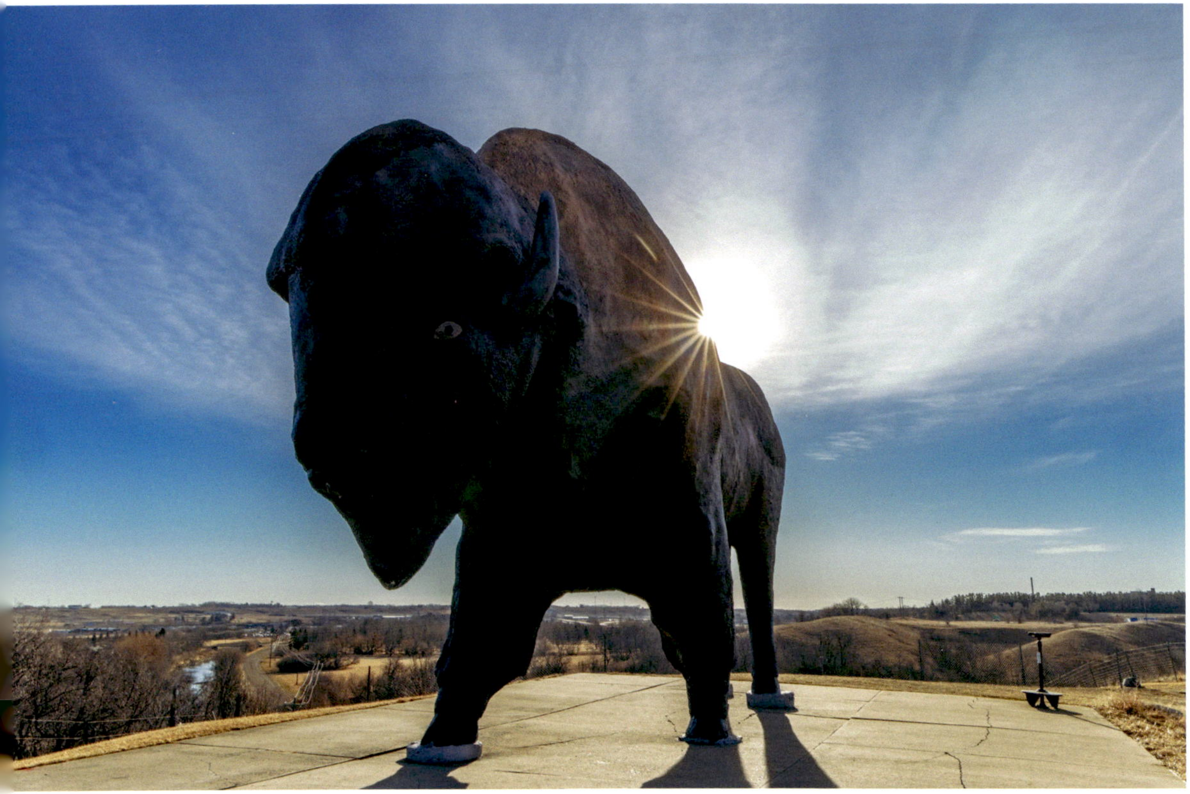

Above: Standing 26 feet tall and 46 feet long and weighing 54 tons, the "World's Largest Buffalo Monument" surveys his domain above Jamestown.

Right: Celebrating the local dairy industry, 38-foot-tall *Salem Sue* stands proudly as the "World's Largest Holstein" on the outskirts of New Salem.

Far right: Snug against the Manitoba border in the Turtle Mountains north of Bottineau, Lake Metigoshe State Park offers boat access to the sprawling lake as well as fishing docks, 13 miles of hiking and mountain biking trails, camping, cabins, and winter sports.

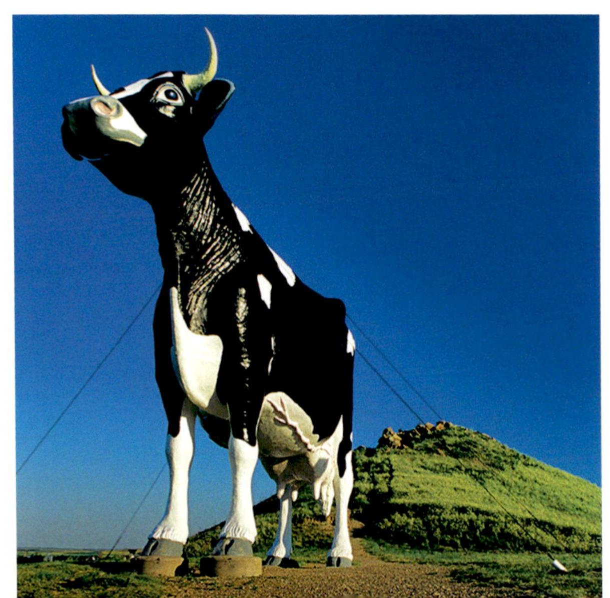

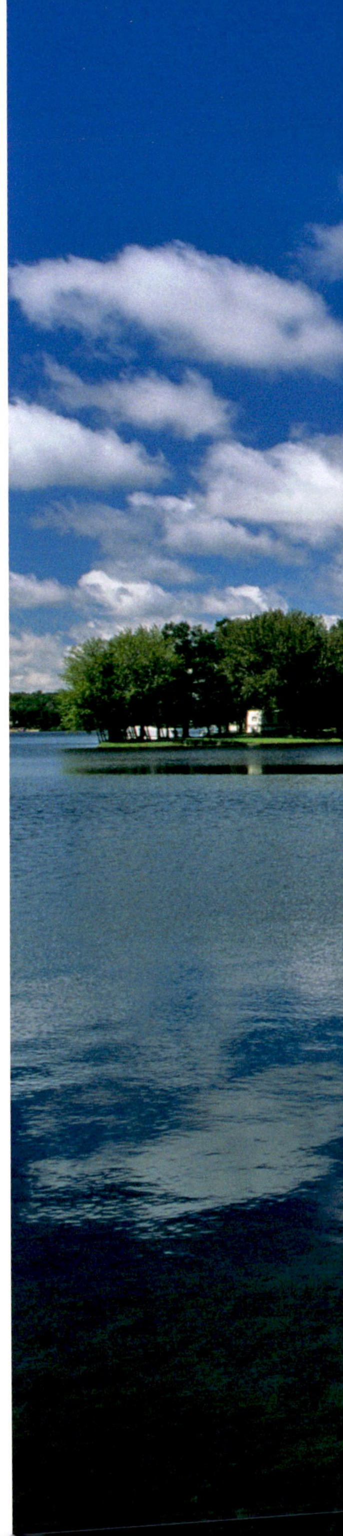

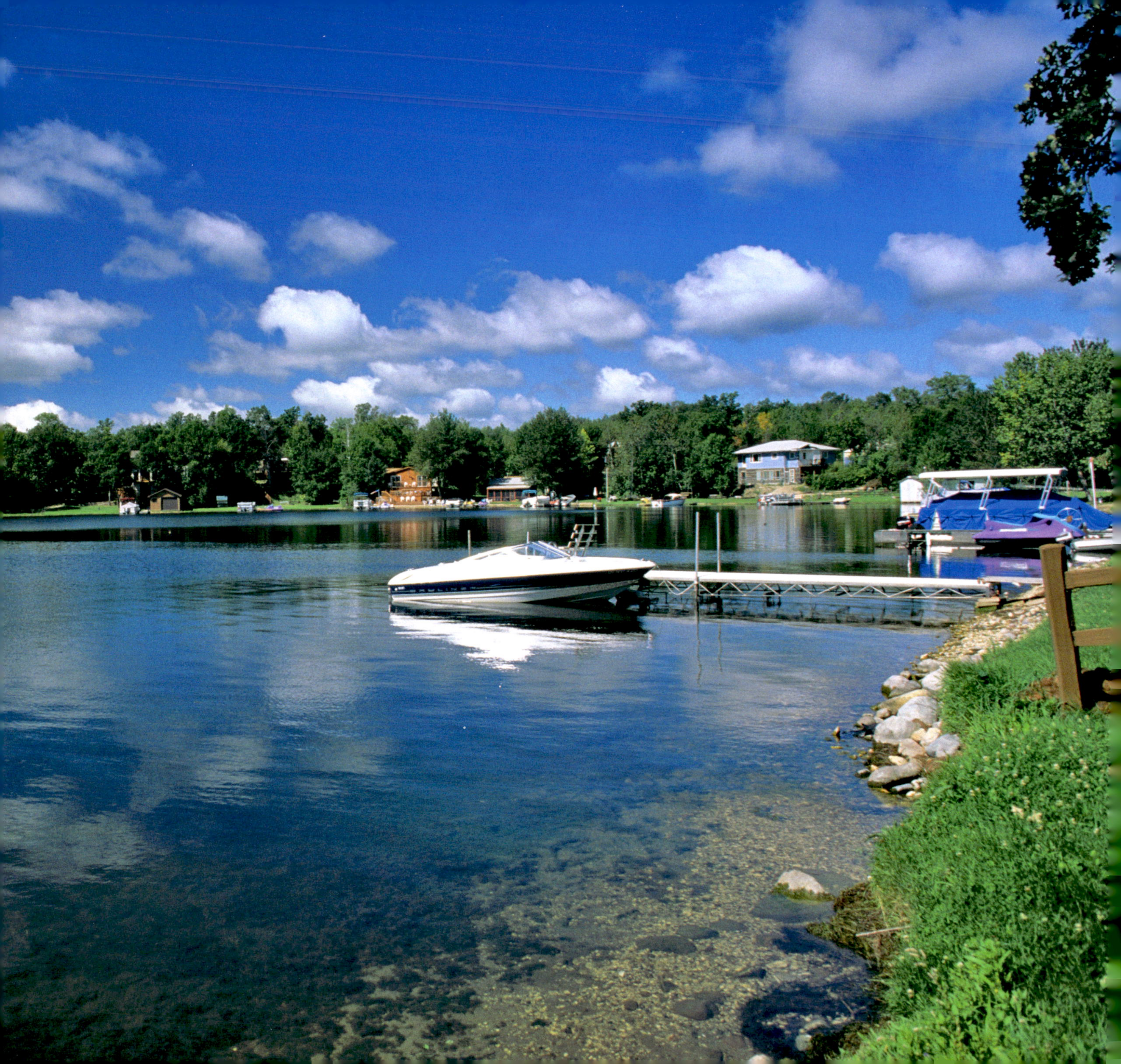

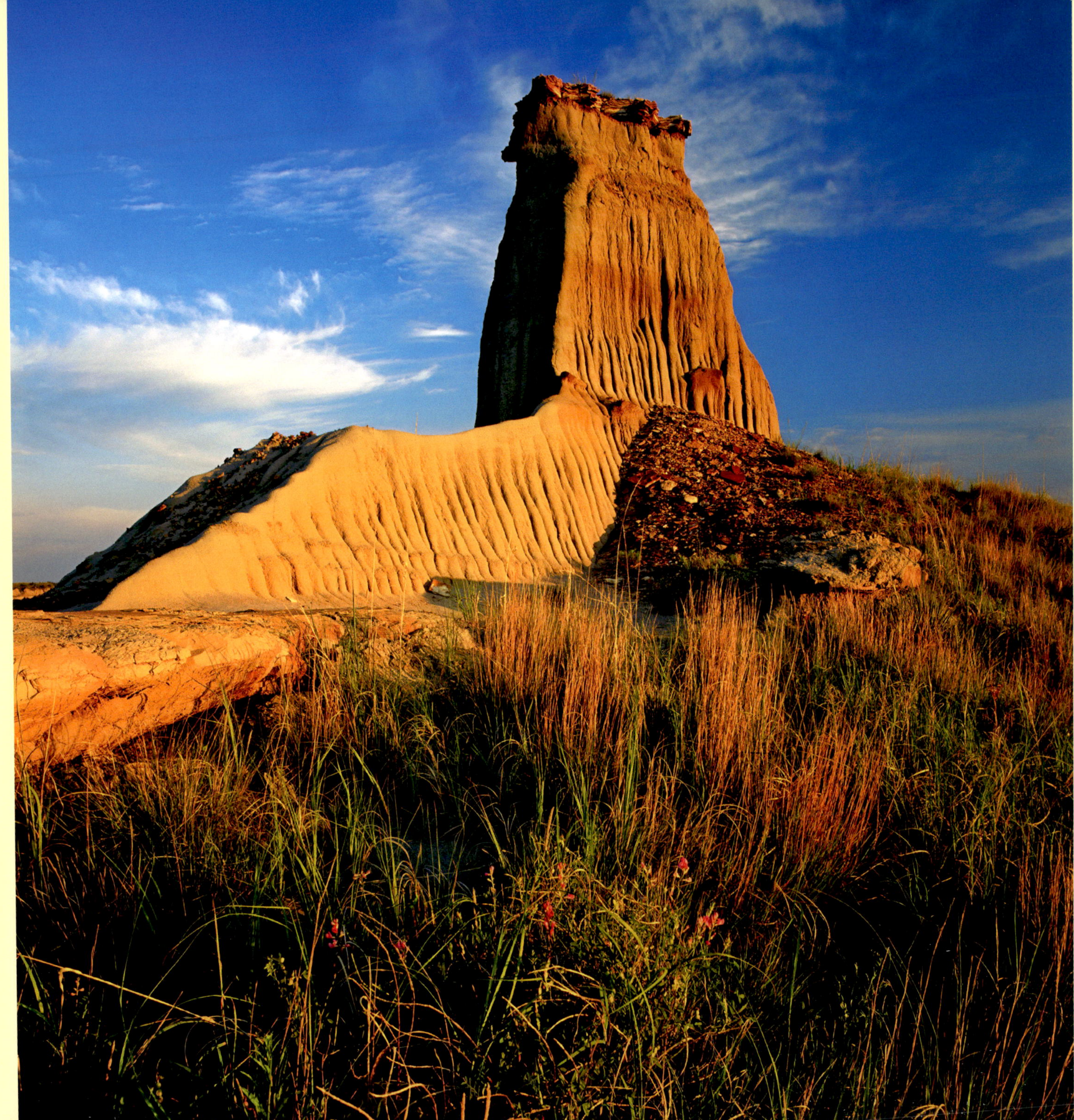

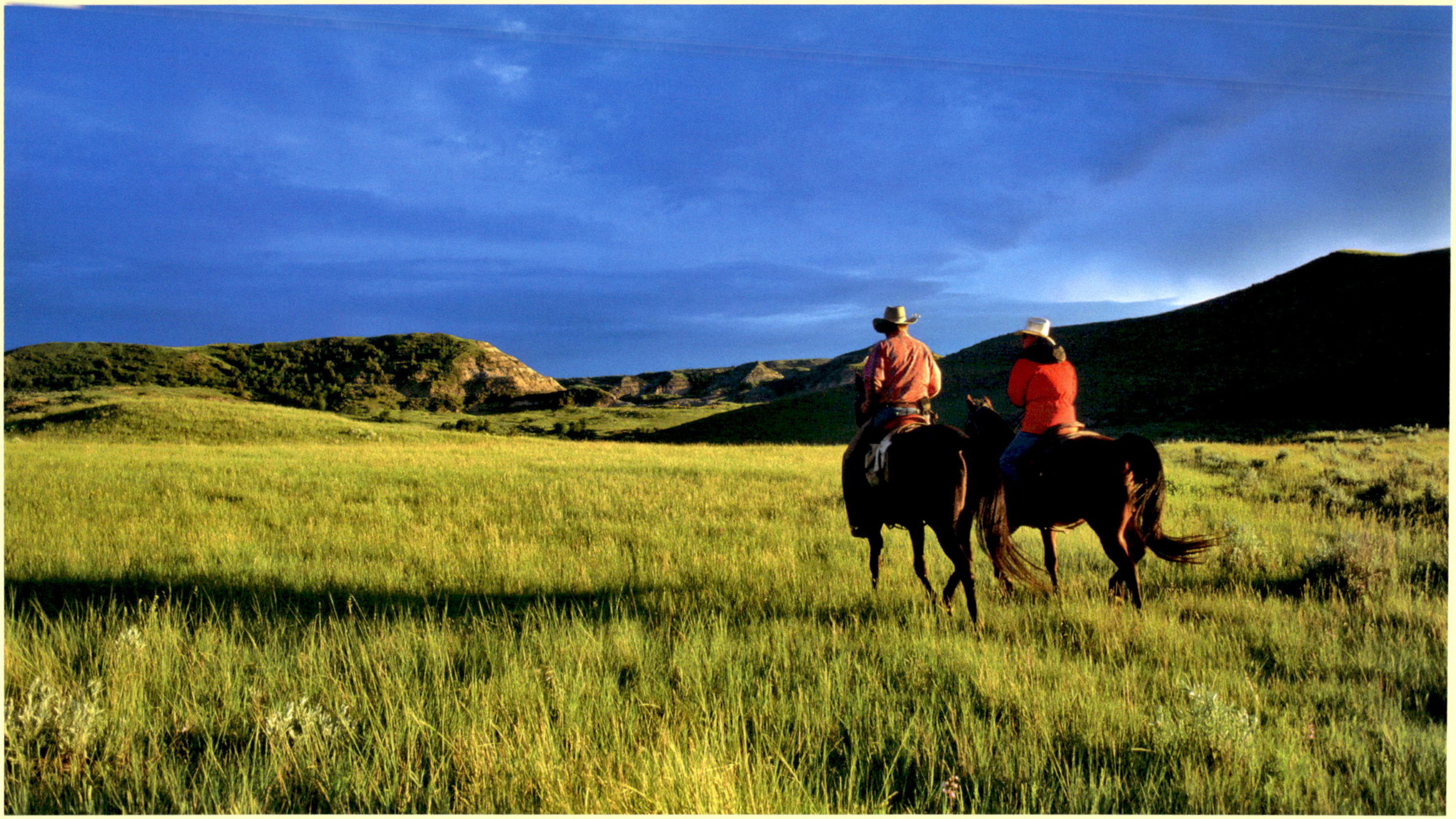

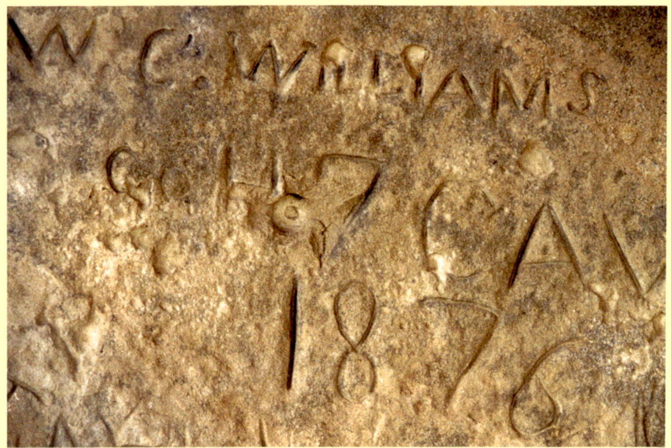

Above: Horseback riders are welcome on the non-motorized-use Maah Daah Hey Trail through Little Missouri National Grassland.

Left: While camped in May 1876 on their way to Montana, two of George Armstrong Custer's soldiers—W. C. Williams and F. Neely—carved their names into a rock in the badlands near present-day Medora. Today, Initial Rock is listed on the National Register of Historic Places. One month after inscribing their names, Williams and Neely survived the Battle of the Little Bighorn.

Facing page: Caprocks shield a badlands sandstone tower in Little Missouri National Grassland.

Right: Leonard Crunelle's 12-foot-tall bronze statue of Sakakawea and her son, Jean Baptiste Charbonneau, stands in a place of honor on the State Capitol grounds in Bismarck.

Far right: Tepees greet the sun at the Knife River Indian Villages National Historic Site near Stanton.

Following pages: The Oxbow Overlook in the North Unit of Theodore Roosevelt National Park affords an expansive vista over the Little Missouri River and adjacent badlands.

Below: Held annually on the second weekend in September, the United Tribes Technical College International Powwow in Bismarck is one of the last large outdoor contest events on the northern Great Plains powwow circuit. More than 900 dancers and musicians gather to celebrate Native American cultures.
PIERRE JEAN DURIEU/SHUTTERSTOCK

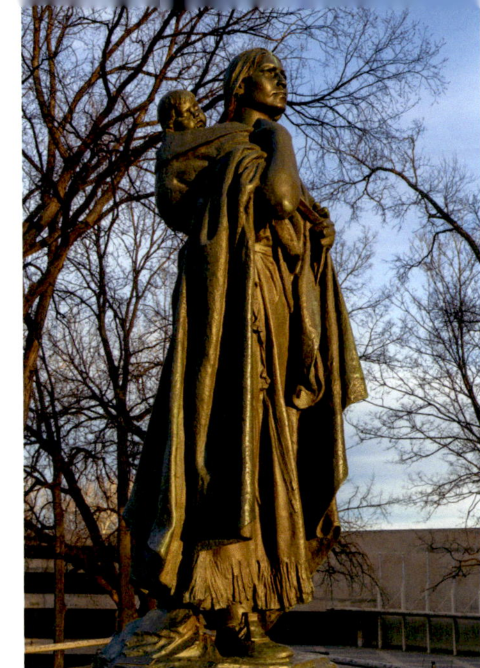

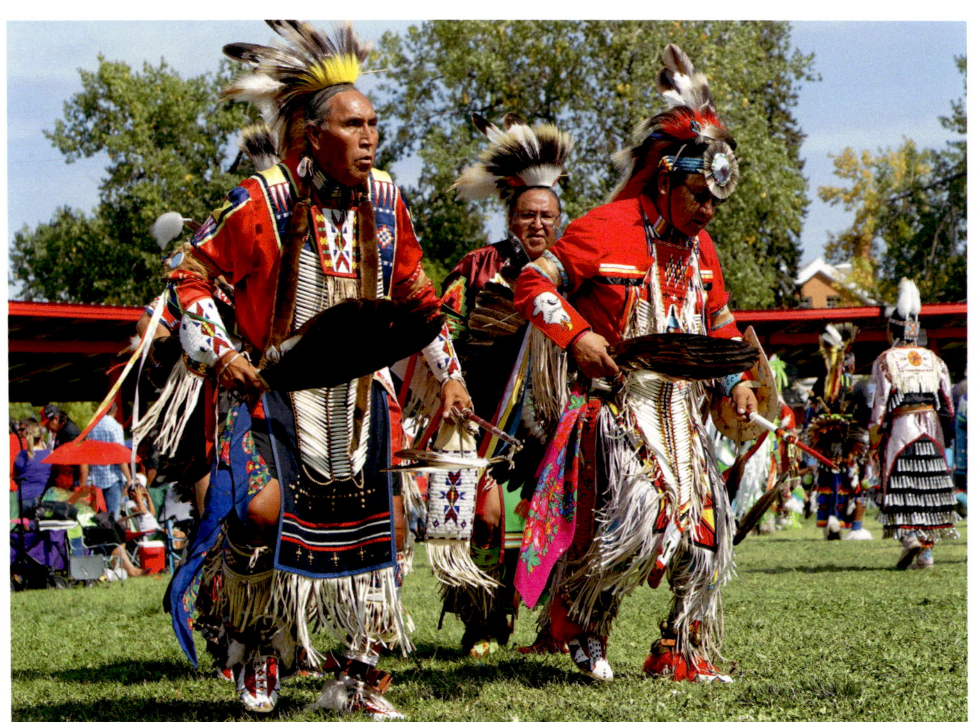

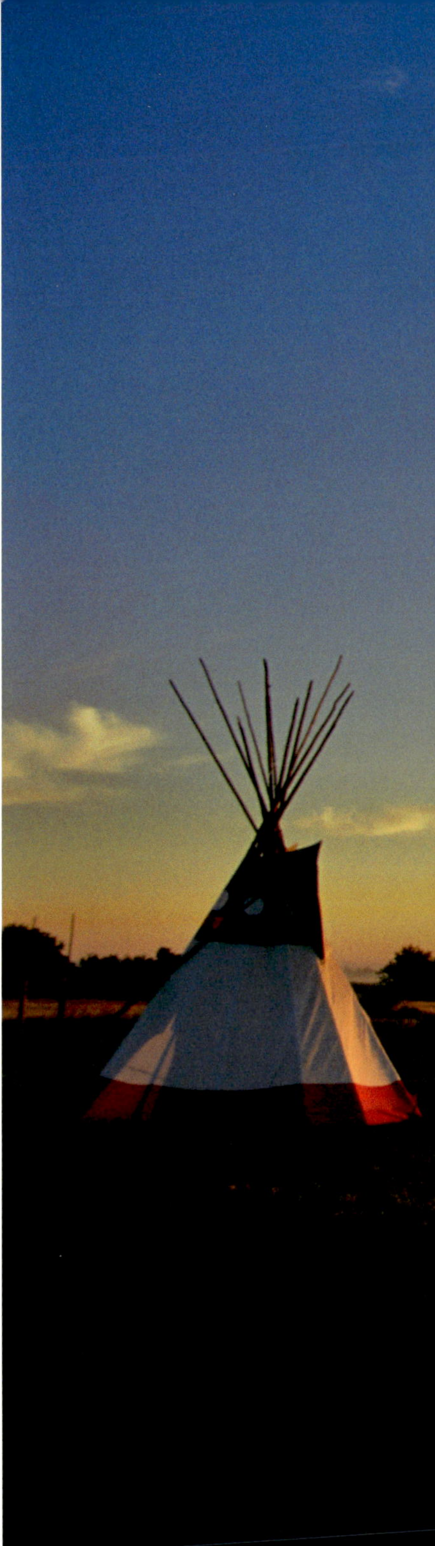

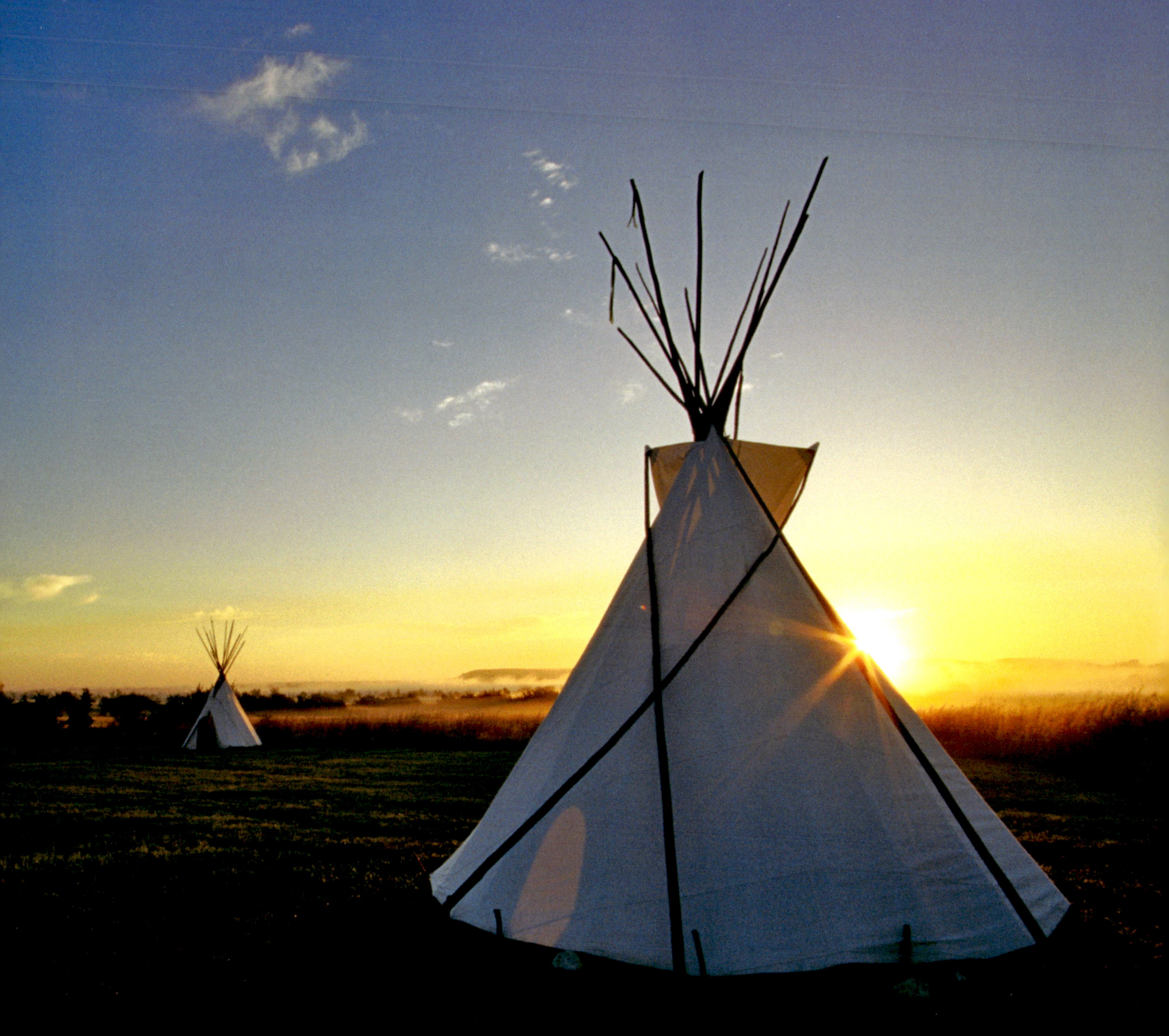

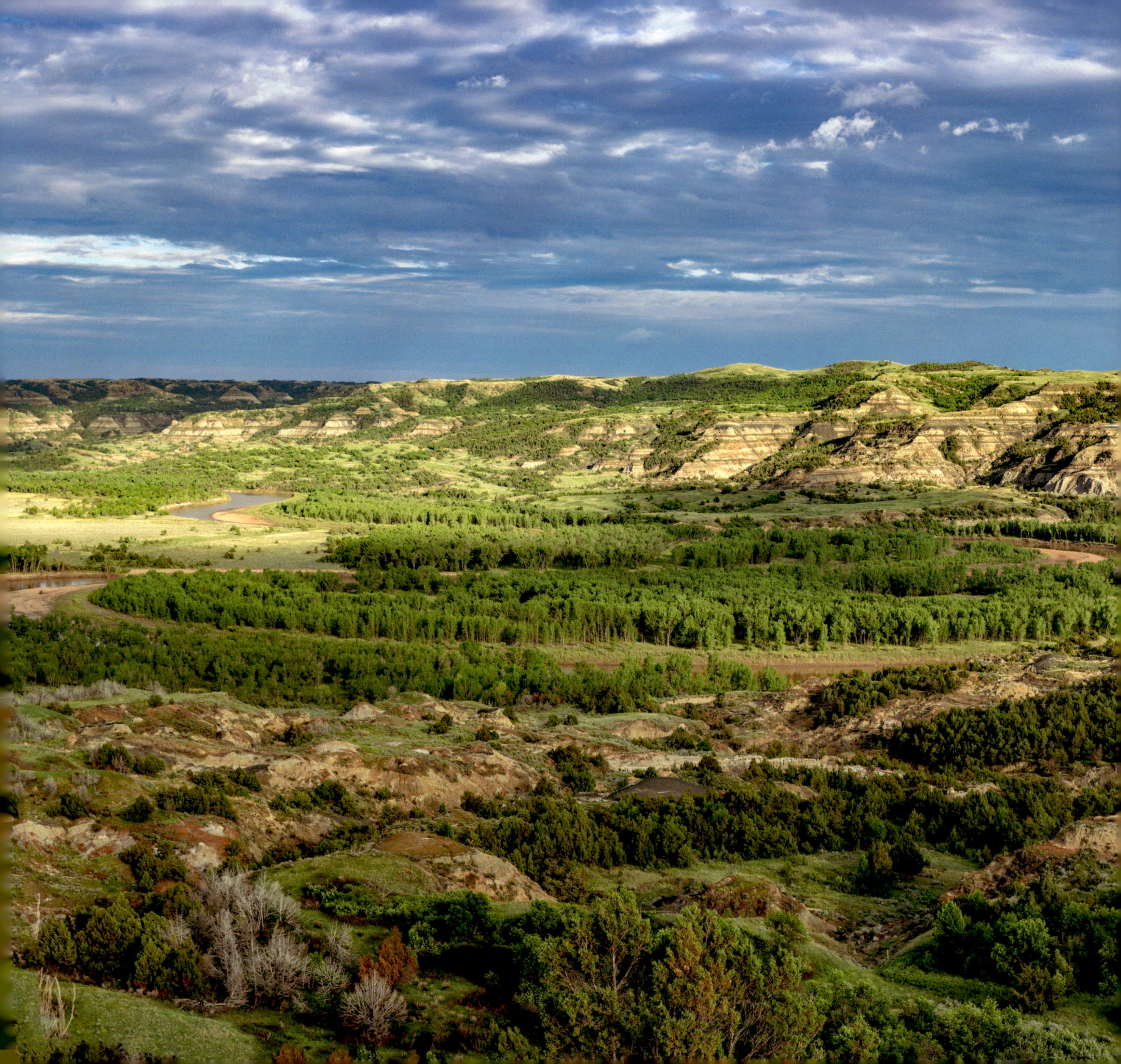

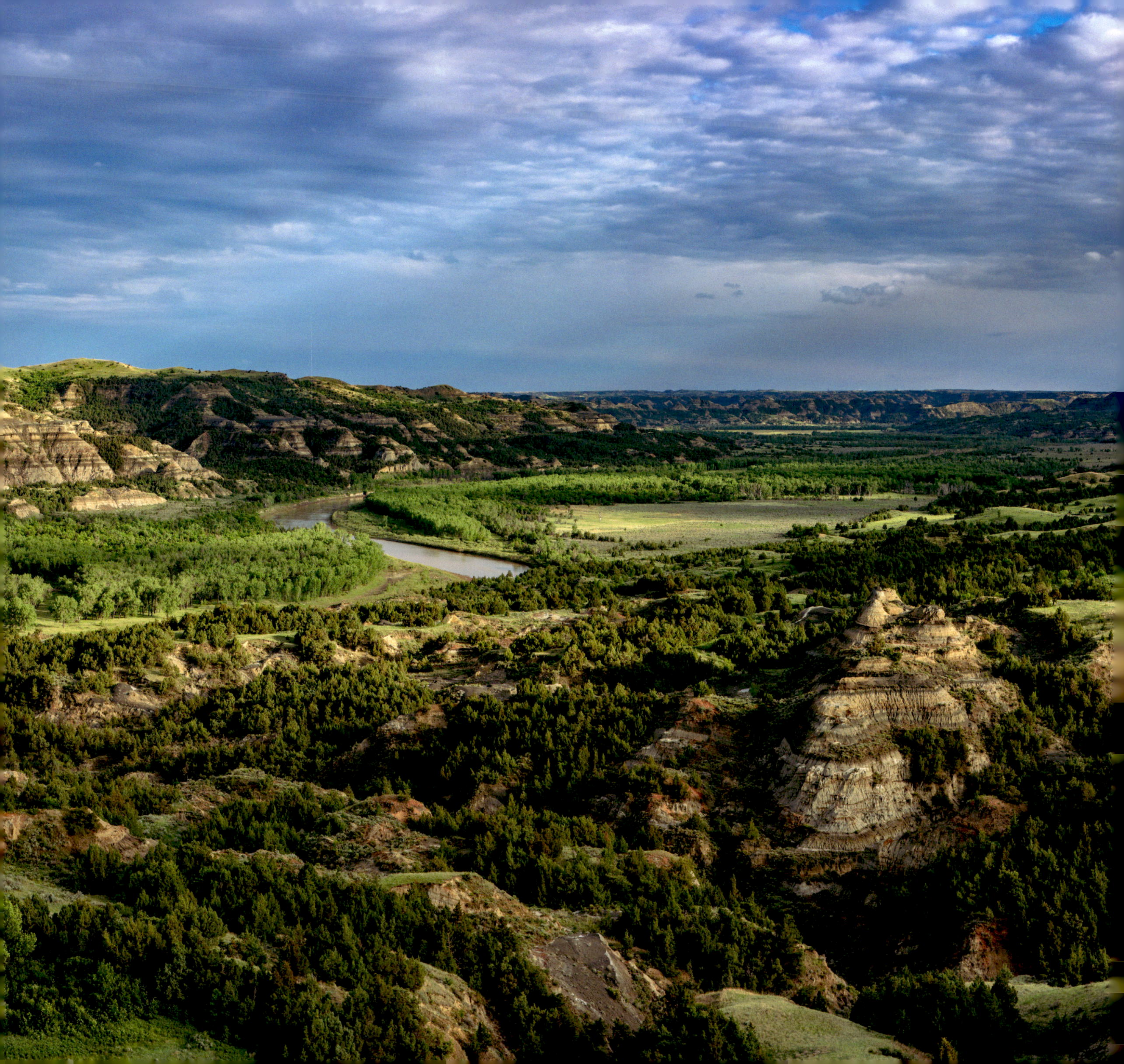

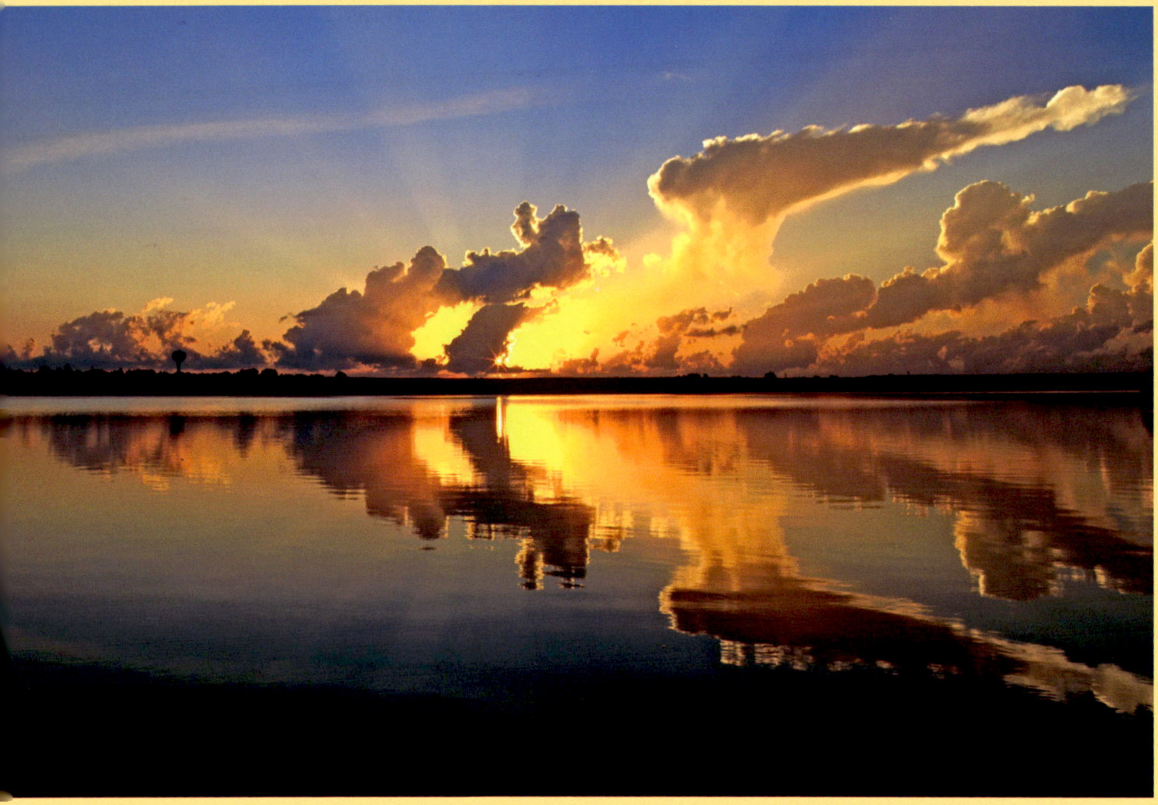

Above: The Little Muddy River near Williston mirrors a prairie sunset.

Right: Sandstone on the north shore of Lake Sakakawea cradles fossilized leaves at Fort Stevenson State Park near the town of Garrison.

Far right: Foxtail barley and the waters of Lake Sakakawea greet a golden sunrise.

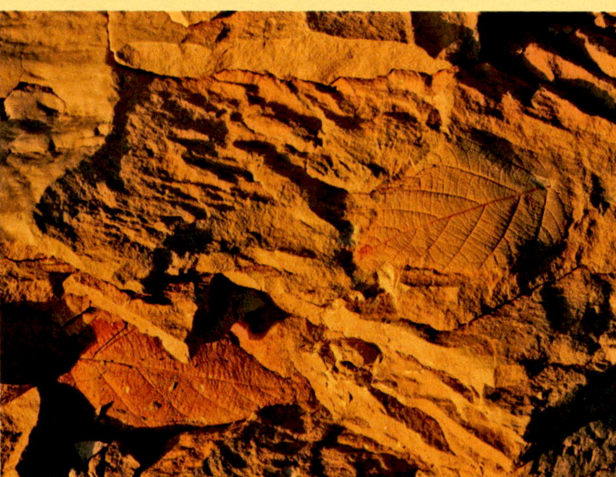

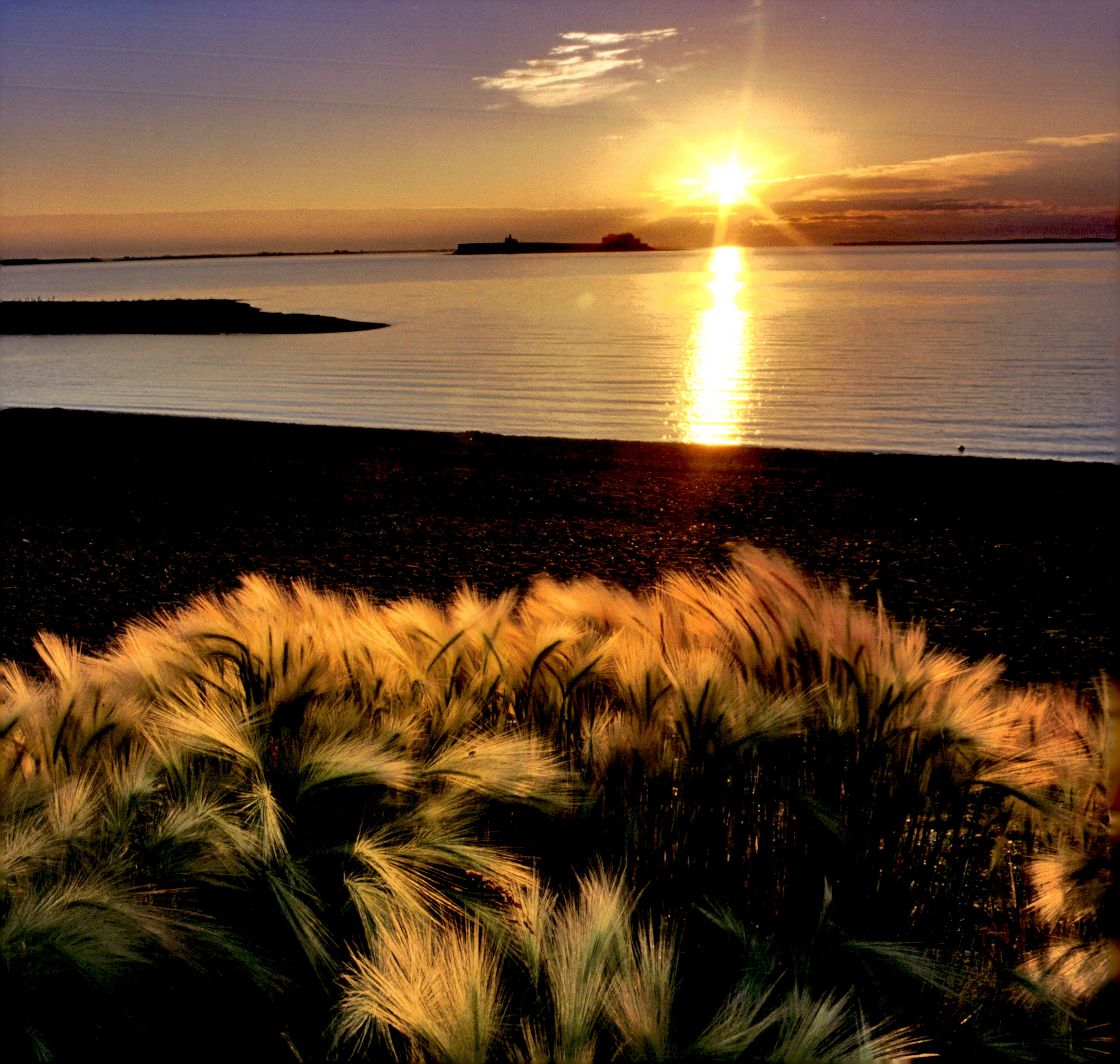

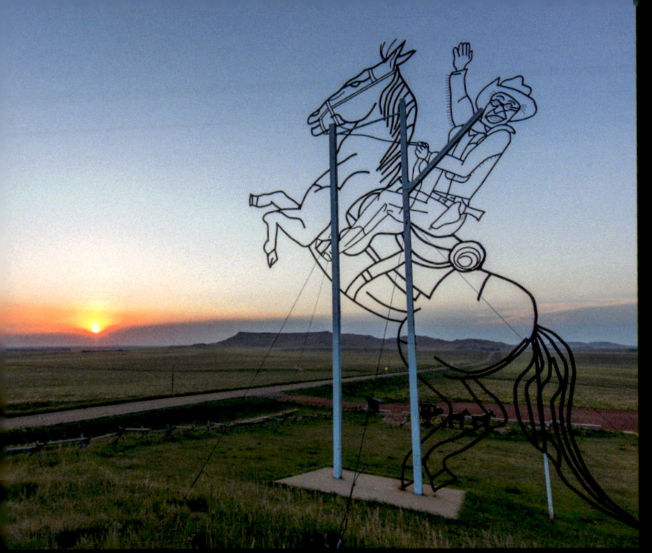

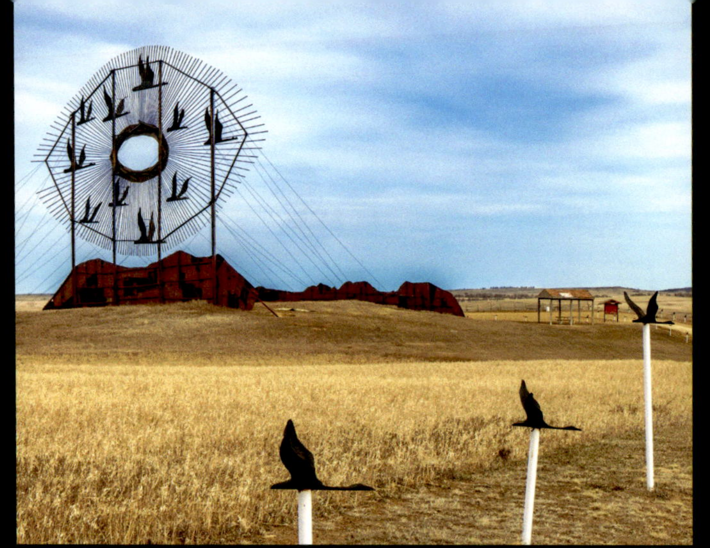

These pages: Starting at Exit 72 on Interstate 94 near Gladstone, the 32-mile Enchanted Highway features seven large metal sculptures before arriving in Regent. Local artist Gary Greff created the whimsical pieces. ***Clockwise from upper left:*** *Teddy Roosevelt Rides Again*, *Geese in Flight*, *Pheasants on the Prairie*, *Fisherman's Dream*, *Tin Family*, *Grasshopper*, and *Deer Crossing*. An eighth sculpture of a dragon in Regent is in progress.

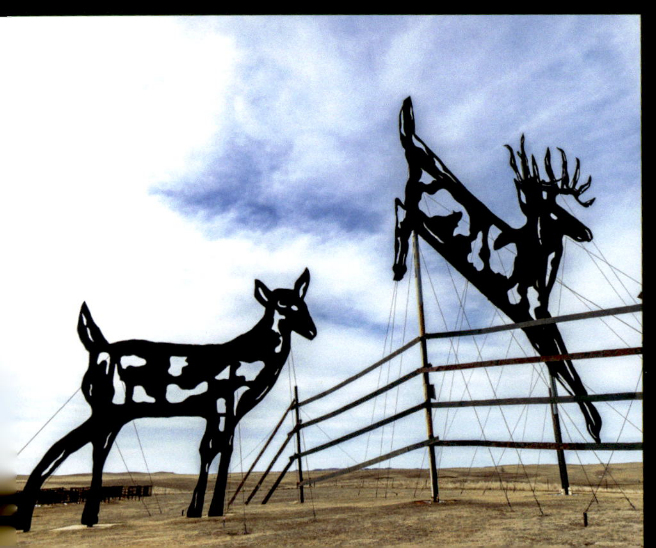

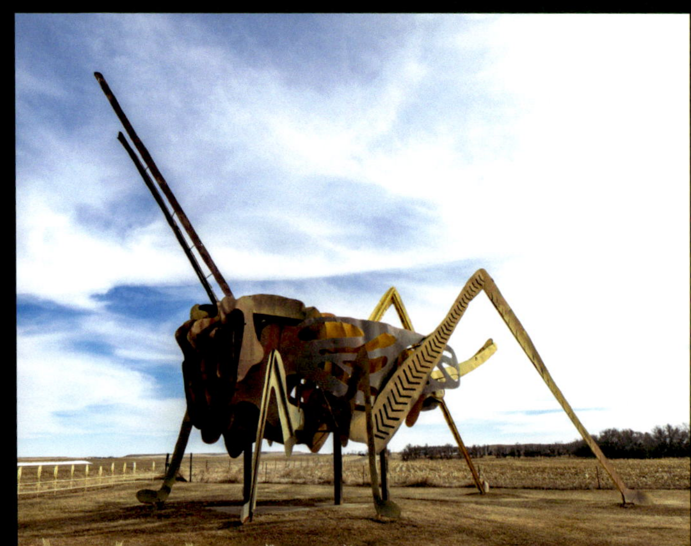

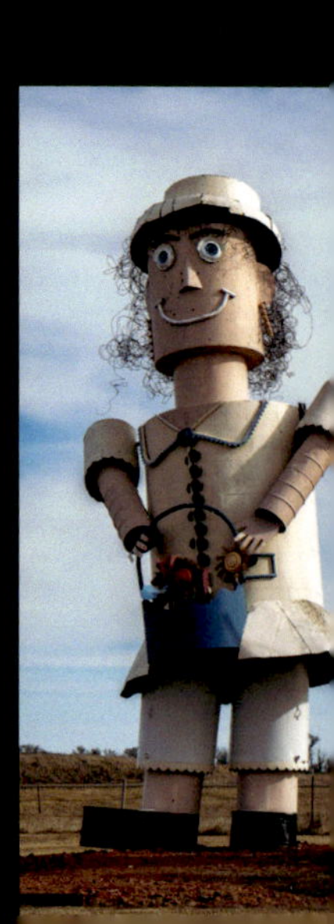

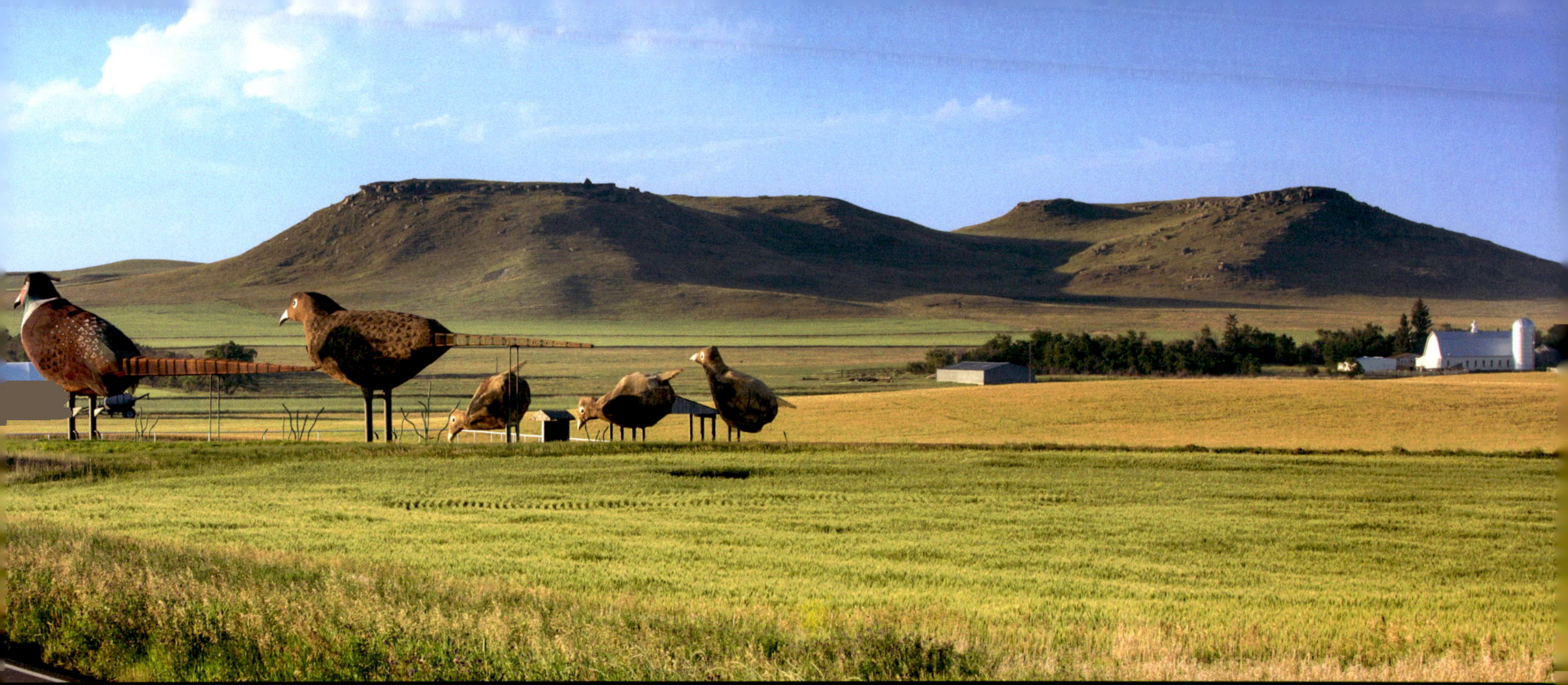

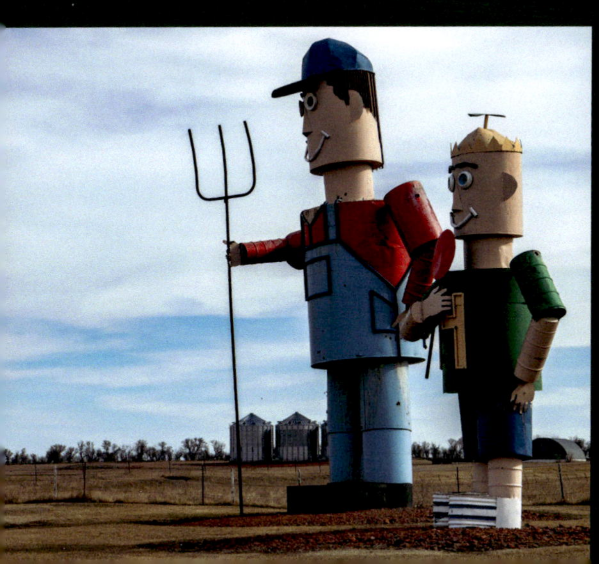

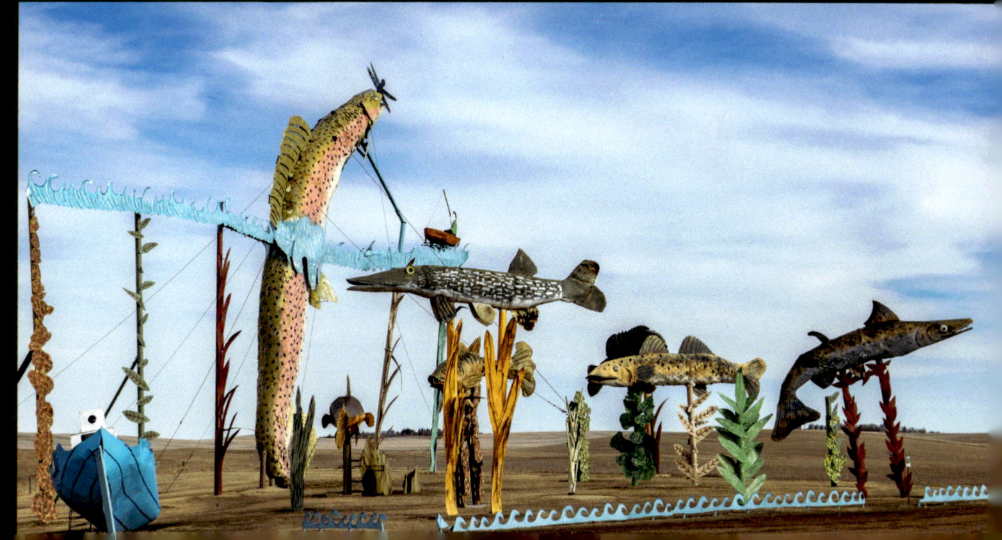

Right: Camp tents glow under the night sky at Burning Coal Vein on the Maah Daah Hey Trail in Little Missouri National Grassland.

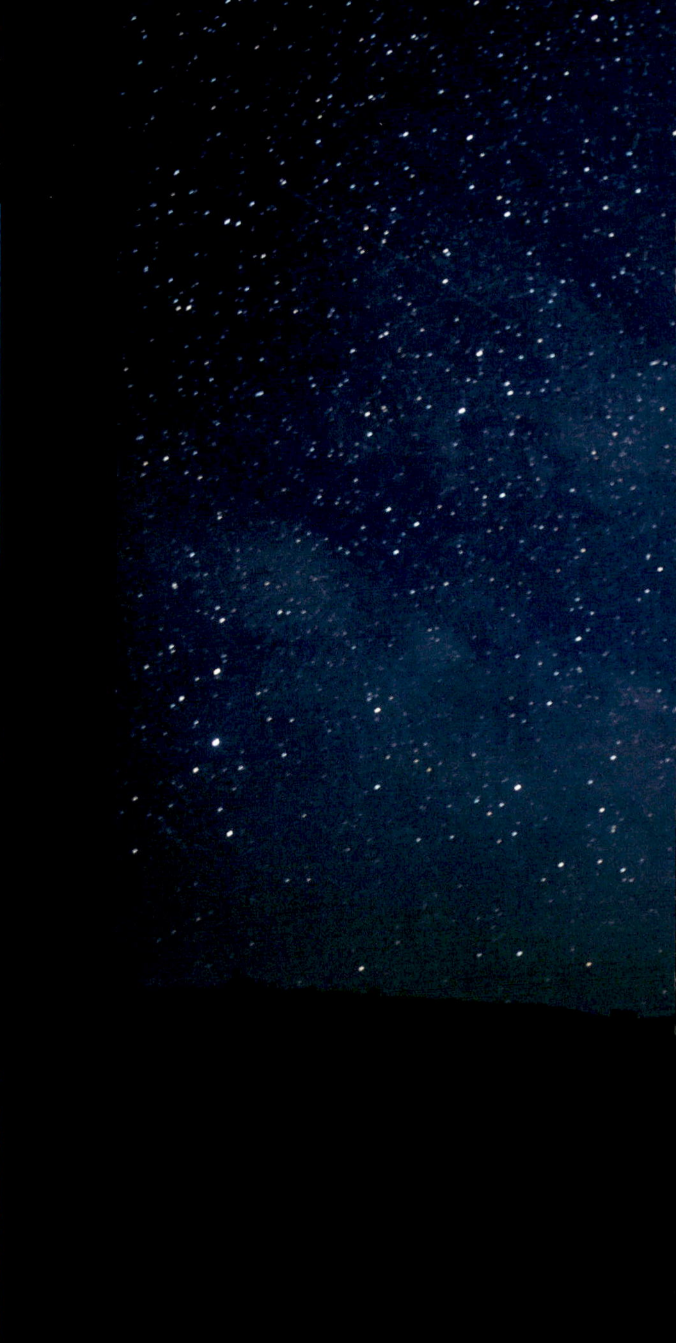

Below: The full moon rises over Standing Rock State Historic Site near Enderlin in Ransom County. The Standing Rock, or *Íyá Bósdata* in Santee Sioux, rises from atop a 2,000-year-old burial mound overlooking the Sheyenne River.

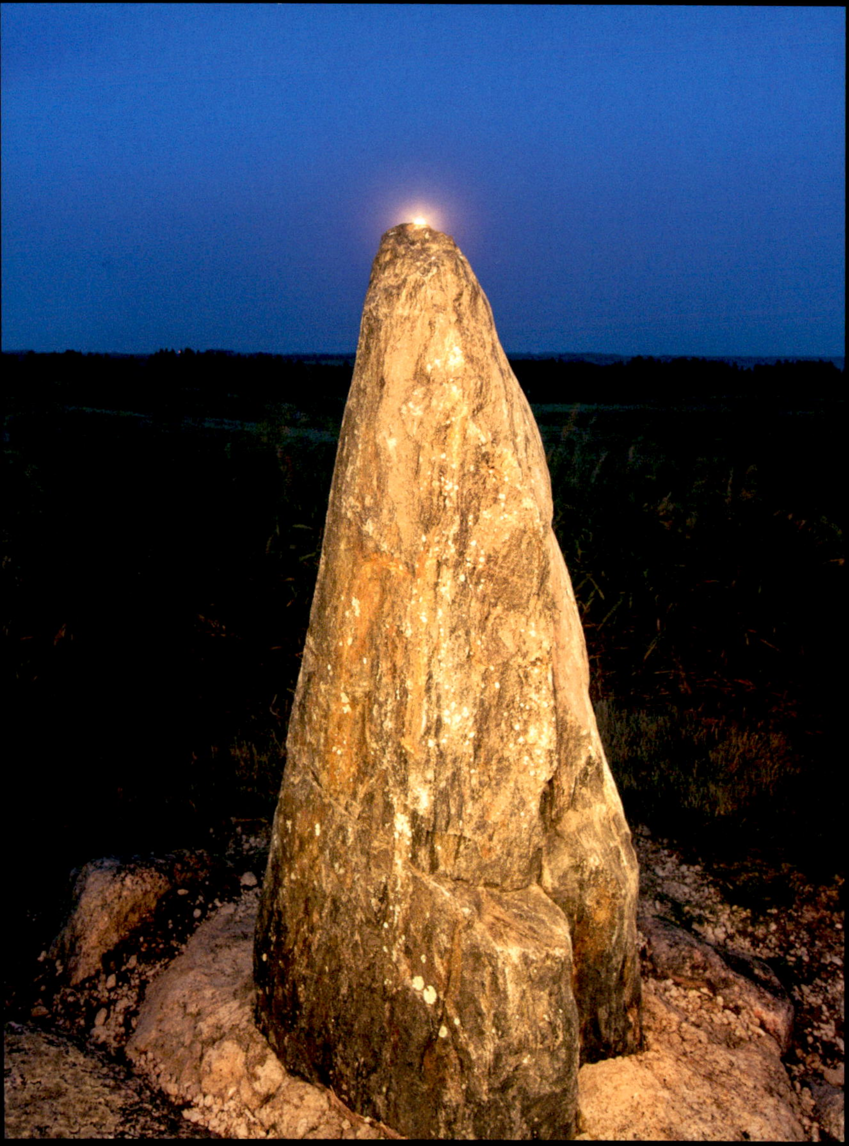

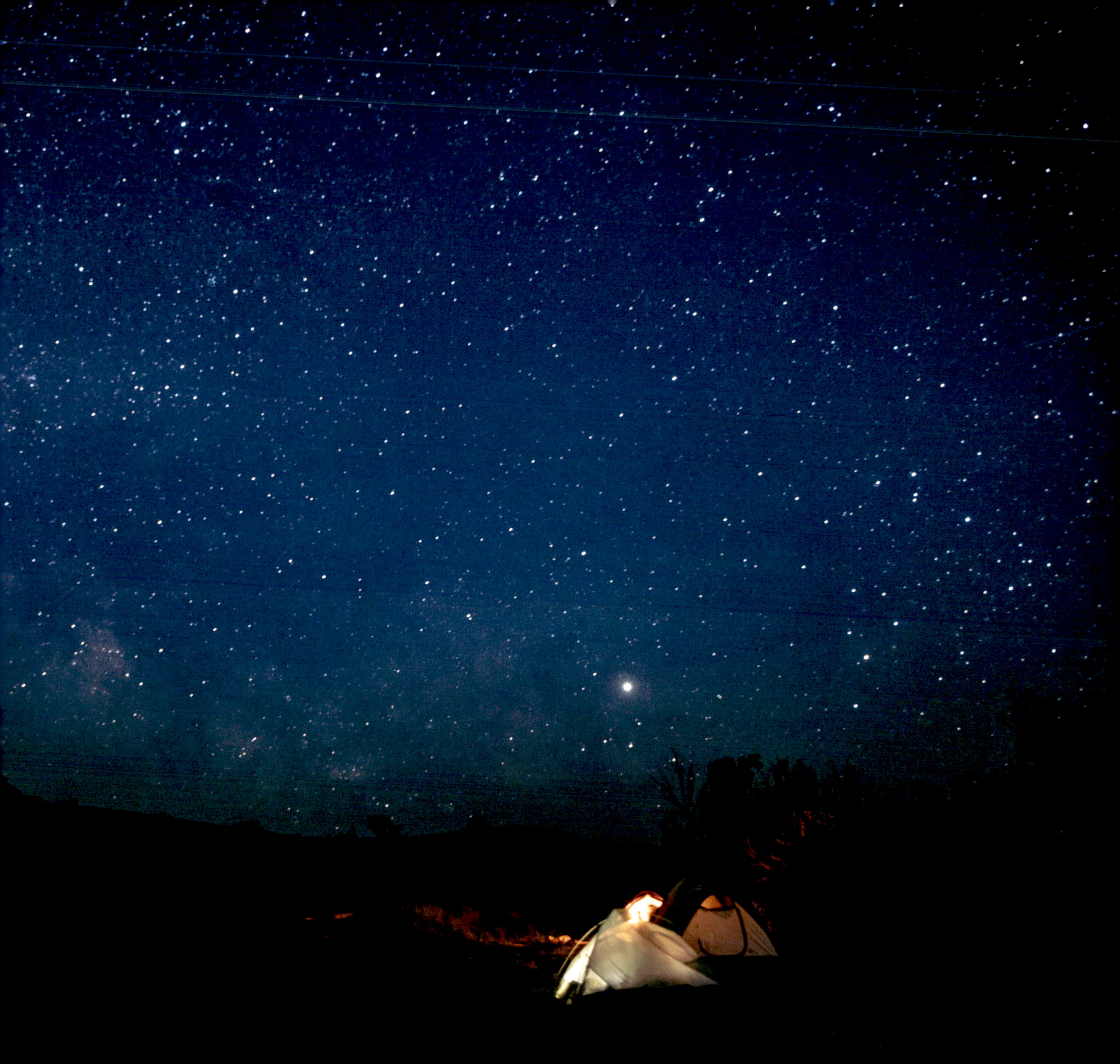

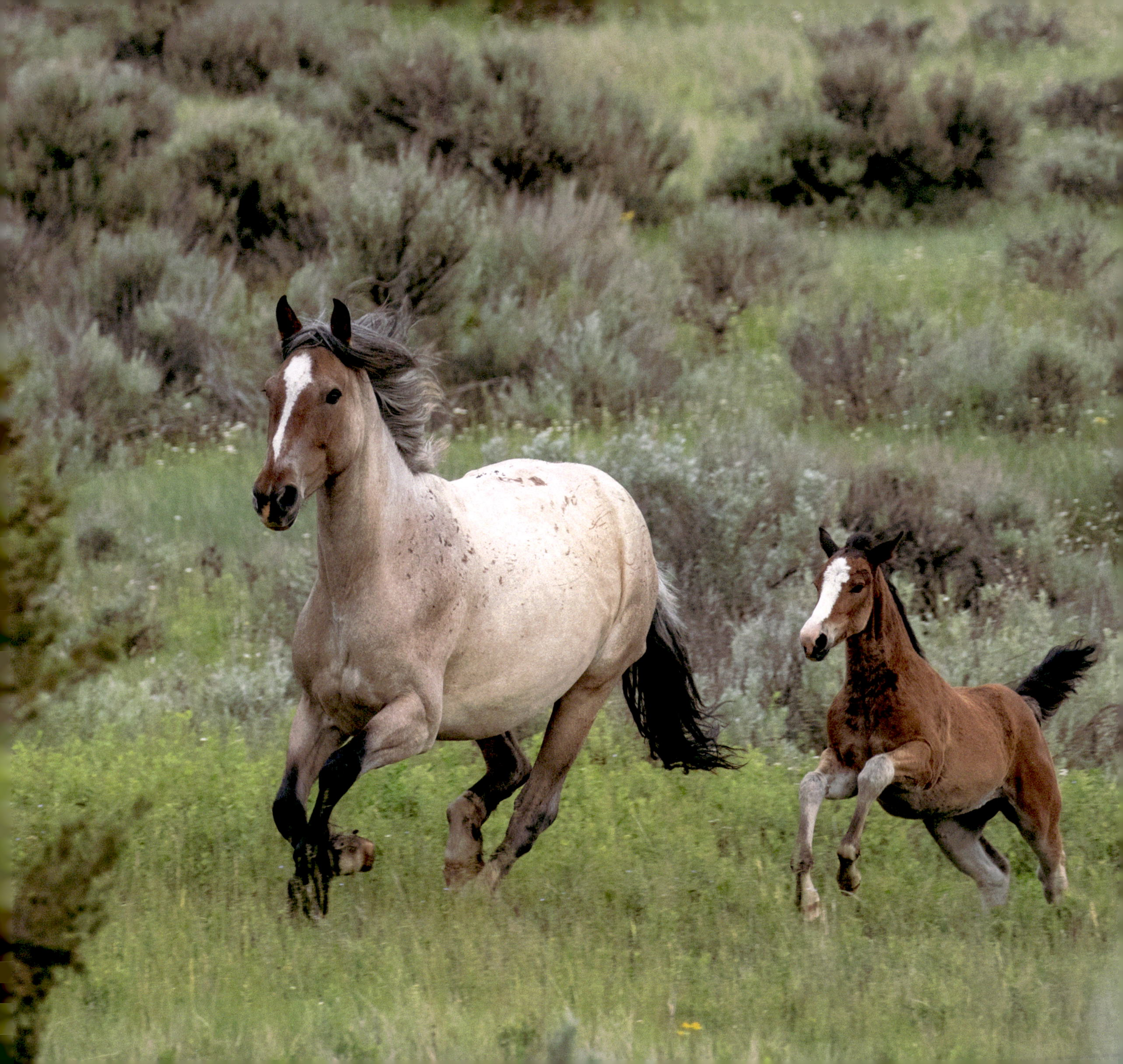

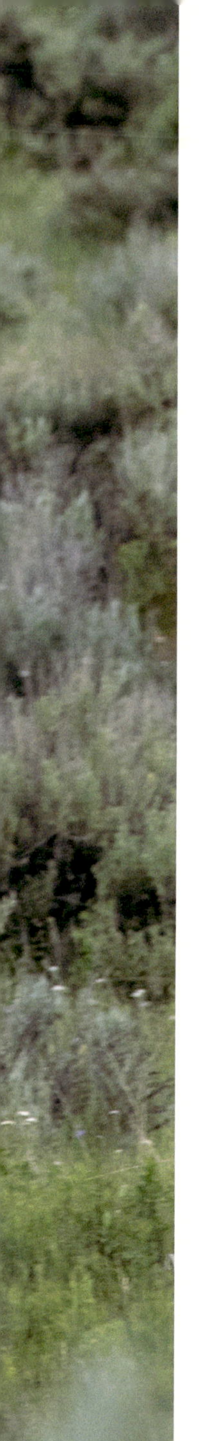

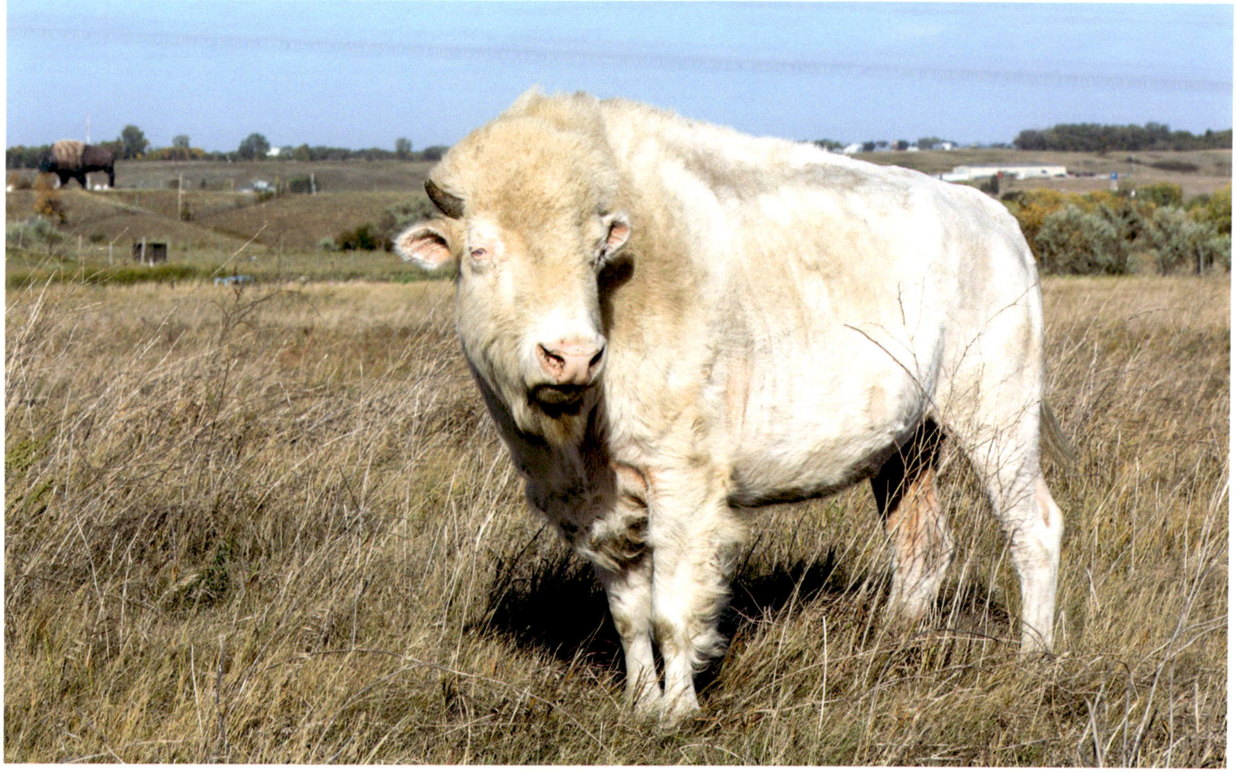

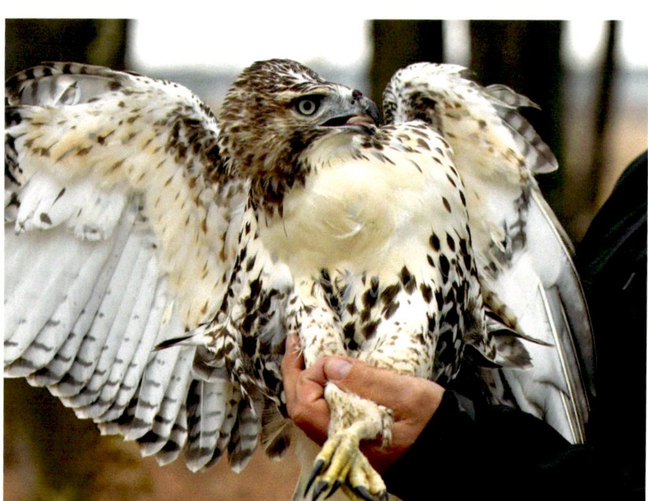

Above: White Cloud, or *Mahpiya Ska,* was a female albino buffalo that roamed a pasture at the North American Bison Discovery Center in Jamestown. She was born in 1996 and died in 2016 at the age of twenty. Today, she stands indoors for viewing by visitors. White bison are exceedingly rare, considered sacred by Native Americans.

Left: Members of the 319th Logistics Readiness Squadron rescued this Swainson's hawk on the Grand Forks Air Force Base. The Dakota Zoo rehabilitated the bird and then released it near Bismarck. These hawks favor native prairies and grasslands, preying on pocket gophers and ground squirrels.
MIKE LALONDE/DAKOTA ZOO/PUBLIC DOMAIN

Far left: A mare and her foal rollick through lush rangeland in Theodore Roosevelt National Park near Medora.

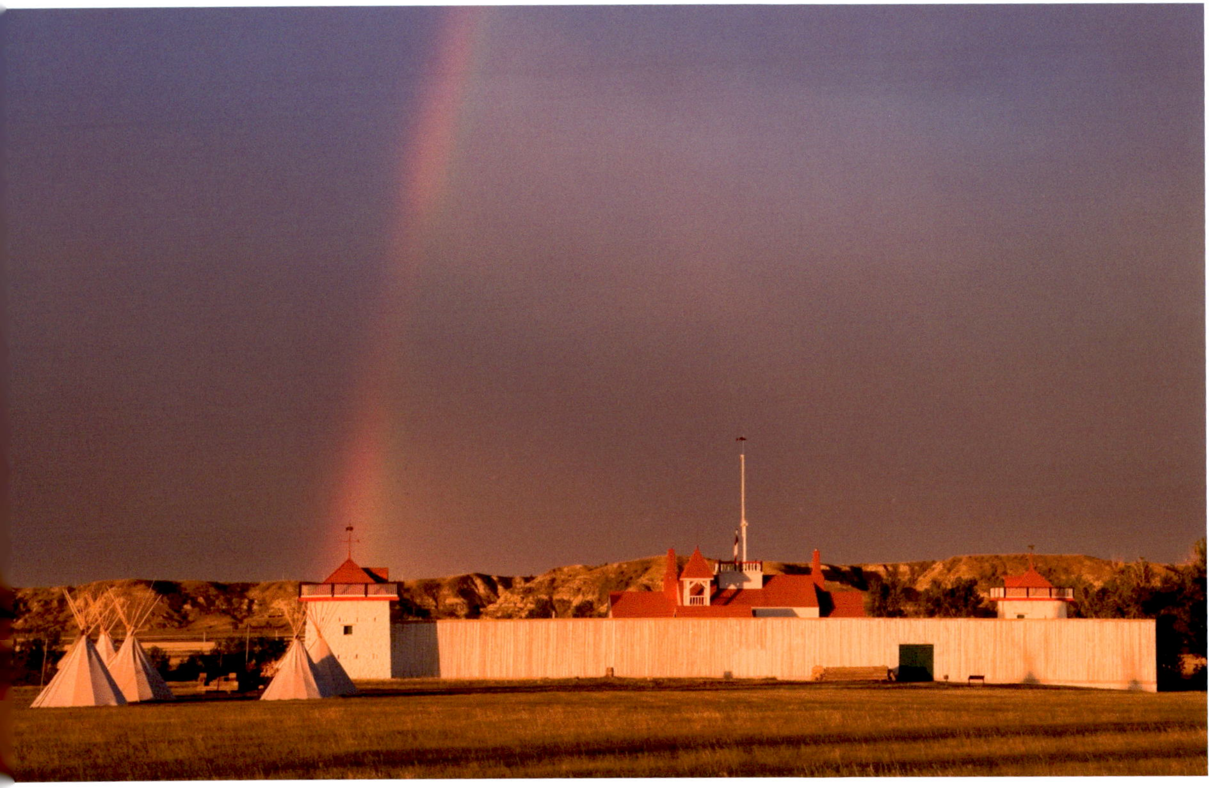

Above: In the early to mid-1800s, Fort Union was the most important trading post on the Upper Missouri River. Today, visitors can tour the reconstructed post and enjoy living history presentations at the national historic site near the Montana-North Dakota border southwest of Williston.

Right: On River Road in Bismarck, Keelboat Park offers a self-guided walking tour to sculptures and a 55-foot replica keelboat like the one that carried the Lewis and Clark Expedition.

Far right: The Missouri and Yellowstone Rivers meet at a tranquil site just southeast of Fort Union, near Williston.

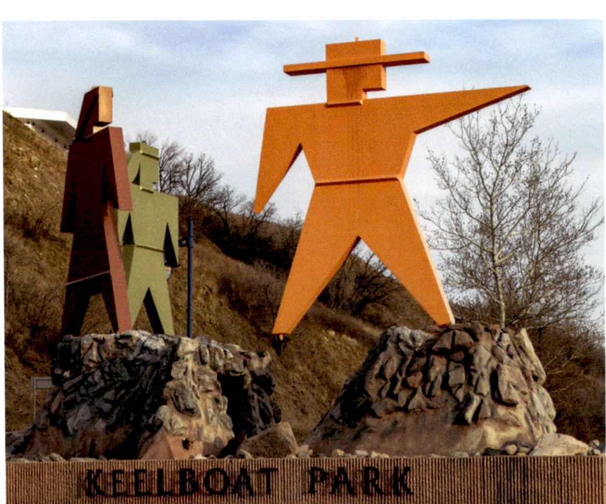

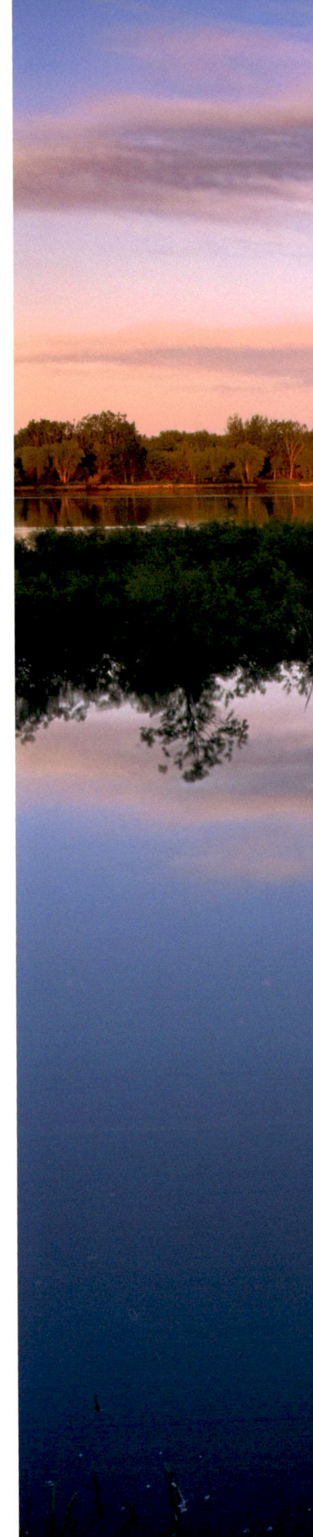

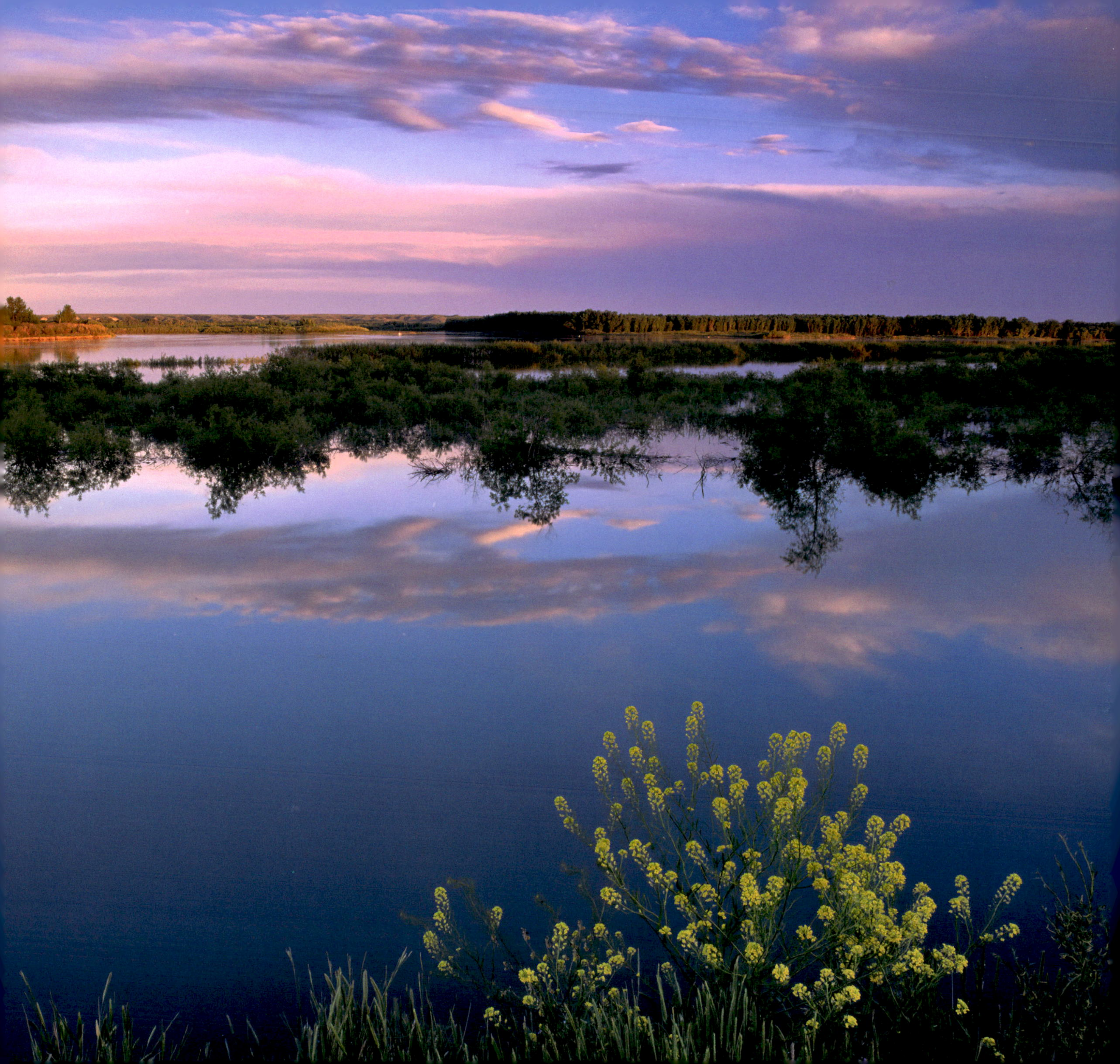

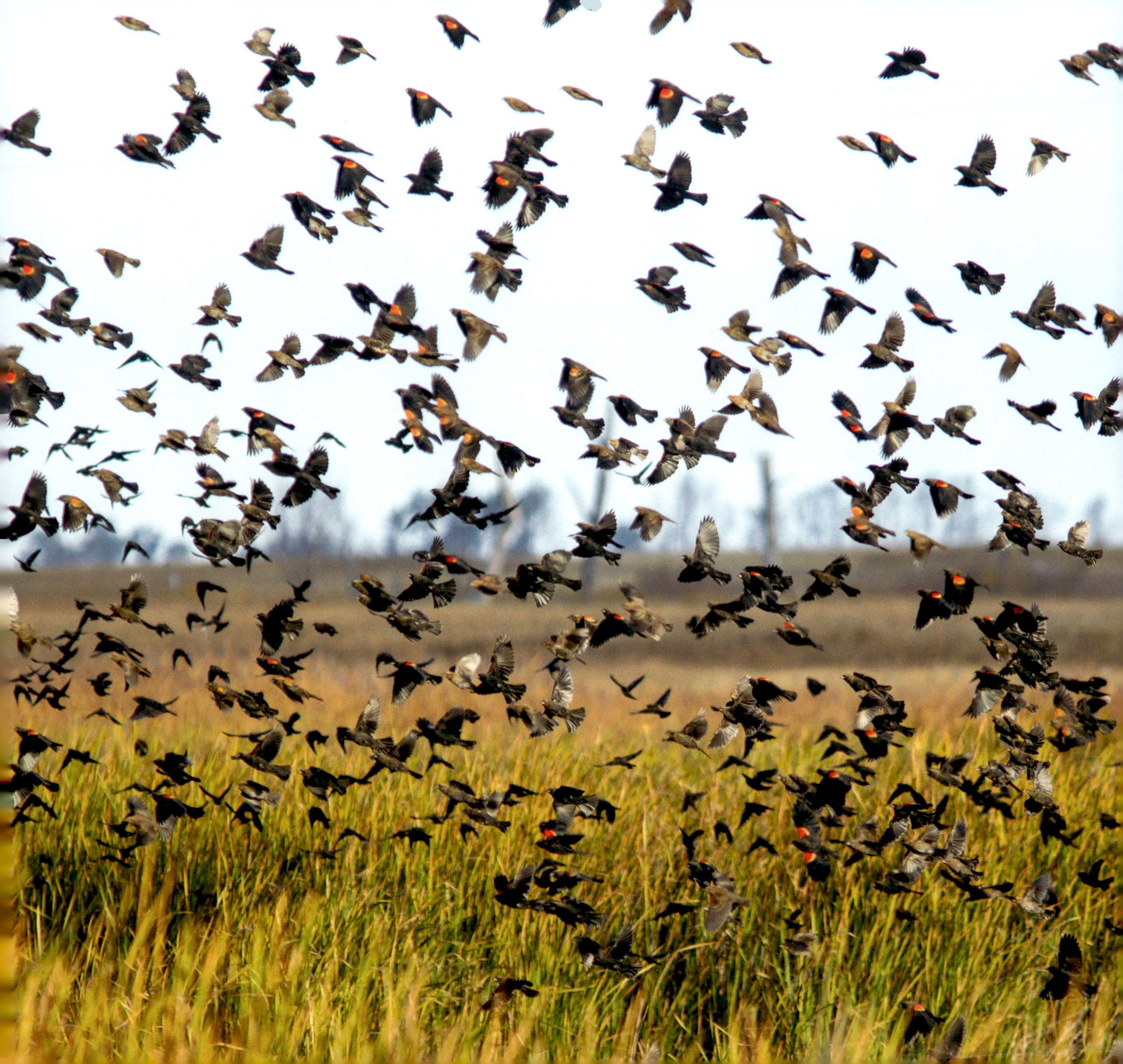

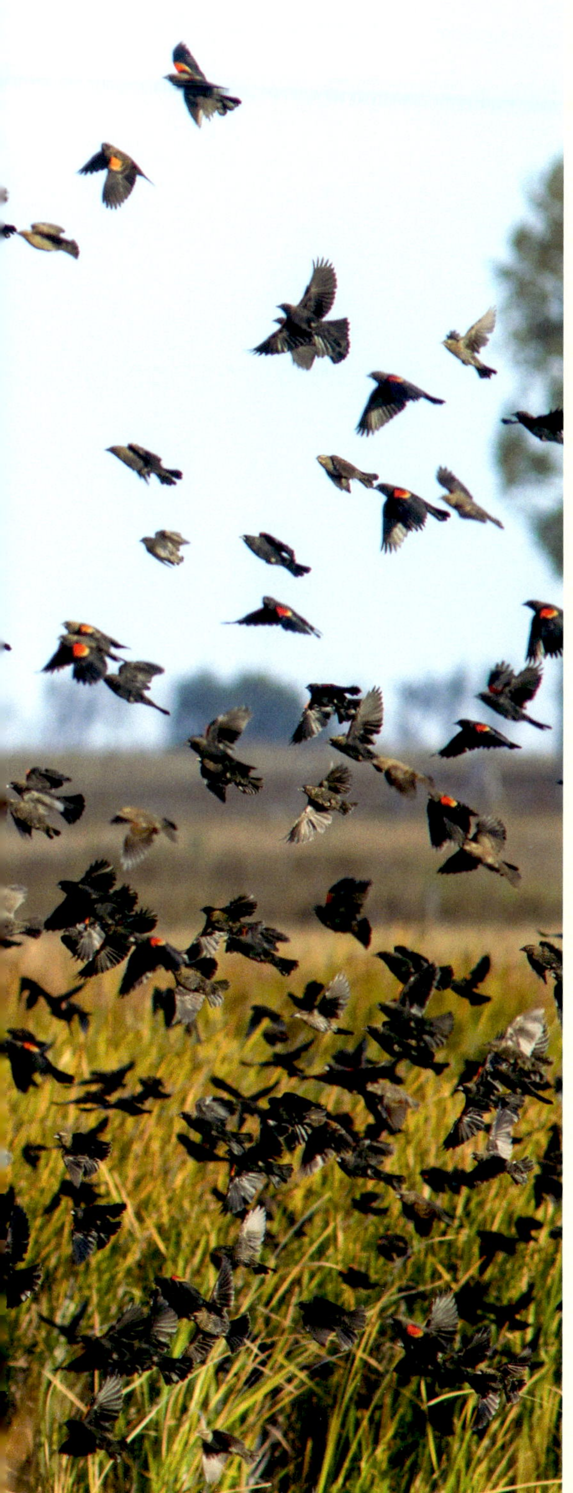

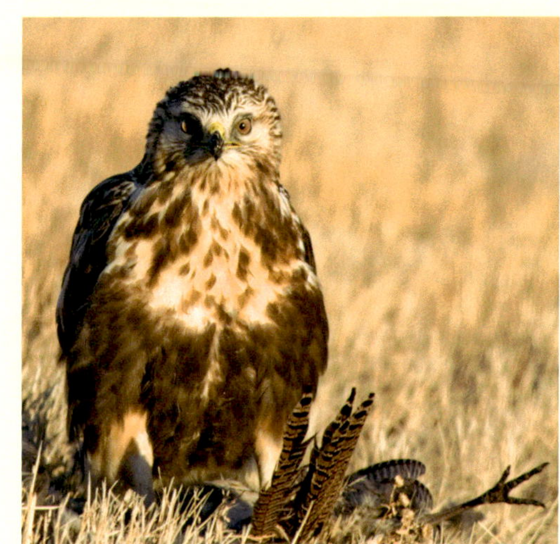

Left: A young rough-legged hawk enjoys a pheasant dinner.

Far left: Red-winged blackbirds take flight at Arrowwood National Wildlife Refuge near Jamestown. Only the males sport a bright red and yellow shoulder patch.

Below: North Dakota often vies with Kansas for the top spot in wheat production. Farmers here specialize in hard red spring wheat, ideal for bread flour, and durum, which is used for premium pastas and couscous.

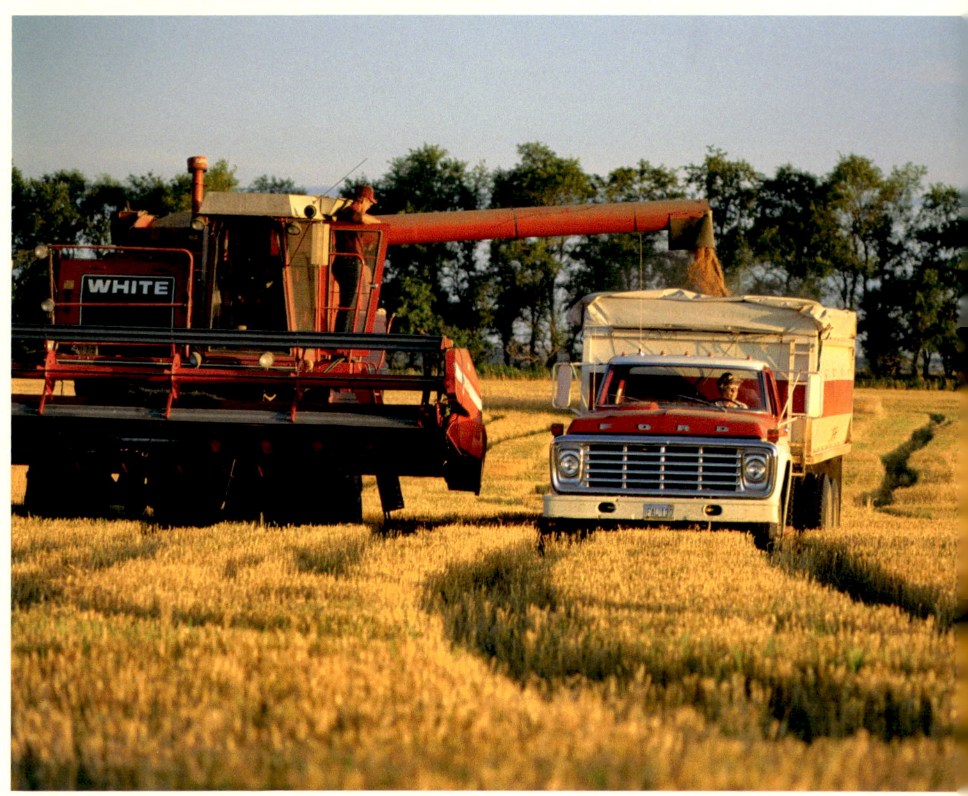

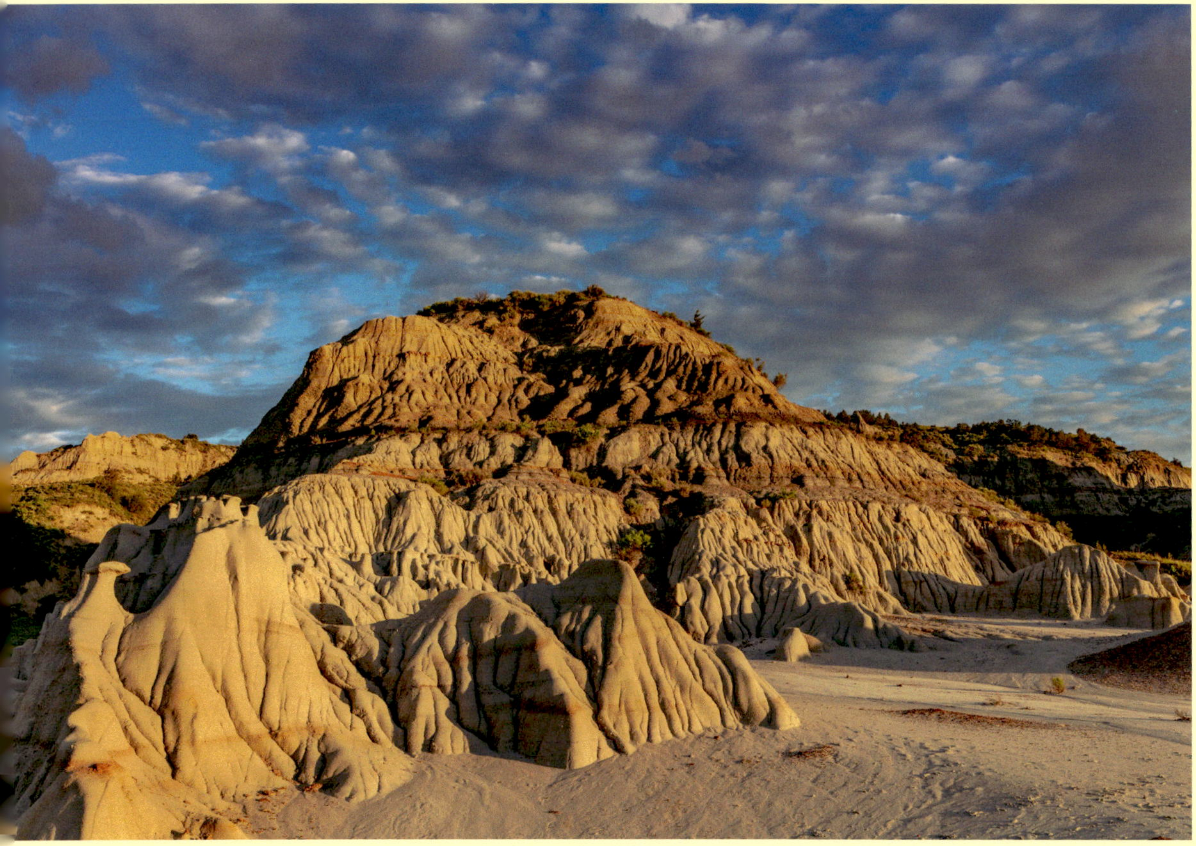

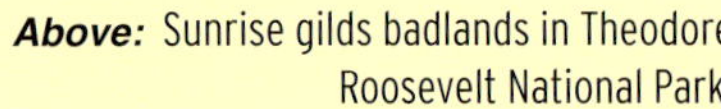

Above: Sunrise gilds badlands in Theodore Roosevelt National Park.

Right: The park is home to black-tailed prairie dogs that live in social colonies or "towns." Each family inhabits multiple burrows spread over as much as an acre of land.

Far right: Near Jones Creek, layers of ancient sand, silt, and ash deposits form sedimentary badlands rich in fossils.

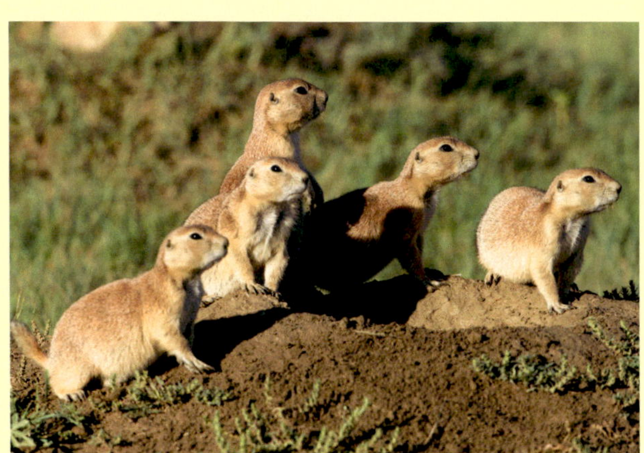

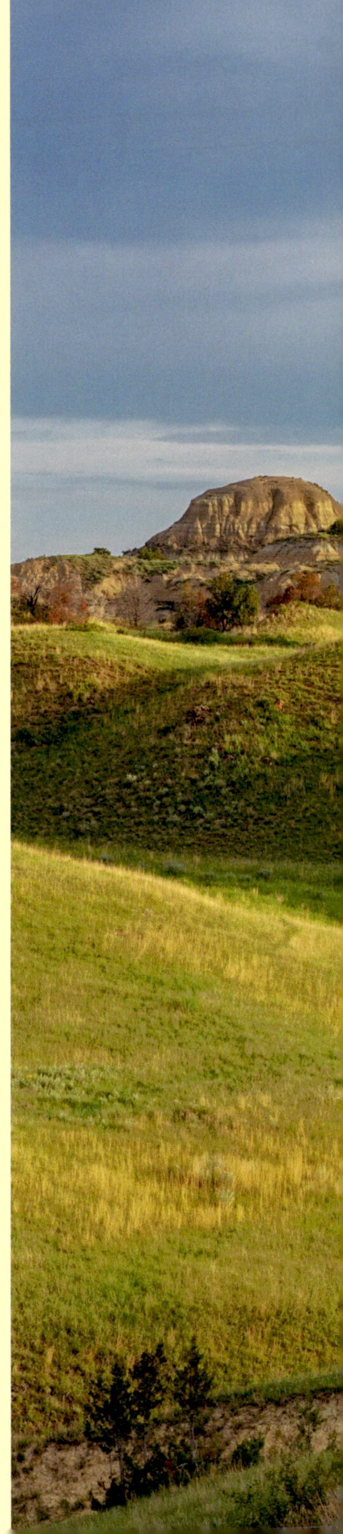

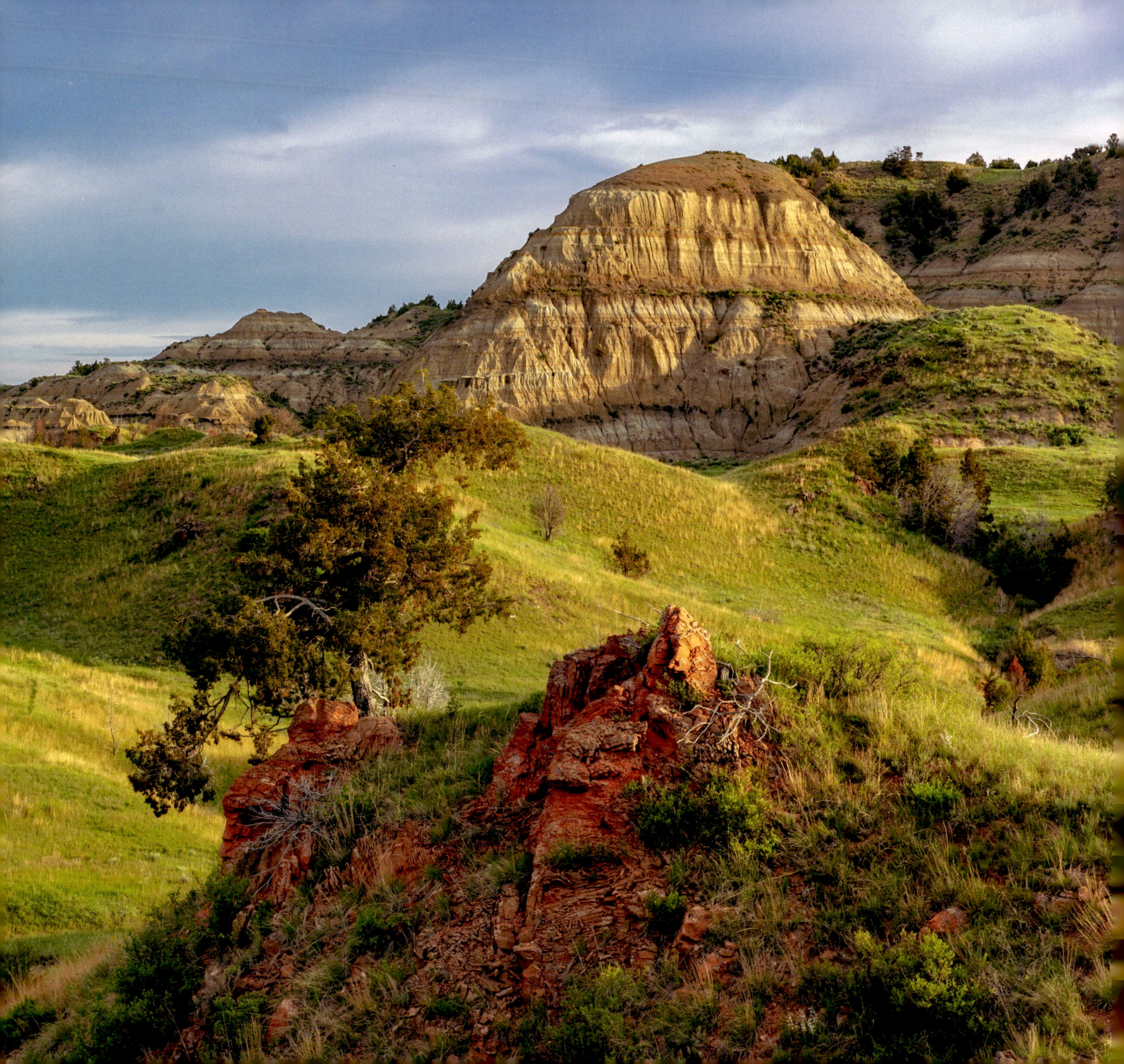

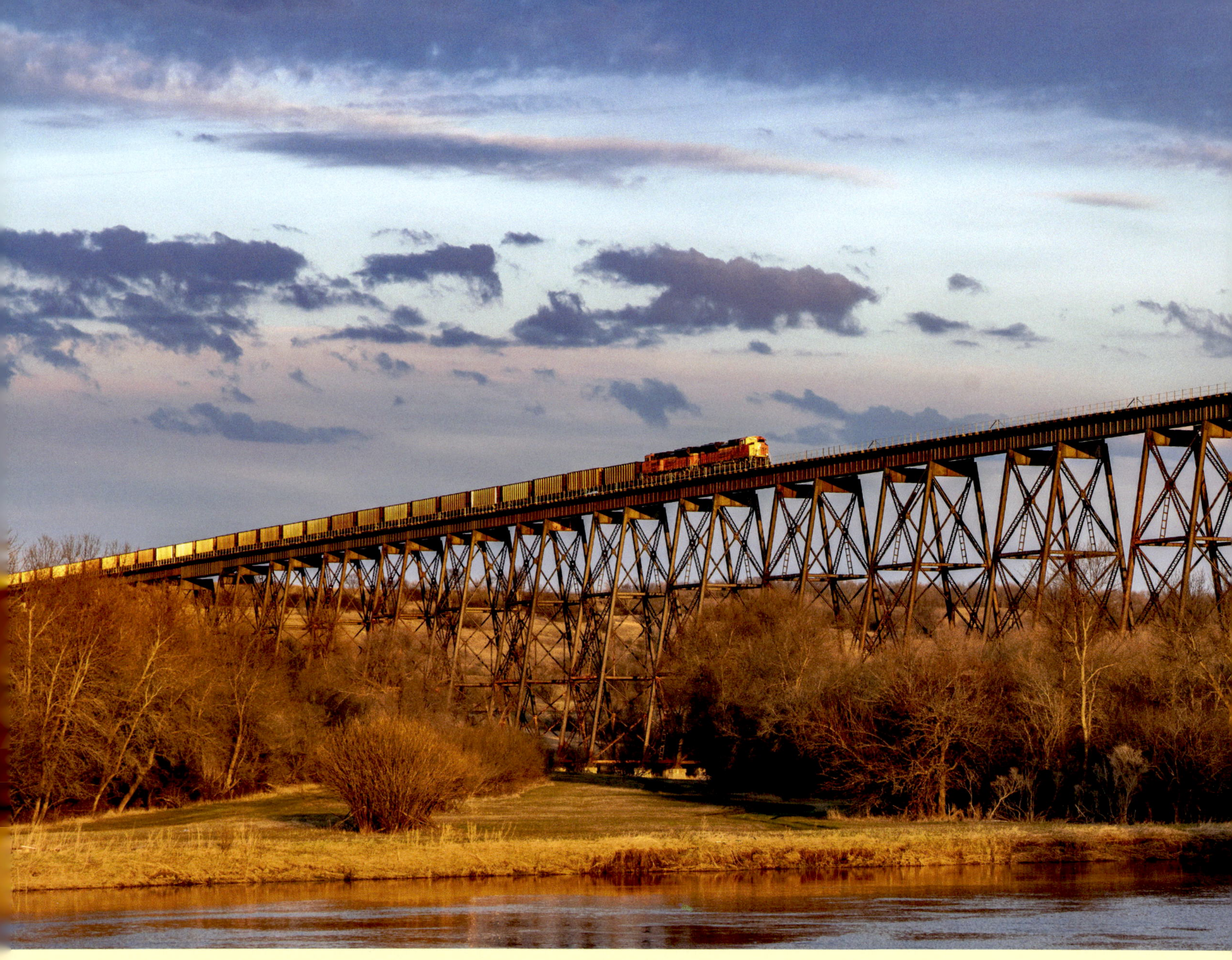

Above: On the north edge of Valley City, about 60 miles west of Fargo, the Hi-Line Railroad Bridge spans the Sheyenne River. One of the longest and highest single-track railroad bridges in the country, the Hi-Line is 3,860 feet long and soars 162 feet above the river. It has been in service since 1908.

Facing page, top: Four Bears Memorial Bridge across Lake Sakakawea on the Fort Berthold Reservation commemorates two chiefs—one Mandan, one Hidatsa—both named Four Bears.

Facing page, bottom: The City Park Footbridge over the Sheyenne River connects the park to Valley City's downtown. Nearby, the handsome Elks Building offers senior housing.

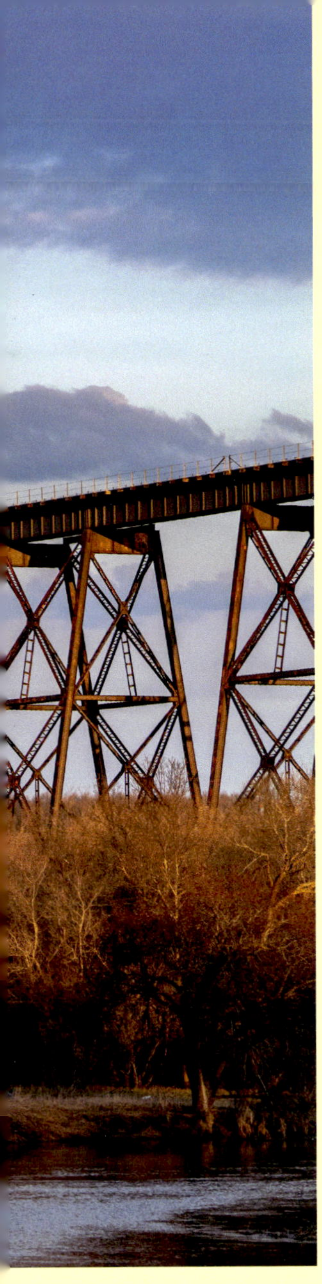

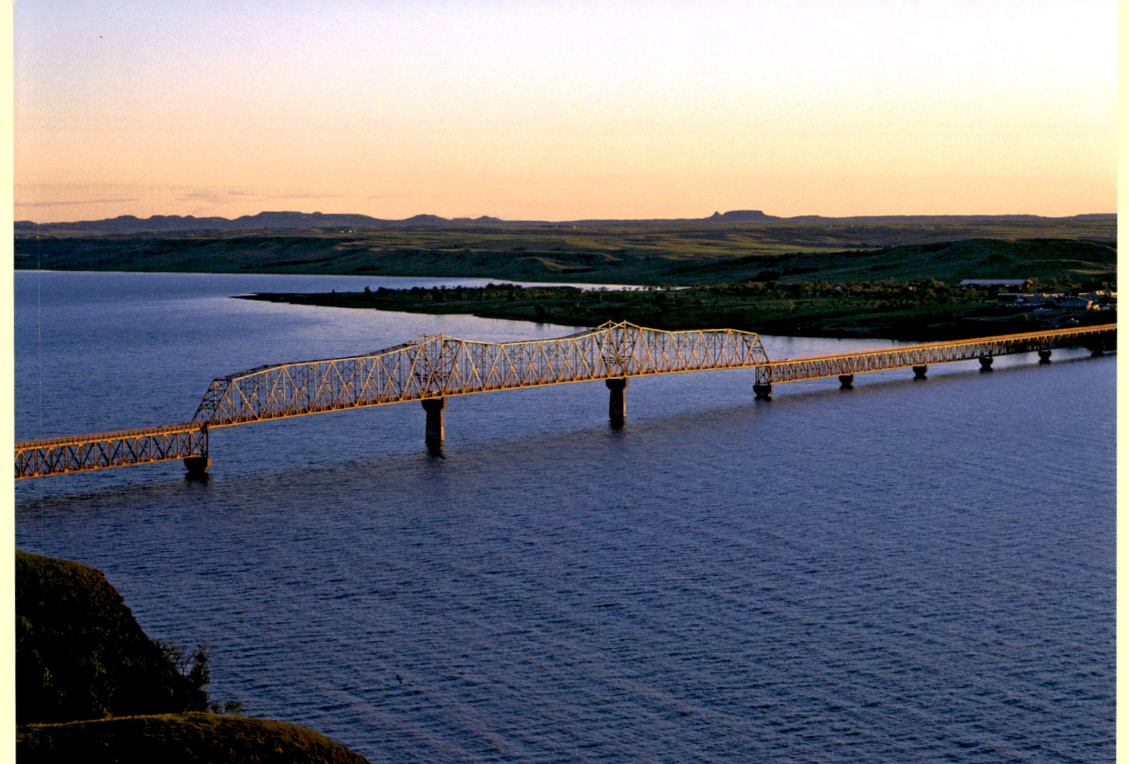

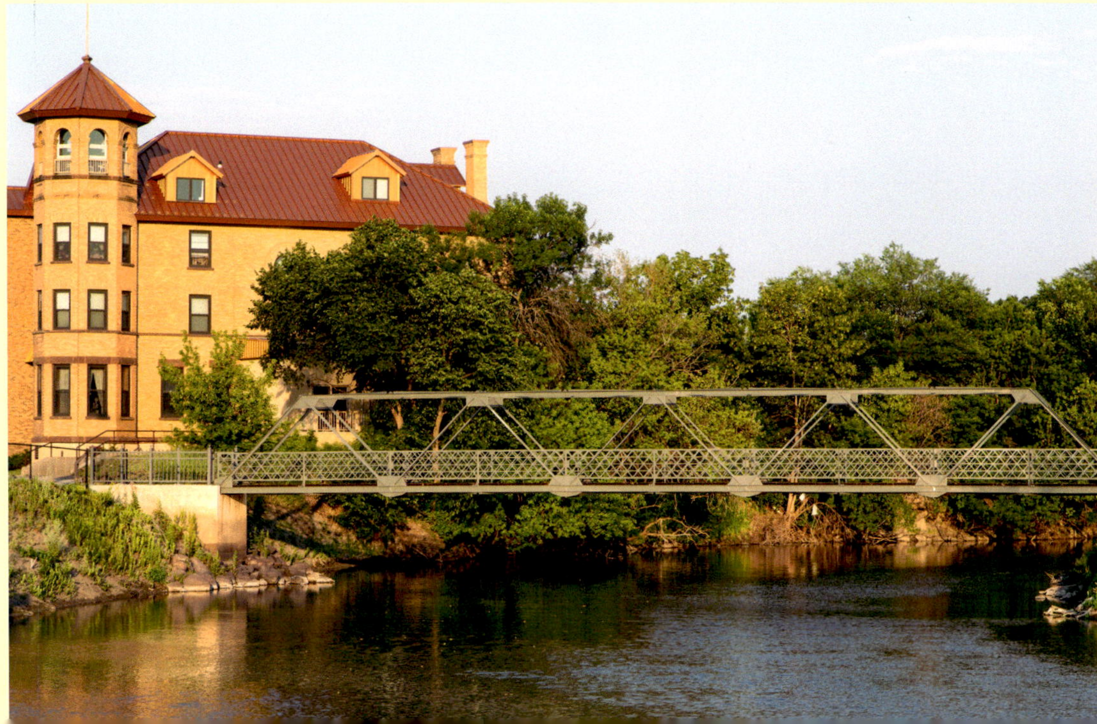

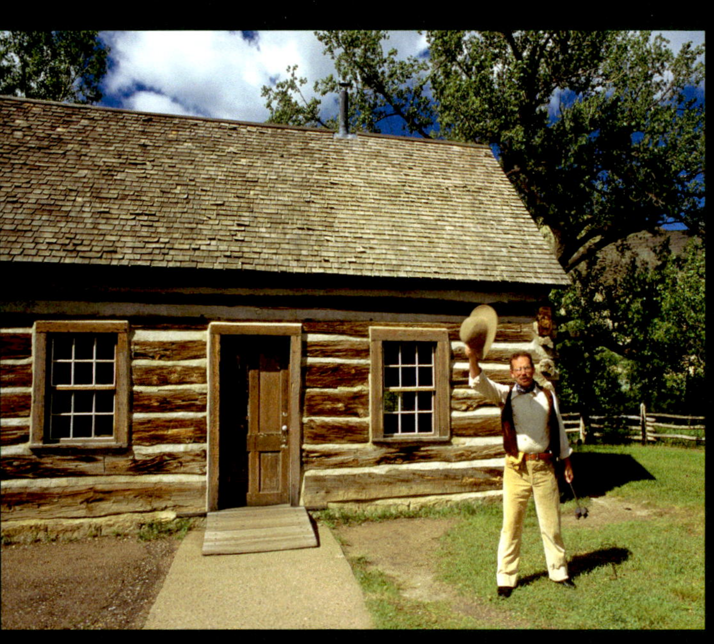

Left: An actor depicts Teddy Roosevelt at the Maltese Cross Cabin on the grounds of the South Unit Visitor Center, Theodore Roosevelt National Park, in Medora.

Right: The historic Slattum Homestead Cabin north of Fort Ransom is one of 41 fascinating interpretive sites along the 63-mile Sheyenne River Valley National Scenic Byway between the Getchell Township Hall north of Valley City and the town of Lisbon.

Following pages: With their orange fur, newborn bison calves freckle the herd in Theodore Roosevelt National Park.

Below: Built in 1876, the Wadeson Homestead Cabin near Kathryn has served as a community hall, country store, pioneer home, and icehouse. Restored in 1981, the hand-hewn oak cabin is now a state historic site on the Sheyenne River Valley National Scenic Byway.

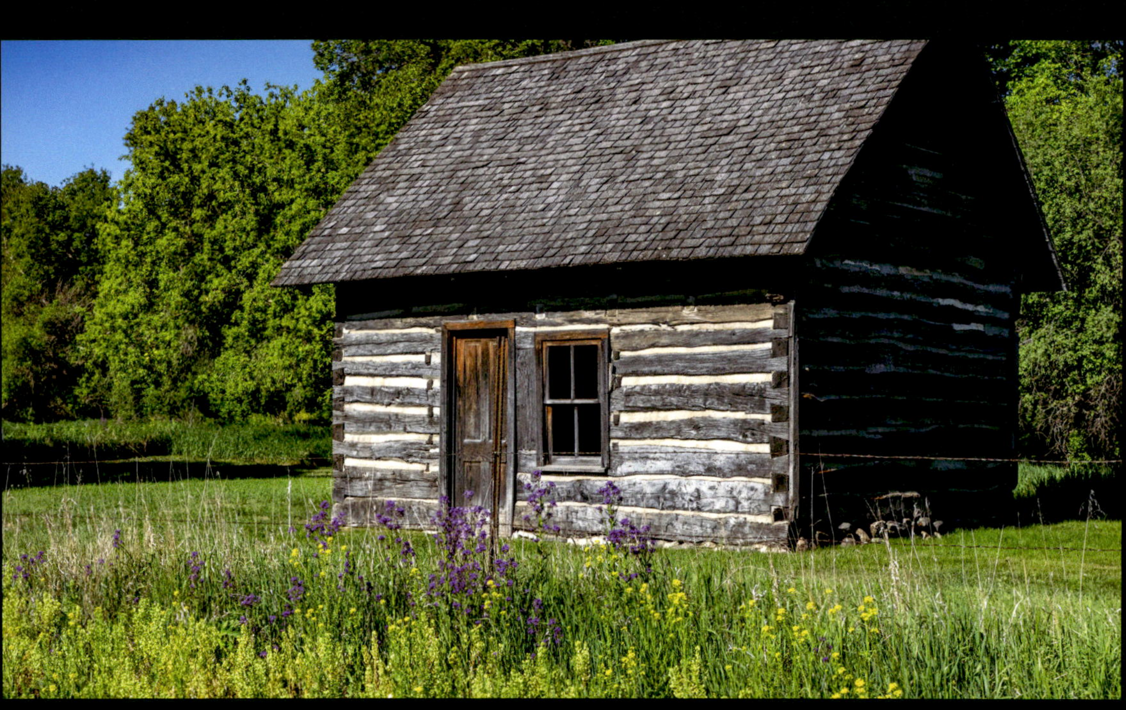

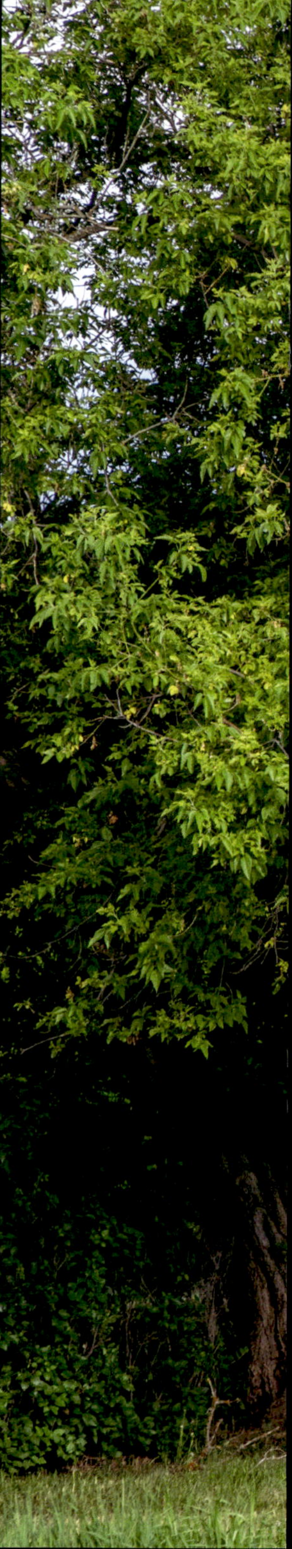

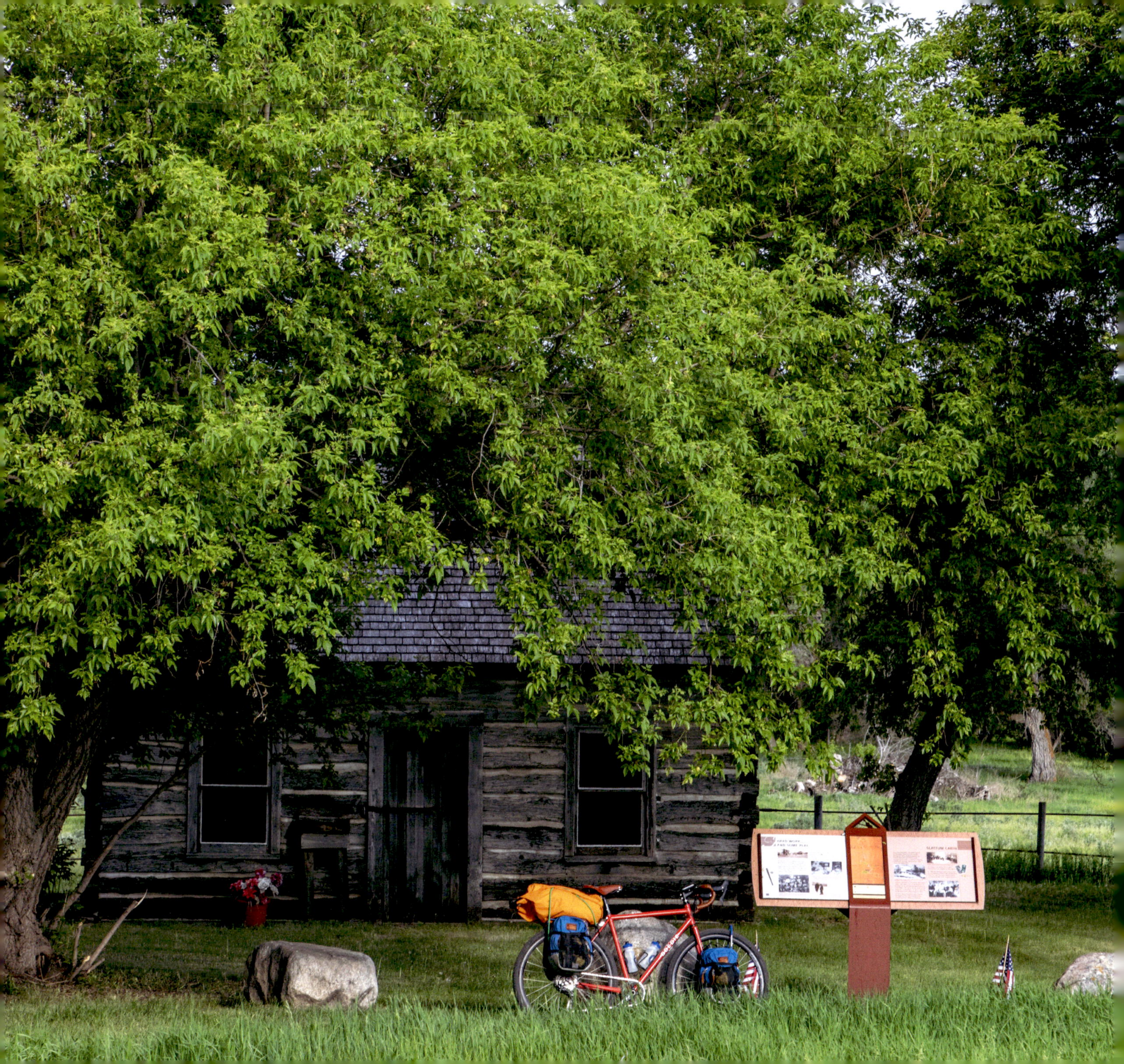

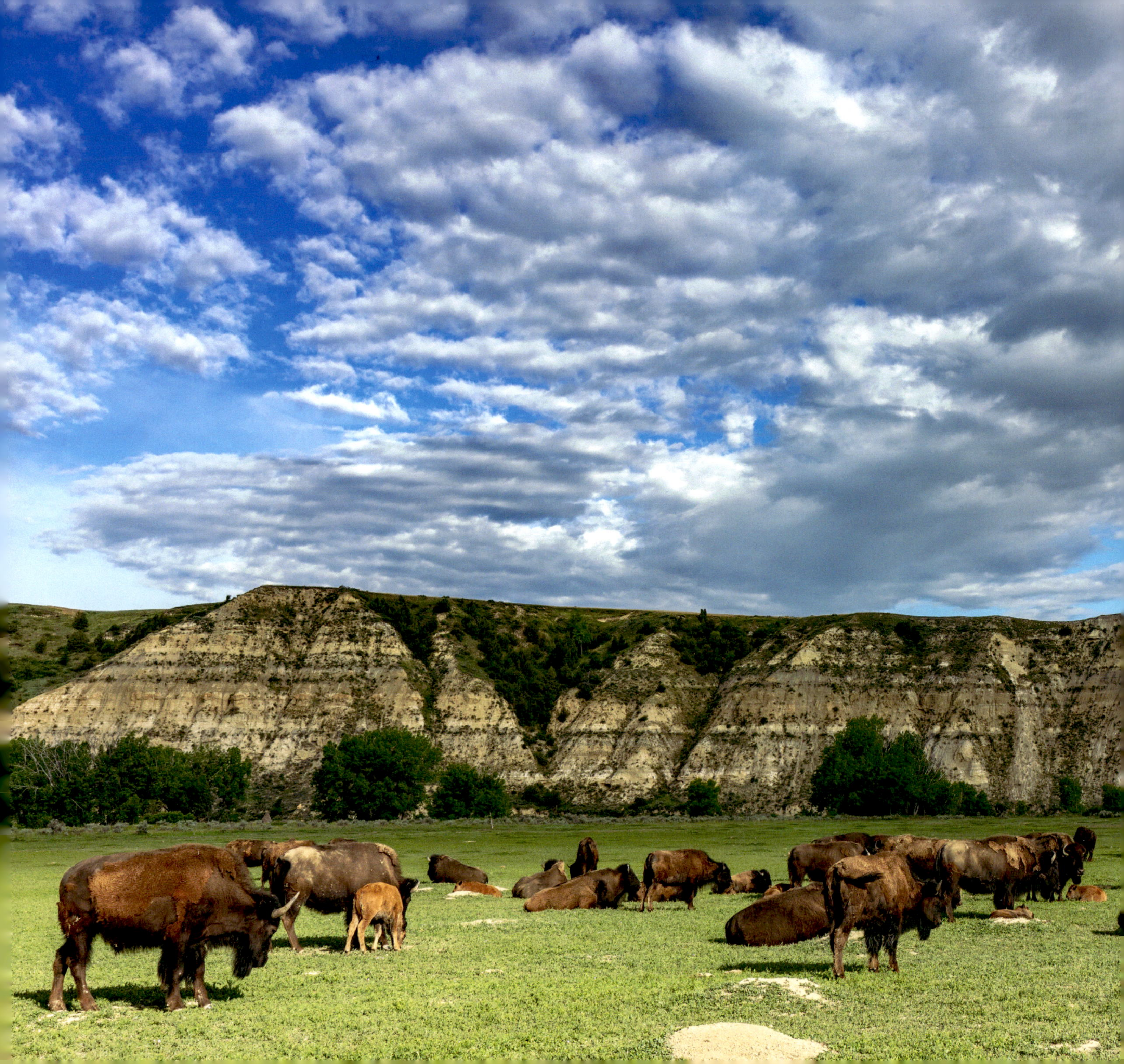

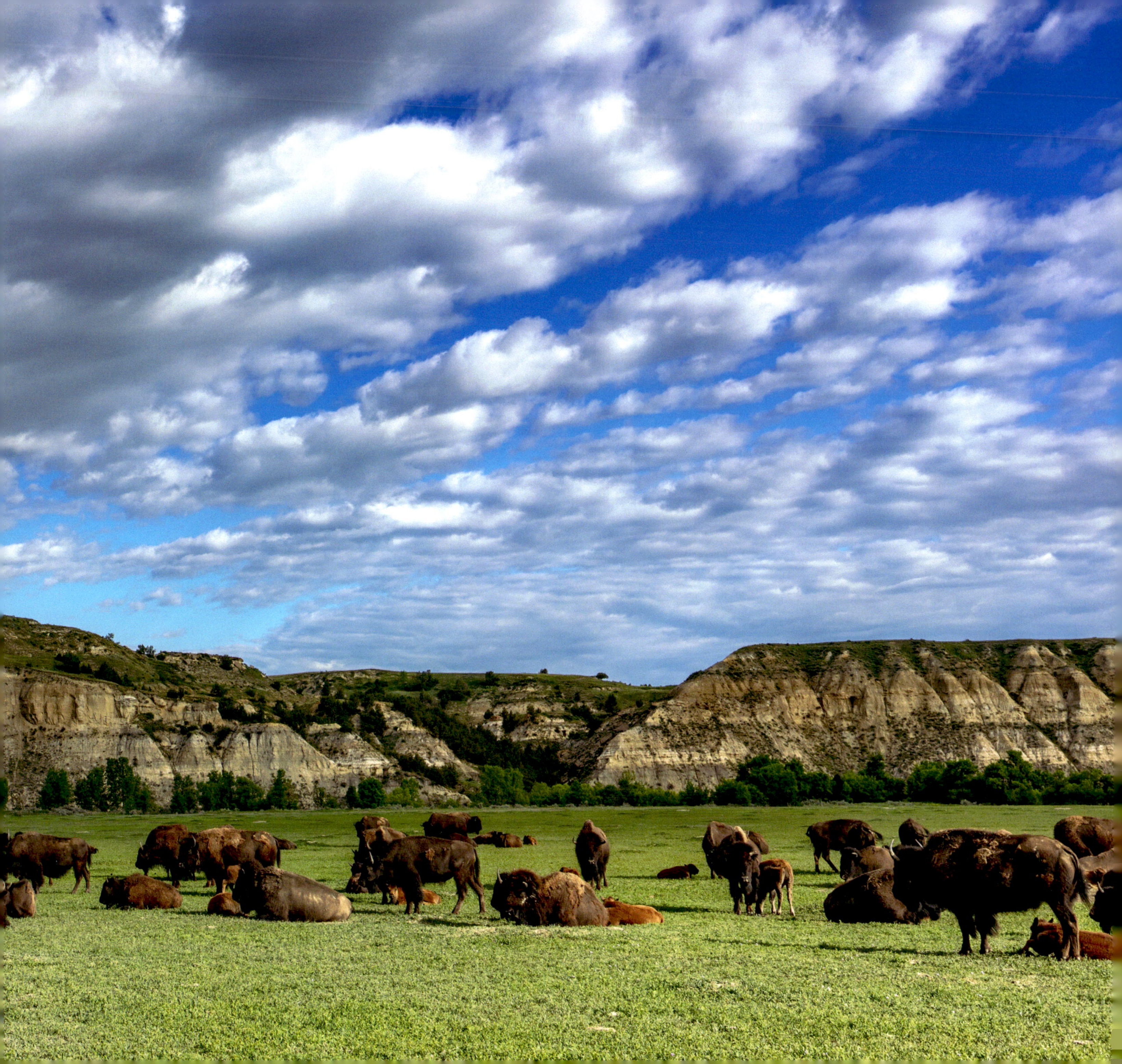

Right: The faintest hint of a black vee on its golden breast marks a young western meadowlark. The official state bird of North Dakota, western meadowlarks are beloved for their bubbling song and their efficiency in devouring grasshoppers and other agricultural pests.

Far right: The Little Missouri River threads between bluffs and badlands in Theodore Roosevelt National Park north of Medora.

Below: The 19,500-acre Des Lacs National Wildlife Refuge near Kenmare provides critical habitat for more than 250 species of waterfowl, shorebirds, songbirds, and upland game birds, as well as deer, moose, and painted turtles.

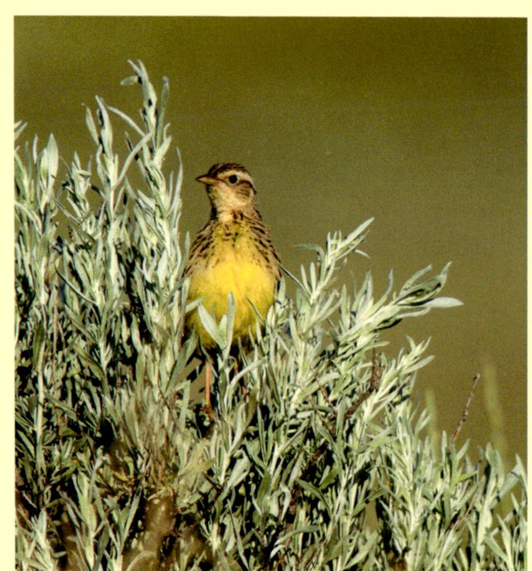

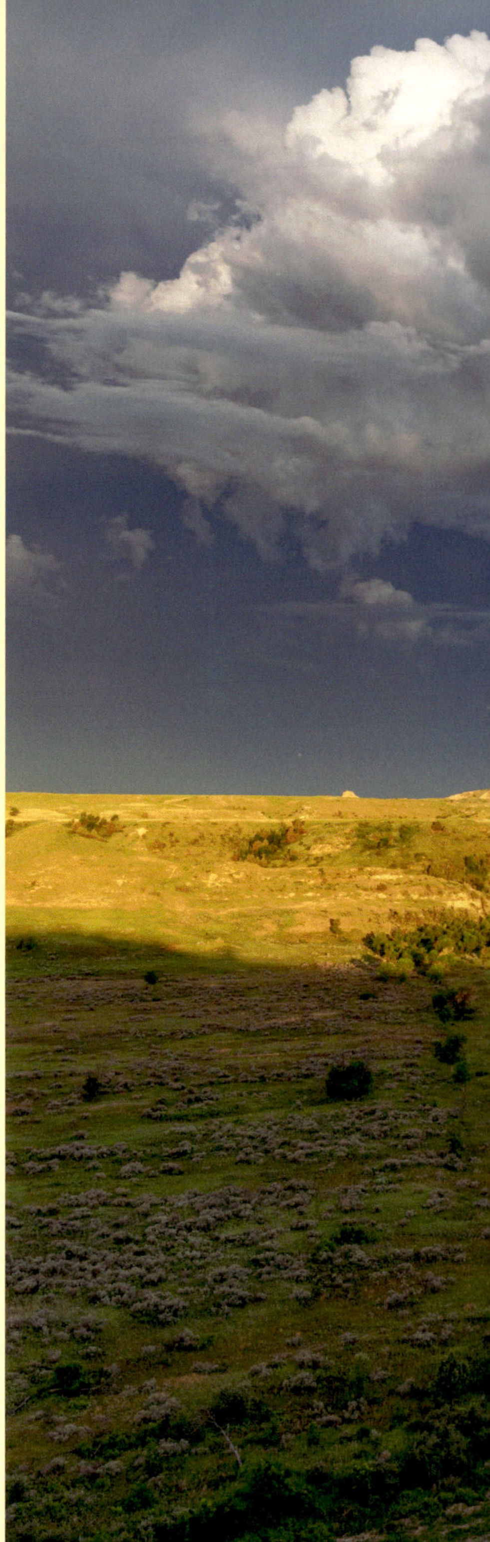

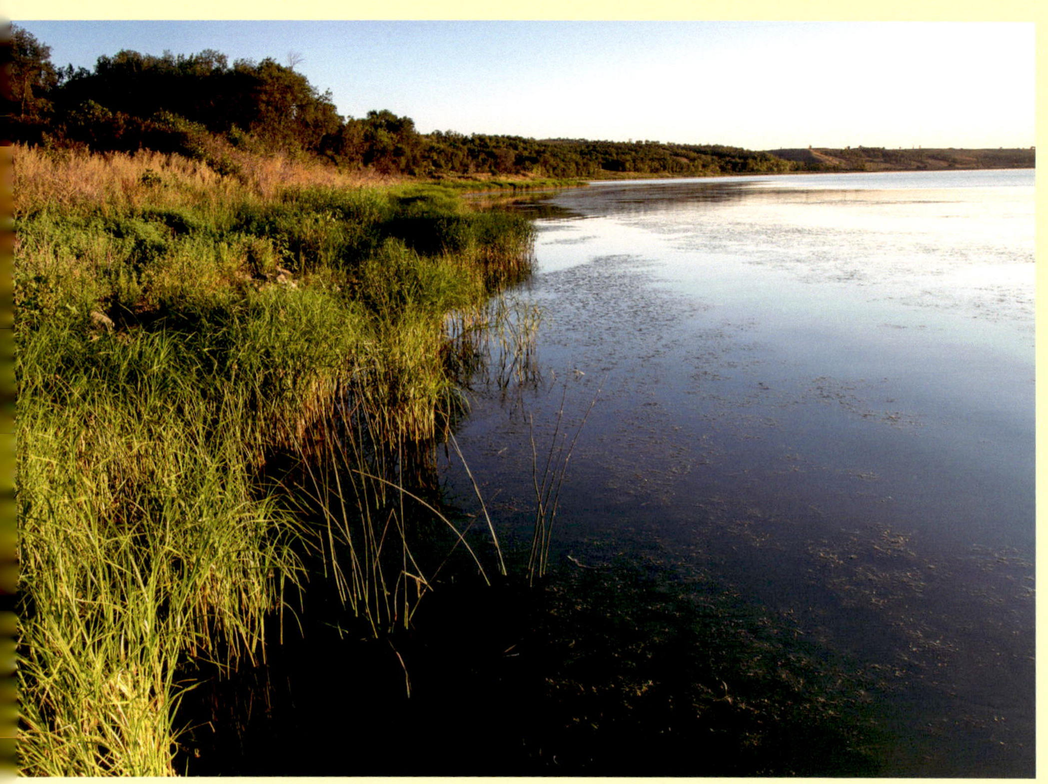

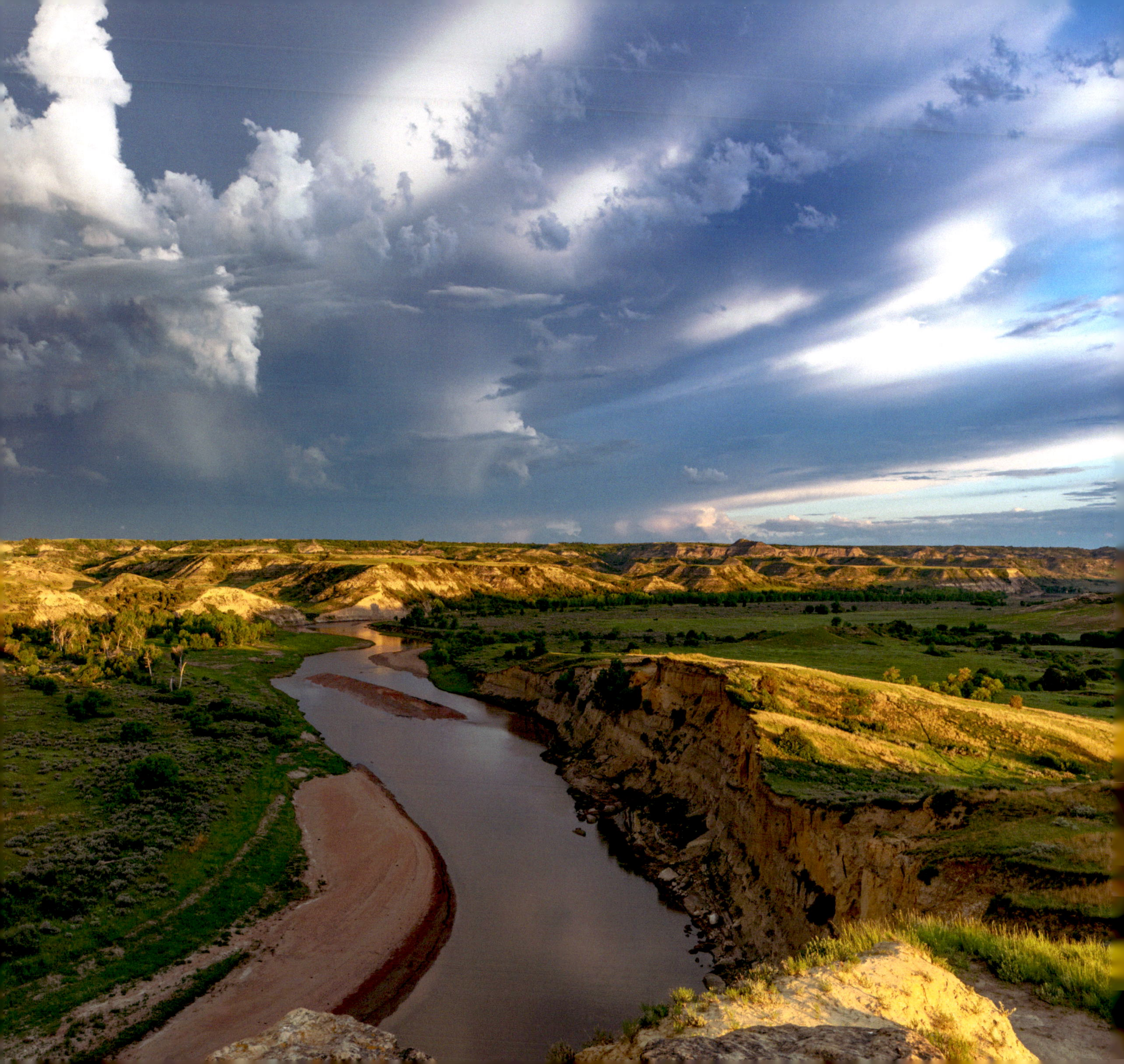

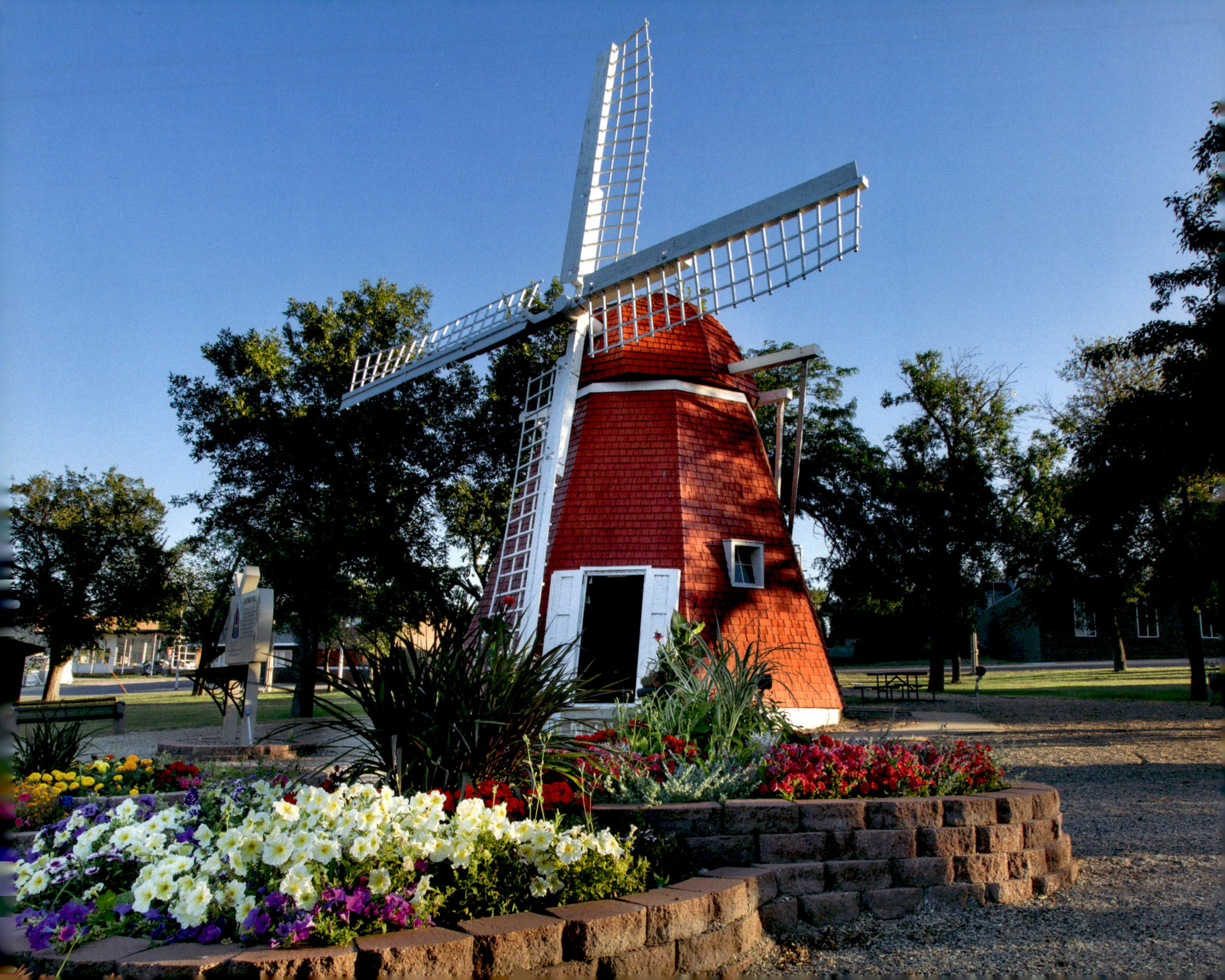

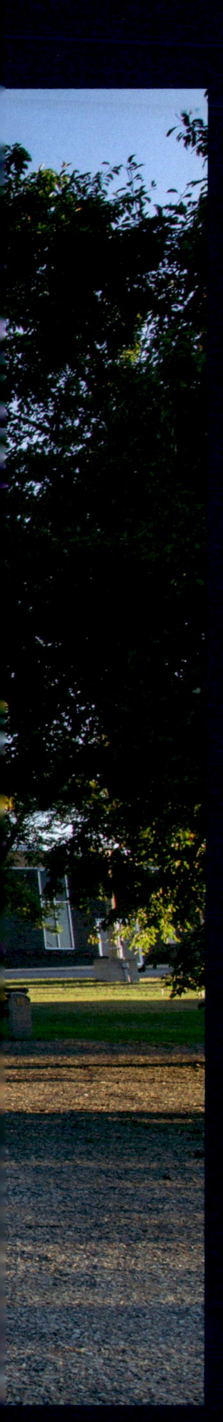

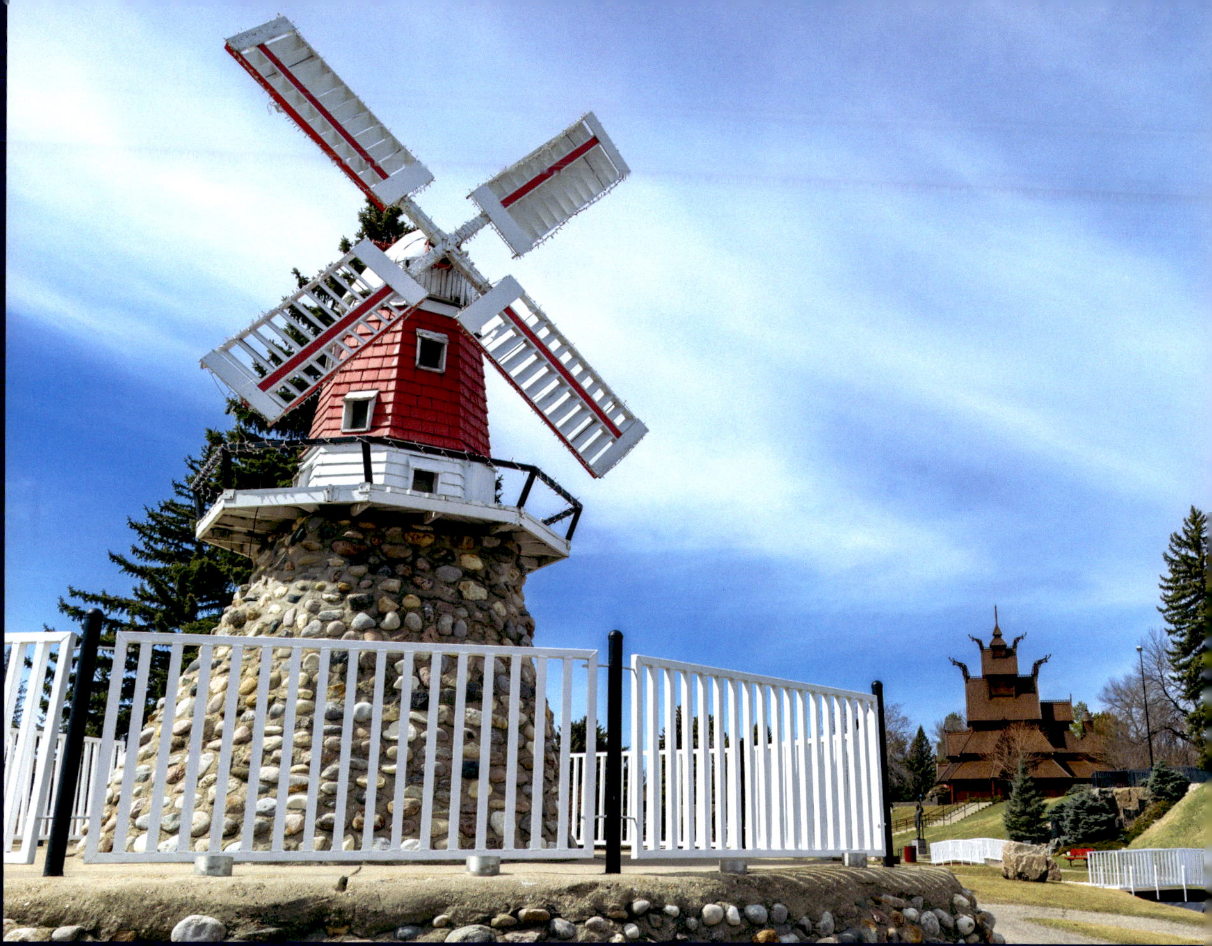

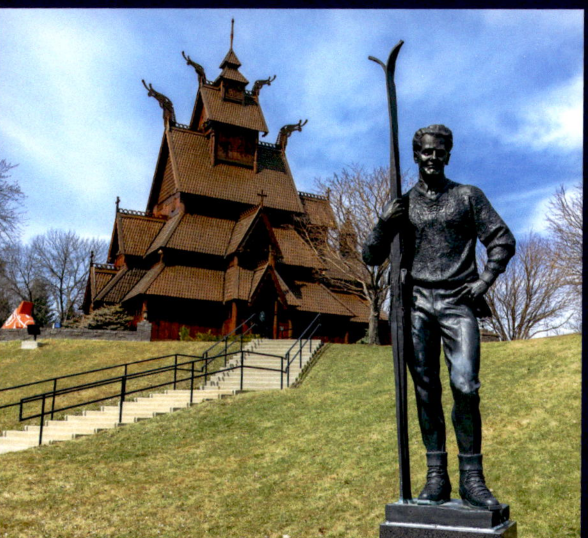

Above: The grounds of the Scandinavian Heritage Center in Minot showcase iconic aspects of several cultures, including a Swedish Dala horse, Finnish sauna, a full-size replica of the Gol Stave Church in Norway (seen here in the background), and this rare example of a Danish windmill.

Left: The Gol Stave Church replica looms behind a bronze statue of Casper Oimoen at the Scandinavian Heritage Center. Oimoen, who immigrated from Norway to Minot, was an American ski jumping national champion. He was inducted into the U.S. Skiing Hall of Fame in 1963.

Far left: The downtown square in Kenmare is home to this Danish grist mill, built in 1902 by Christian Jensen, who ground 200 sacks of grain per day into flour. Dutch windmills are common, but Kenmare boasts that its Danish mill is one of only three in the country.

Right: In 1931, the U.S. Geological Survey declared that the geographical center of North America was in Rugby. The town quickly erected a stone monument at the intersection of North Dakota Highway 3 and U.S. Highway 2. Subsequent calculations suggest North America's actual center may be 140 miles south in Center, so named in 1902 because it's the geographical center of Oliver County. But Rugby stands by its claim to fame.

Far right: The 32,000-acre Upper Souris National Wildlife Refuge north of Minot is a key stopover and breeding ground for migratory birds on the Central Flyway.

Below: Next to the geographical center monument in Rugby, a playful signpost notes mileages to distant points of North America. Nearby, flags of the United States, Canada, and Mexico flutter in the breeze.

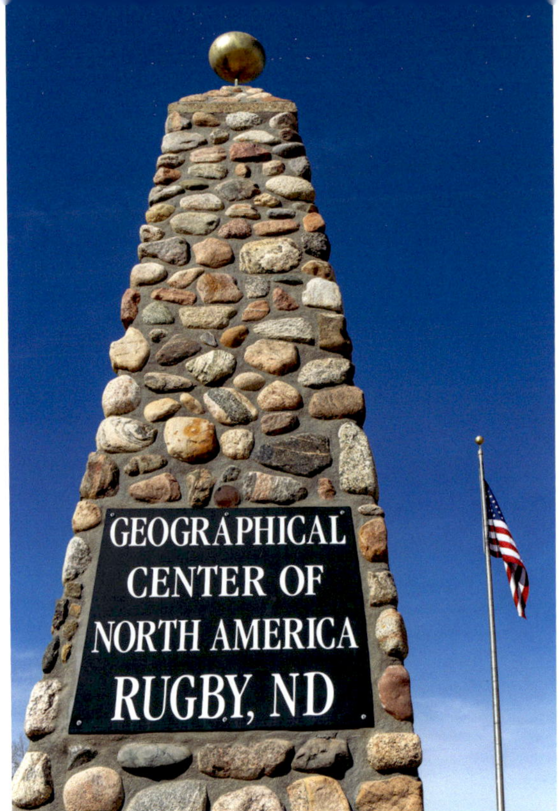

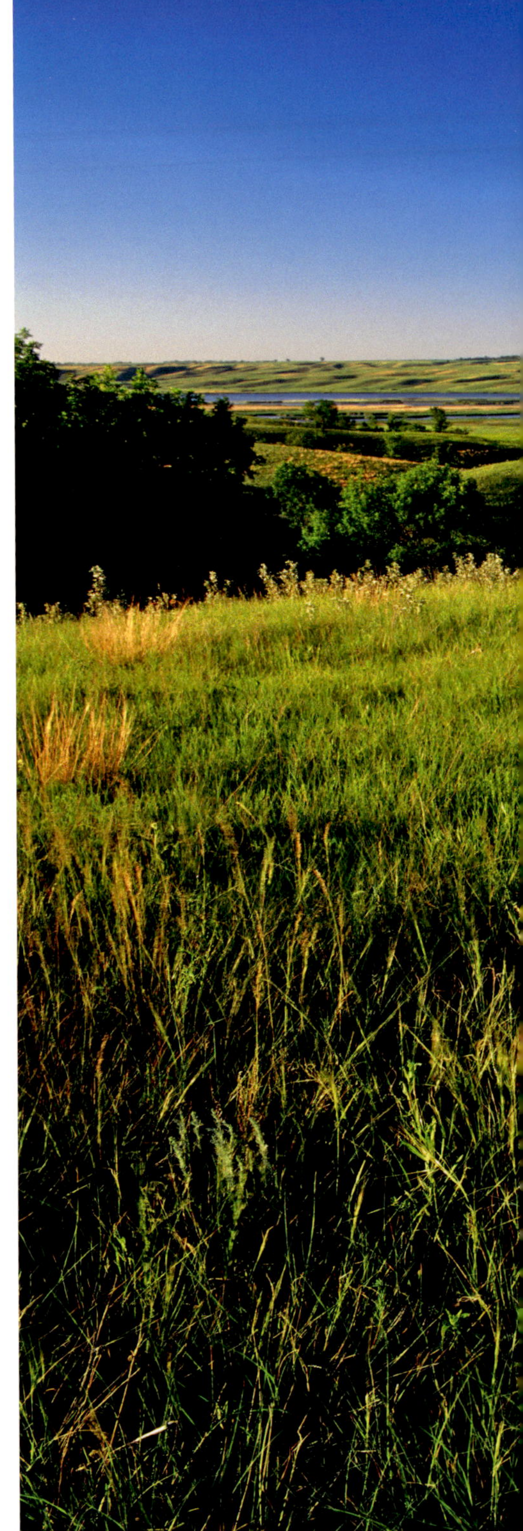

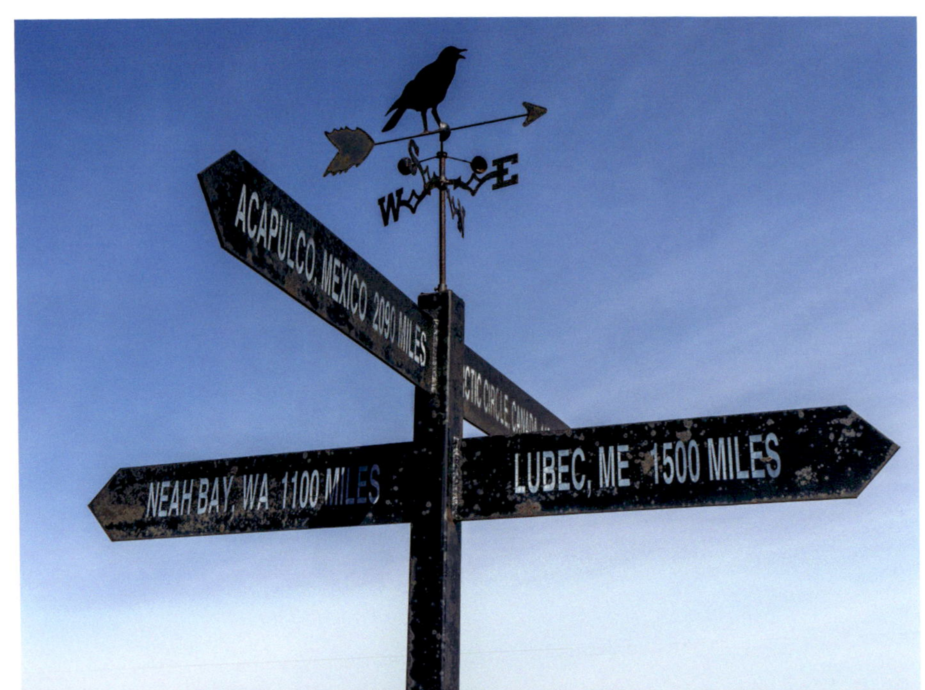

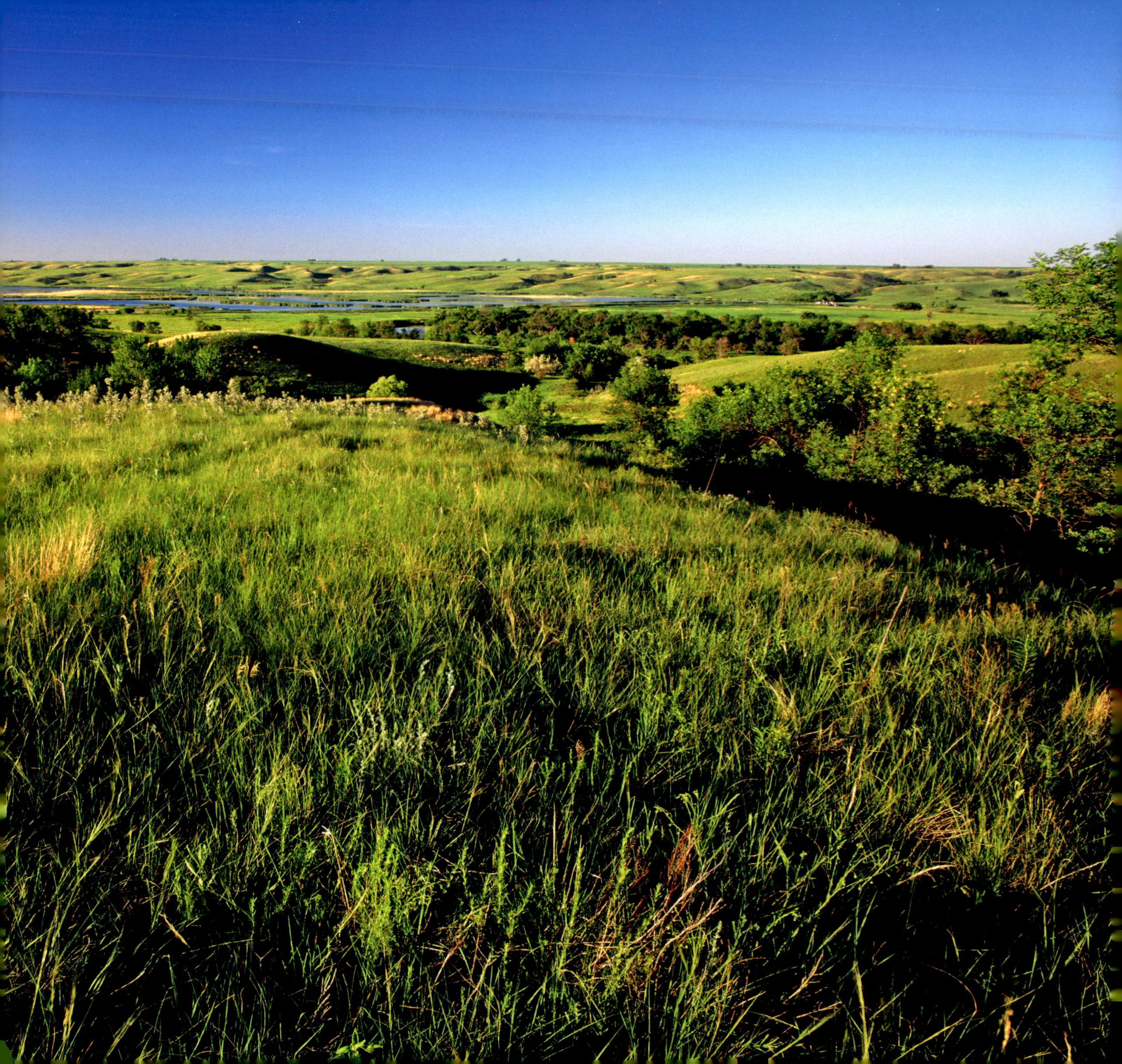

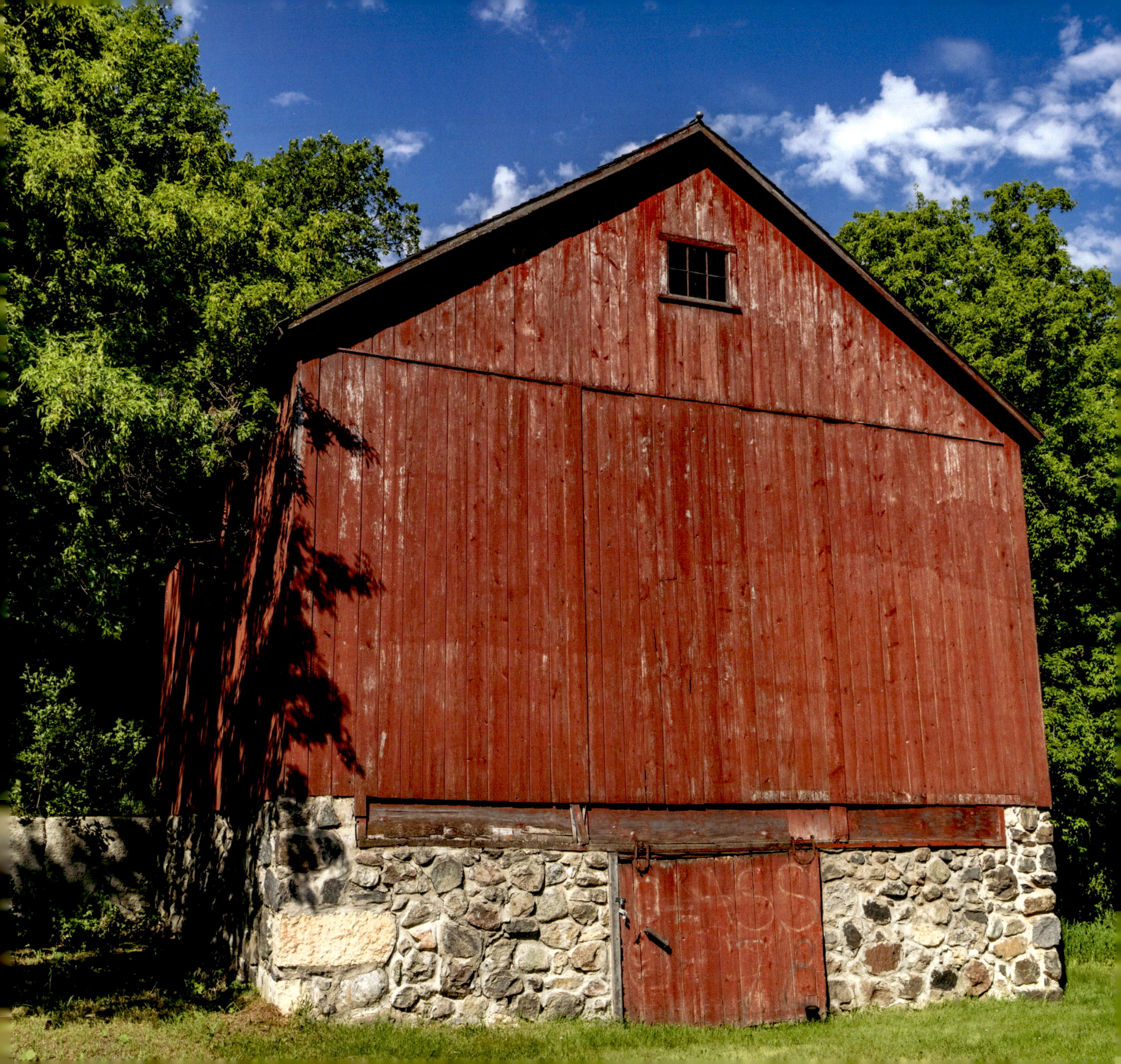

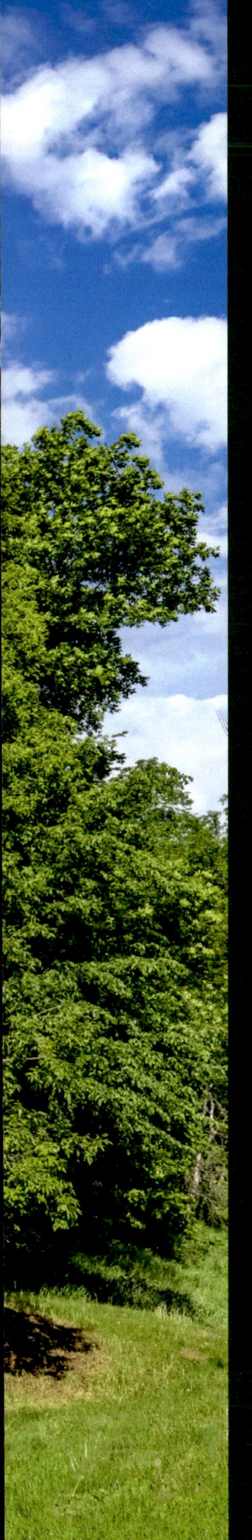

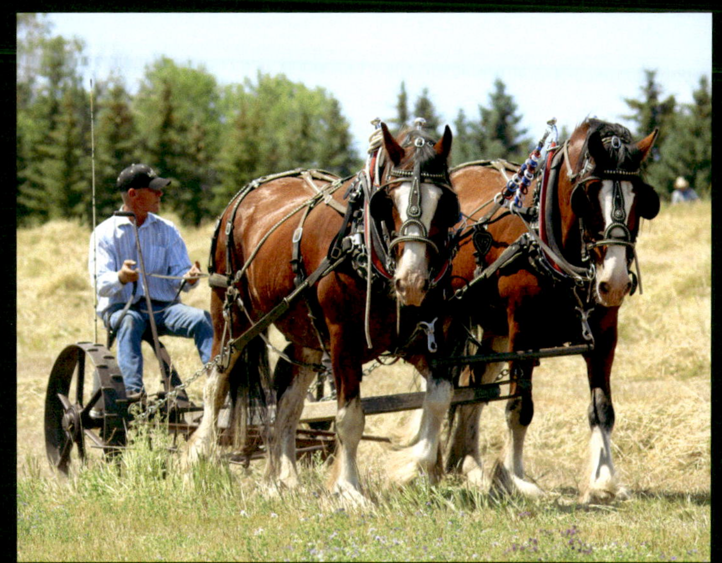

Left: Before the invention of the tractor, farmers used draft horses to pull plows and other heavy machinery. Today, enthusiasts still raise and train draft breeds like this Clydesdale team. JMROCKEMAN/PIXABAY

Far left: In the early 1900s, pioneer merchant and miller Tyler James Walker settled on the banks of the Sheyenne River in the town of Fort Ransom. His two-story barn features a fieldstone foundation and mortise-and-tenon wooden beams. Nearby, T. J. Walker's store now houses the Ransom County Historical Museum.

Below: Sugarbeet farming is big business in North Dakota, ranked third in the country for sugarbeet production. Beet sugar is no different than cane sugar—the bags on your local grocer's shelves may have come from North Dakota beets!

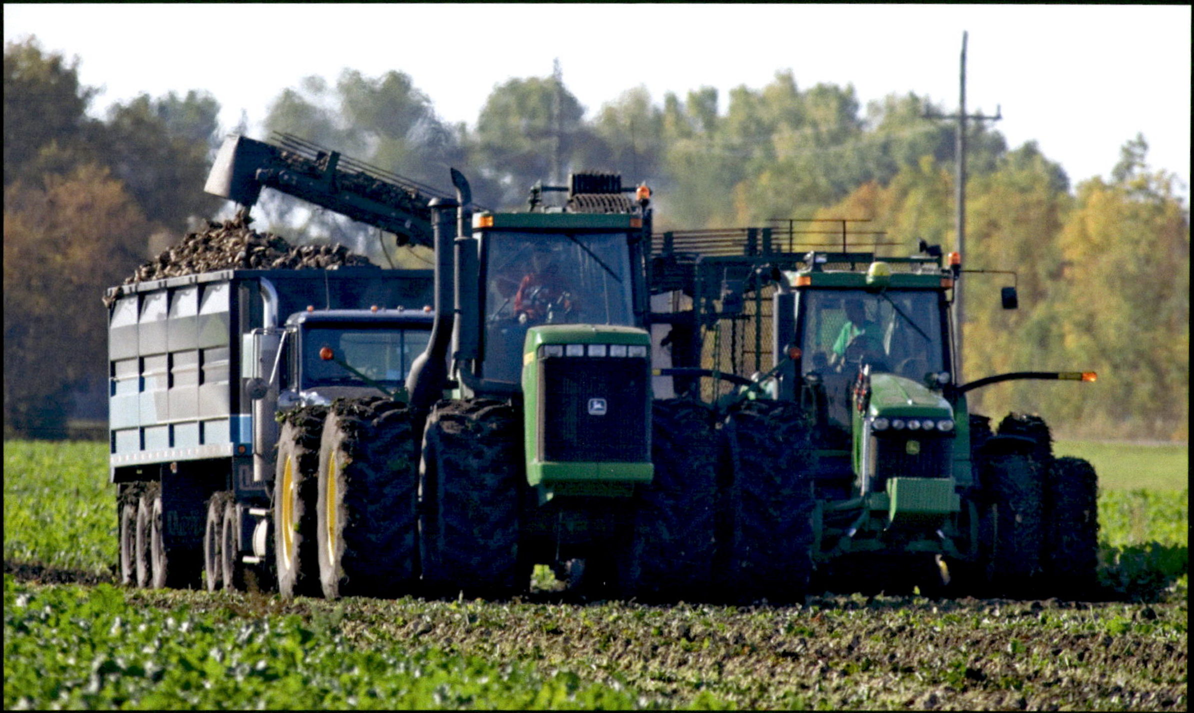

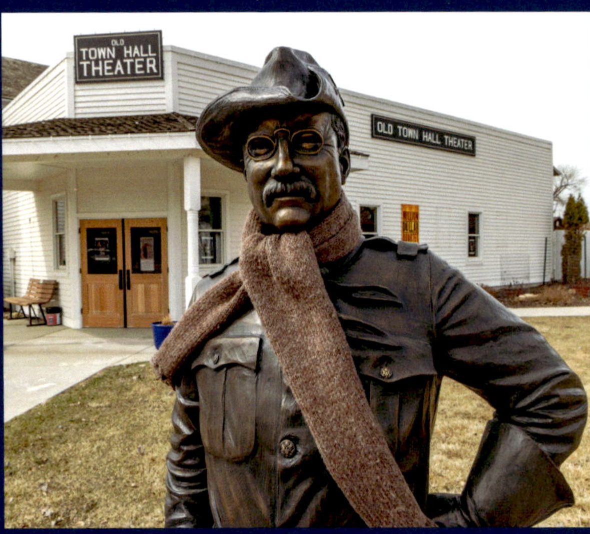

Right: The loan of a scarf on a brisk spring day warms a life-size (five-foot, nine-inch) bronze of Teddy Roosevelt by renowned artist John Lopez. The statue stands in front of the Old Town Hall Theater in Medora.

Far right: Cowboys lead horses across a small suspension bridge over the Knife River at the Knife River Ranch near Golden Valley.

Below: A bull rider clings to his spirited draw at a rodeo in Fort Ransom.

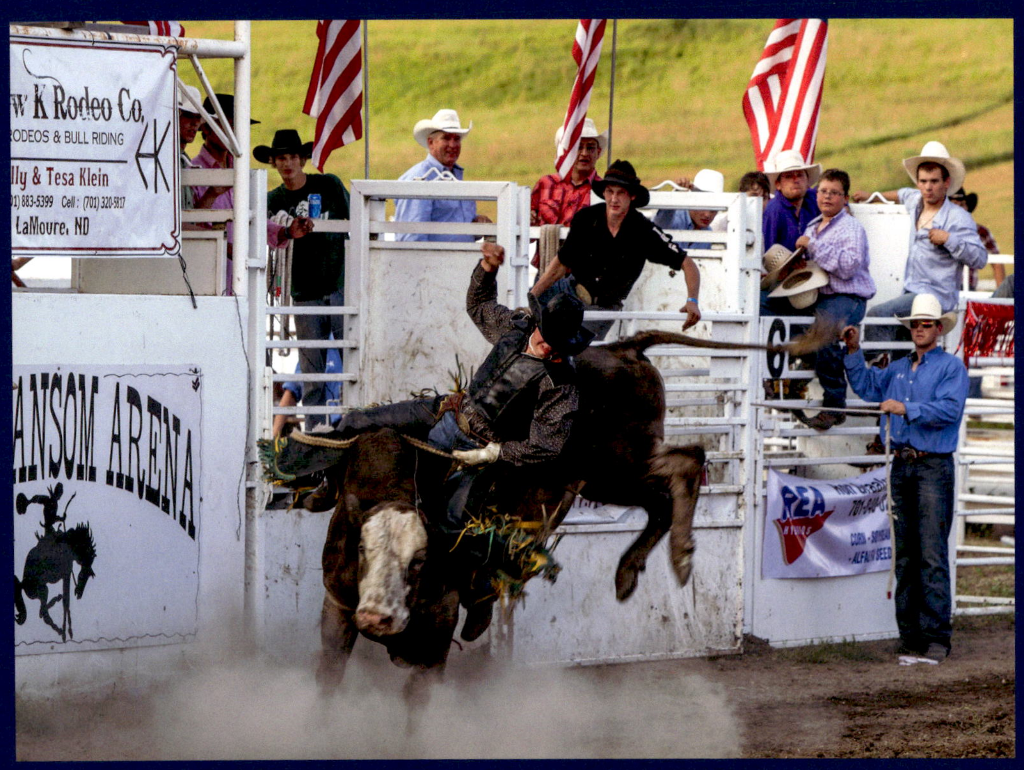

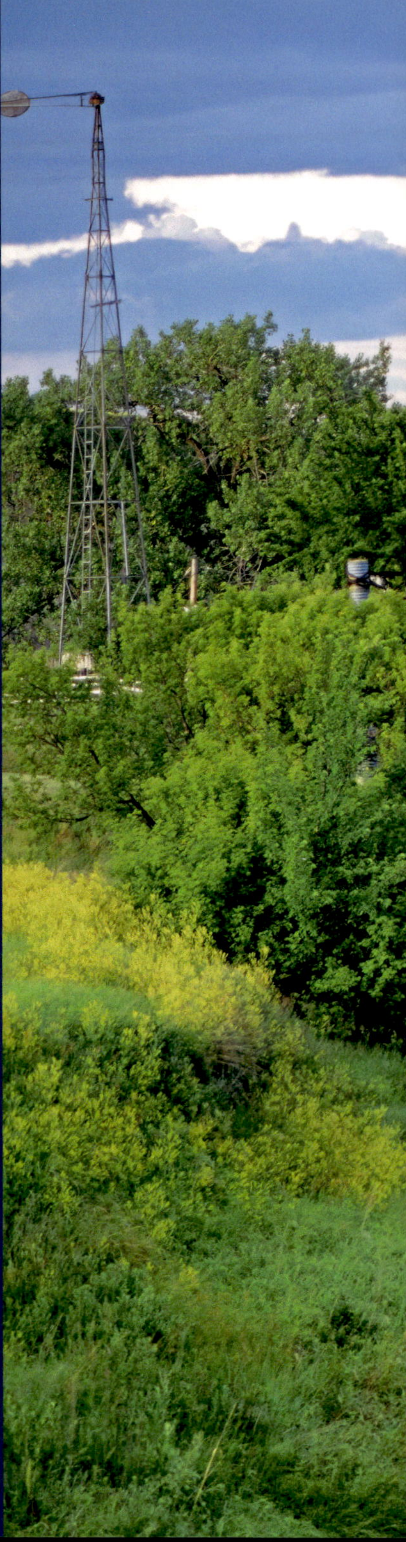

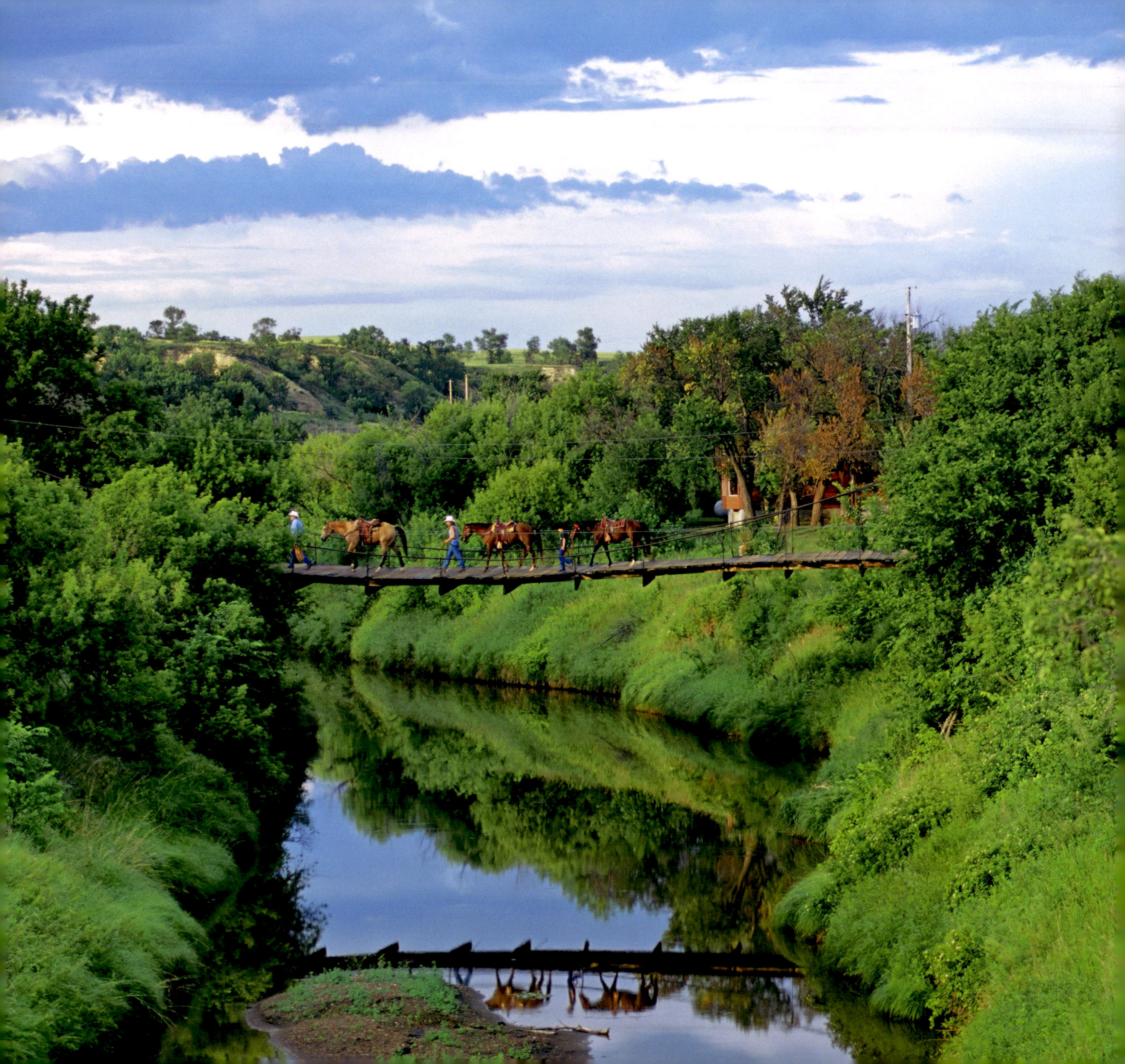

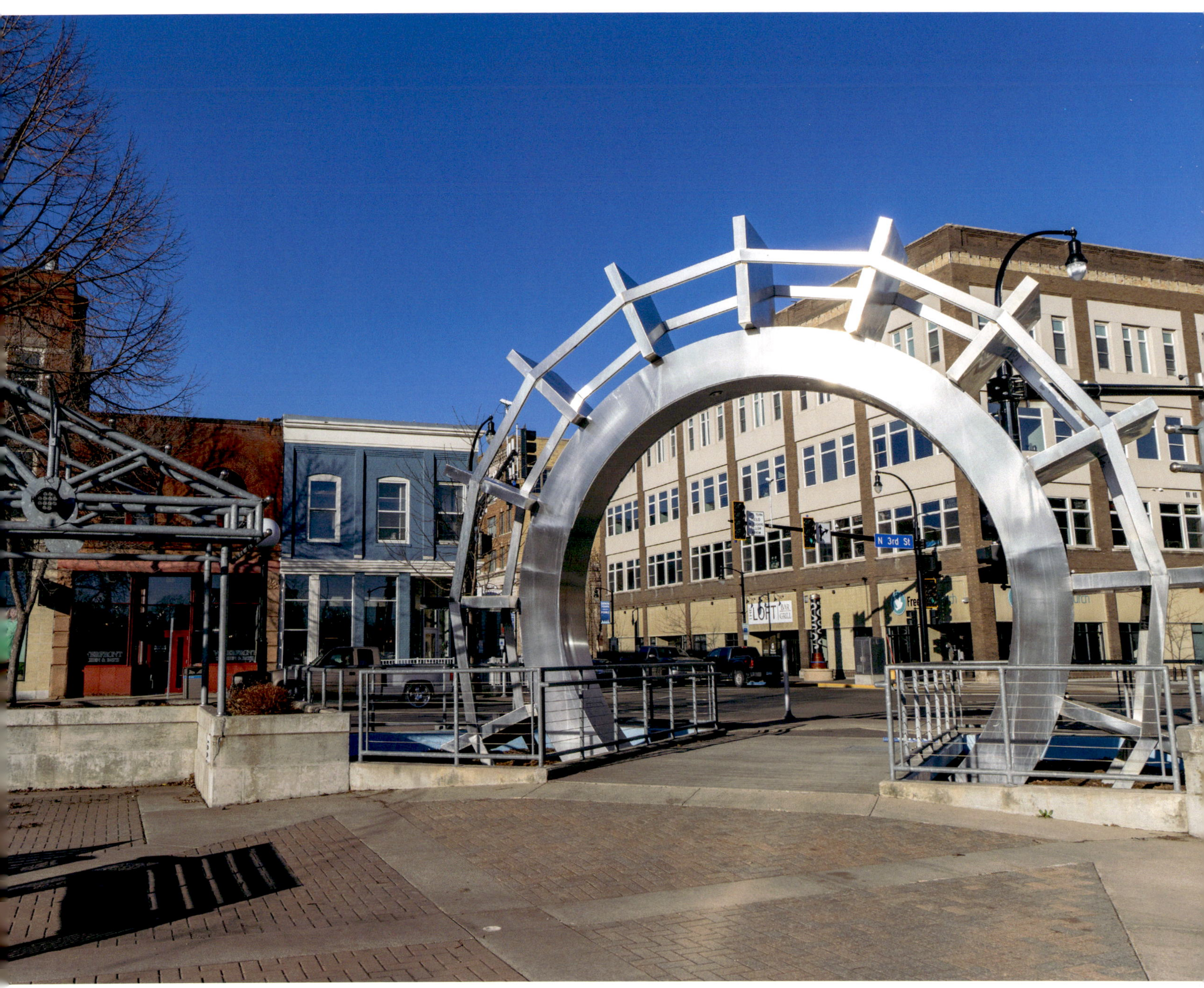
N 3rd St

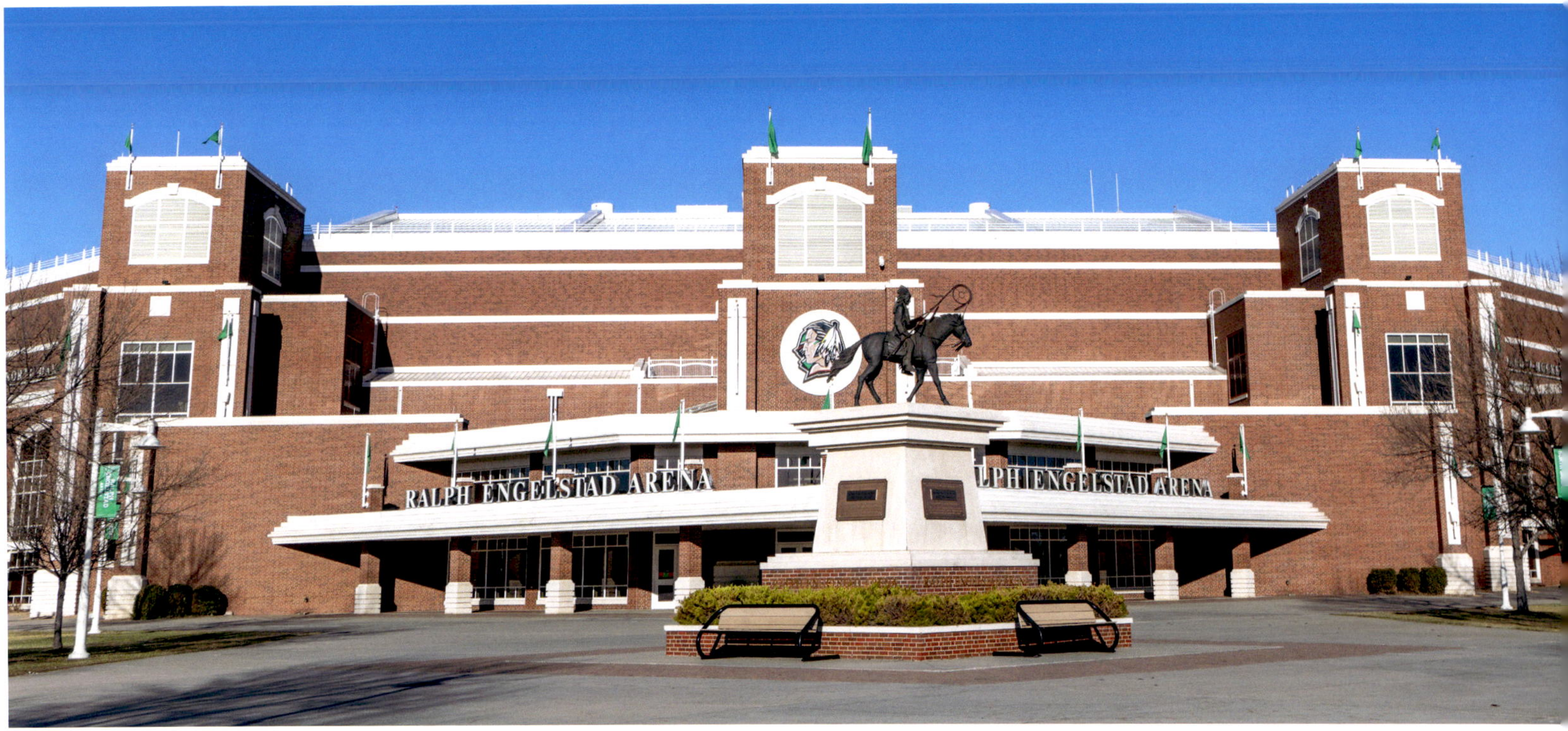

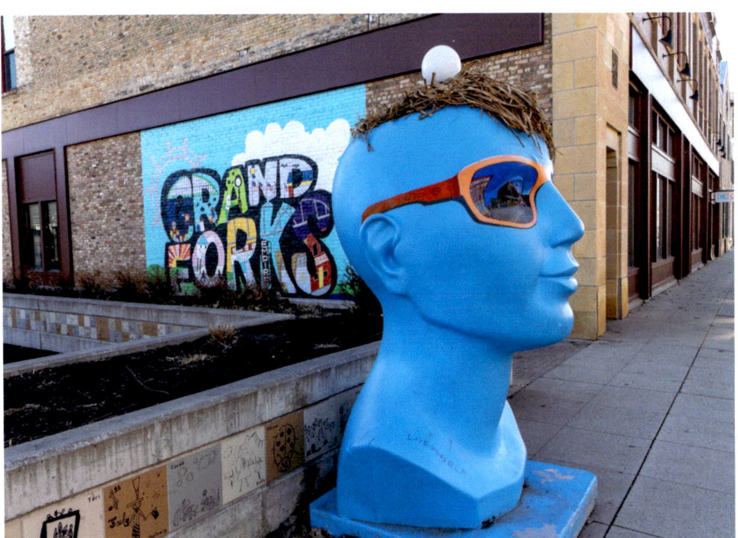

Above: Nicknamed the "Taj Mahal of Hockey," the $104 million Ralph Engelstad Arena in Grand Forks is home ice for the University of North Dakota's men's hockey team. The venue also hosts basketball and concerts.

Left: Grand Forks is home to more than 165 pieces of public art, including *Collassal Head I* by Katie Bergeron Brown. The six-foot-tall polychrome concrete bust doubles as a planter.

Facing page: The steamboat paddlewheel sculpture at the entrance to Grand Forks' Town Square, installed in 2000, was a team effort. The architecture and engineering firm Widseth Smith Nolting designed the piece, and McFarlane Sheet Metal built the wheel, spending three months welding and polishing the stainless-steel components to look like a single block of metal.

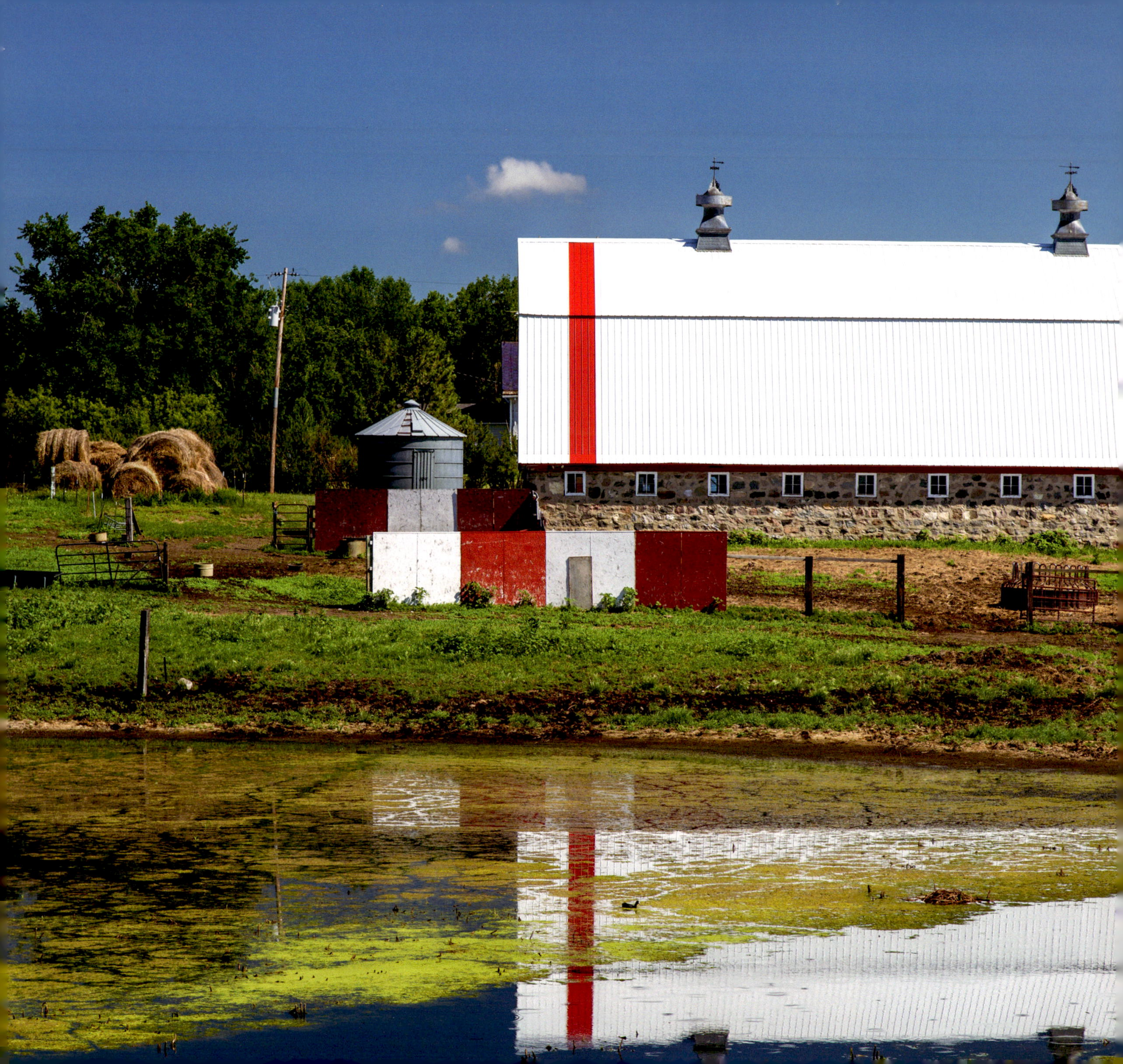

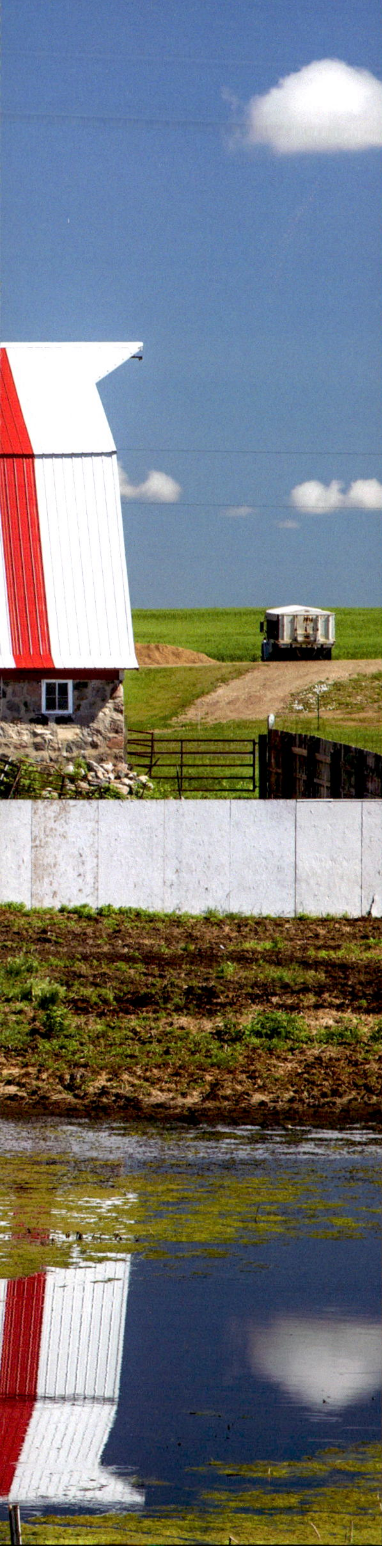

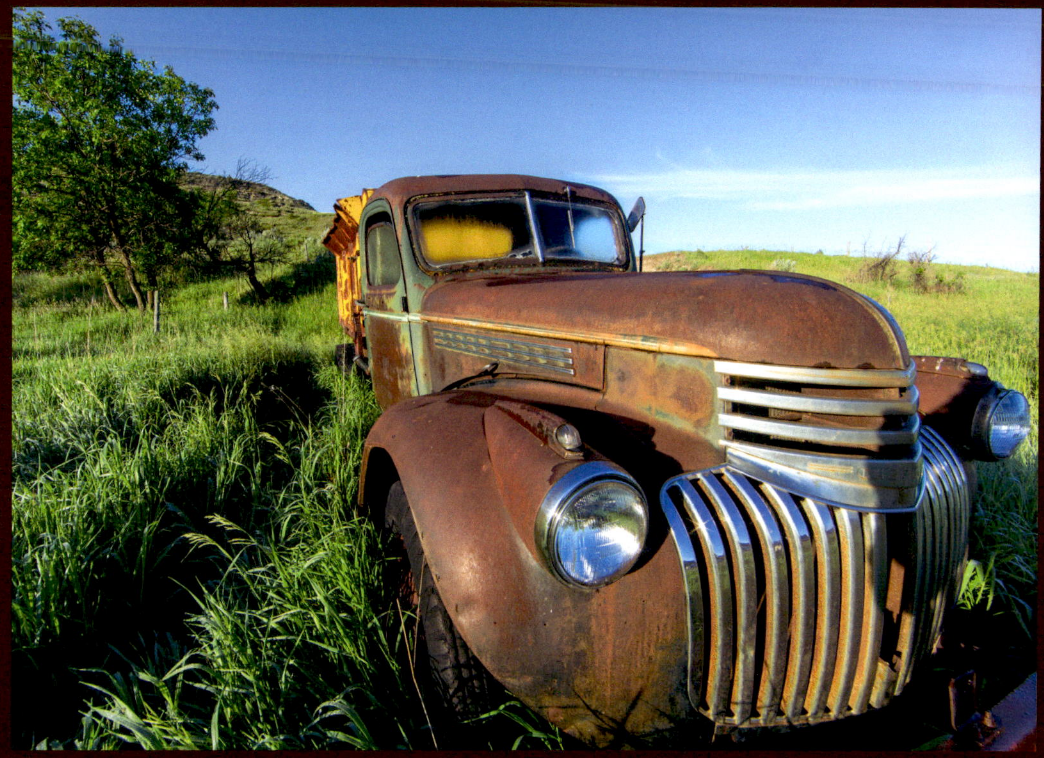

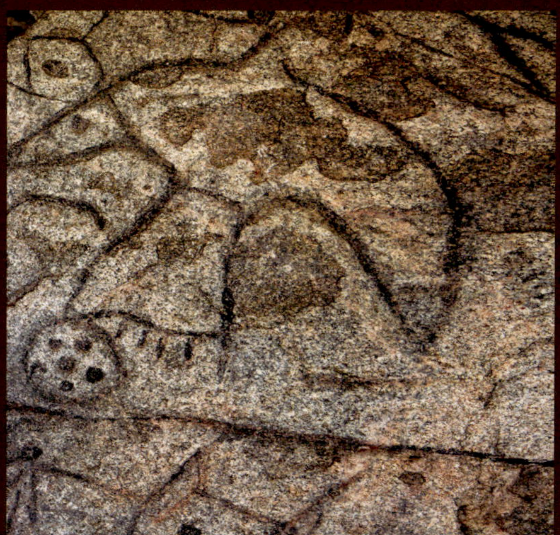

Above: Put out to pasture, this old feed truck enjoys a peaceful retirement.

Left: Thunderbird figures and other tribal petroglyphs inscribe a granite boulder at Writing Rock State Historic Site near Grenora and the Montana border.

Far left: A 1914 fieldstone barn near Grenora sports a new metal roof, ready to serve a thriving farm for another century.

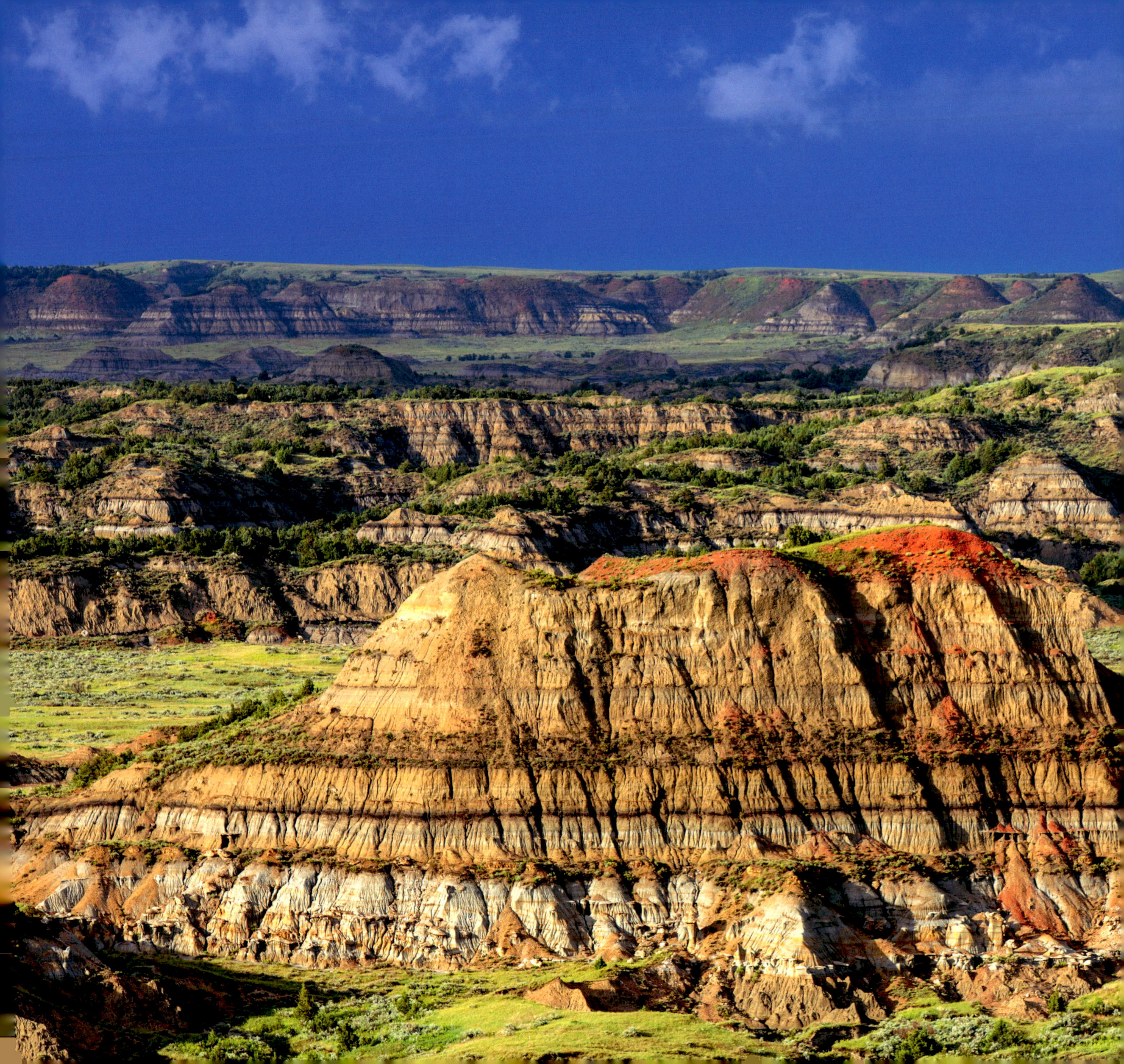

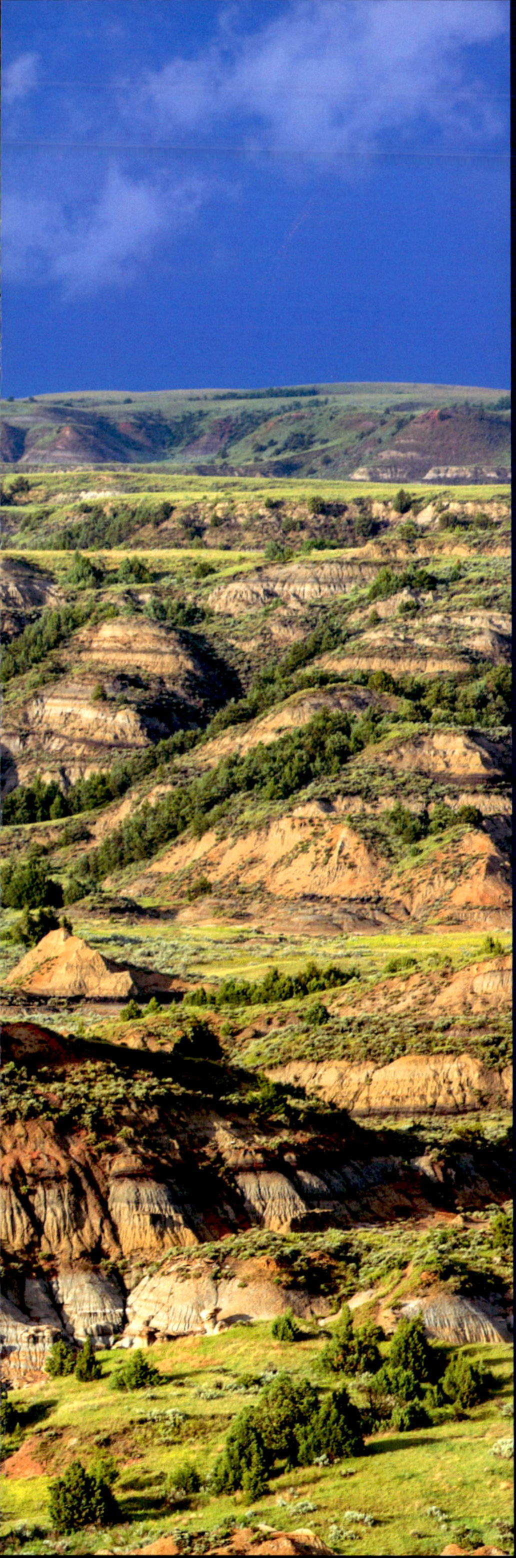

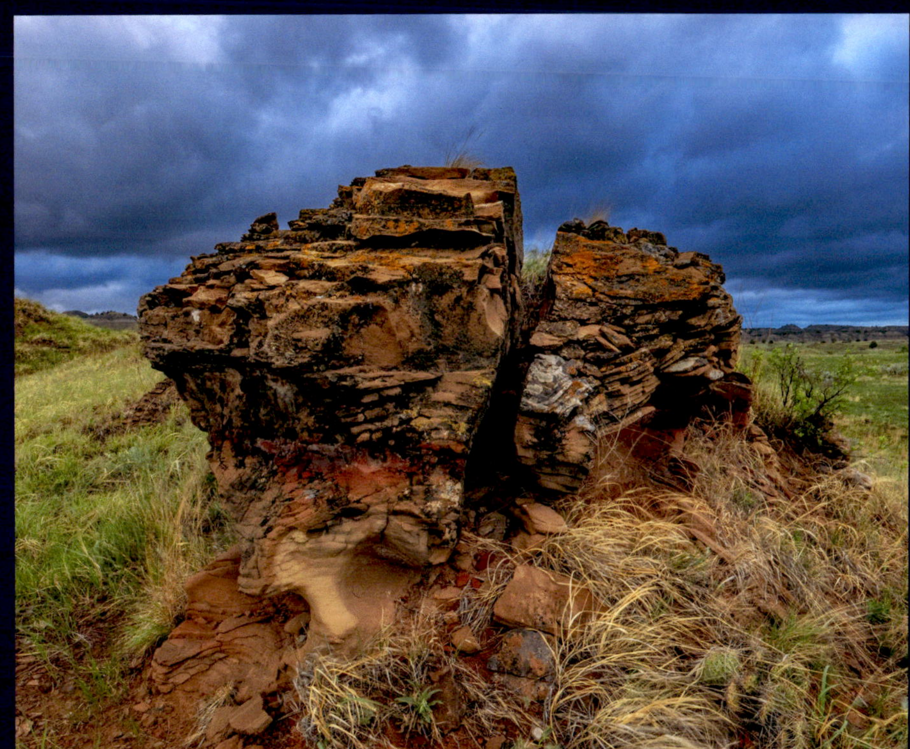

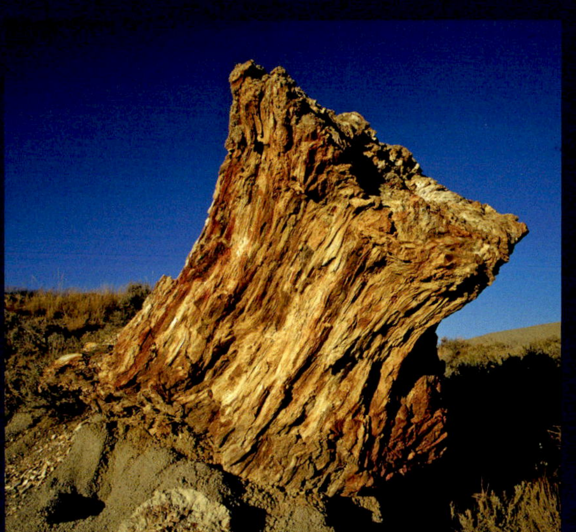

Above: Time and weather split a sandstone rock on the prairie of western North Dakota.

Left: Fossilized trees are scattered along the Petrified Forest Trail in the South Unit of Theodore Roosevelt National Park.

Far left: Tiers of sedimentary layers form buttes and badlands at Painted Canyon in Theodore Roosevelt National Park.

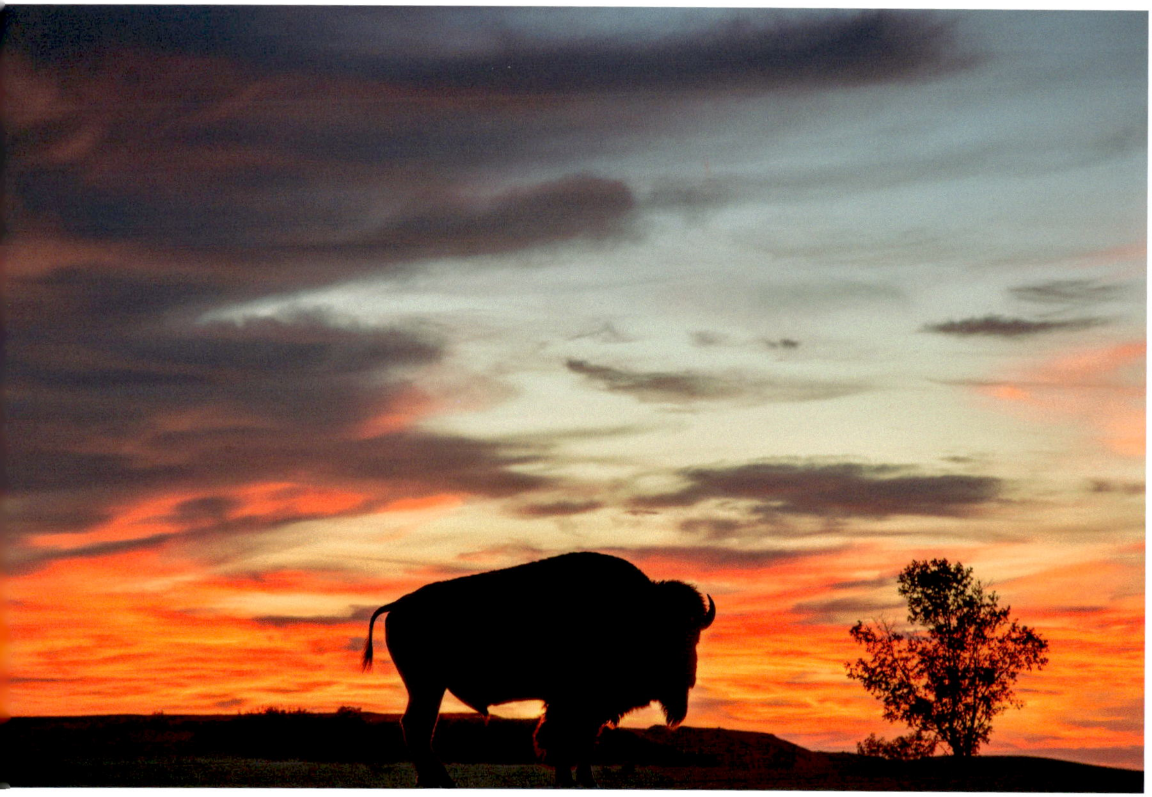

Above: A bull bison in Theodore Roosevelt National Park seems entranced by a brilliant sunset.

Right: Bull elk, their antlers still in velvet, greet a North Dakota sunrise.

Far right: The *Black Viking* statue by William Warll oversees the town of Fort Ransom from atop 100-foot Pyramid Hill.

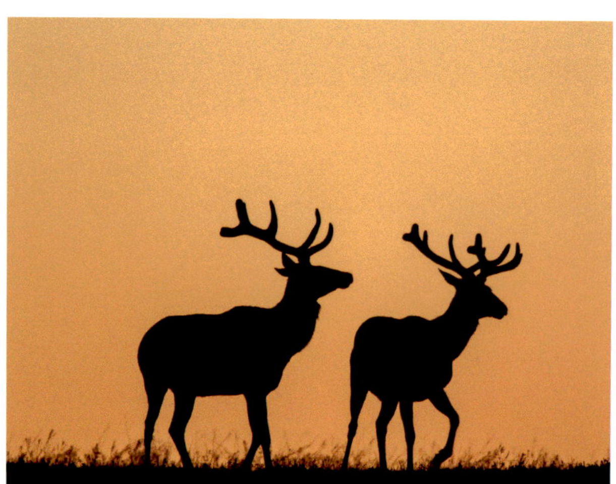

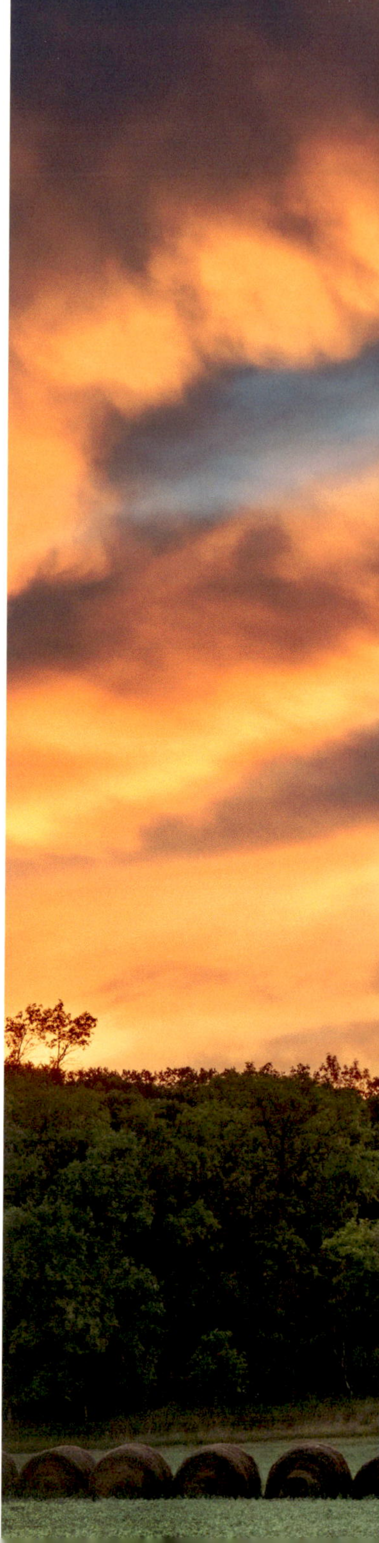

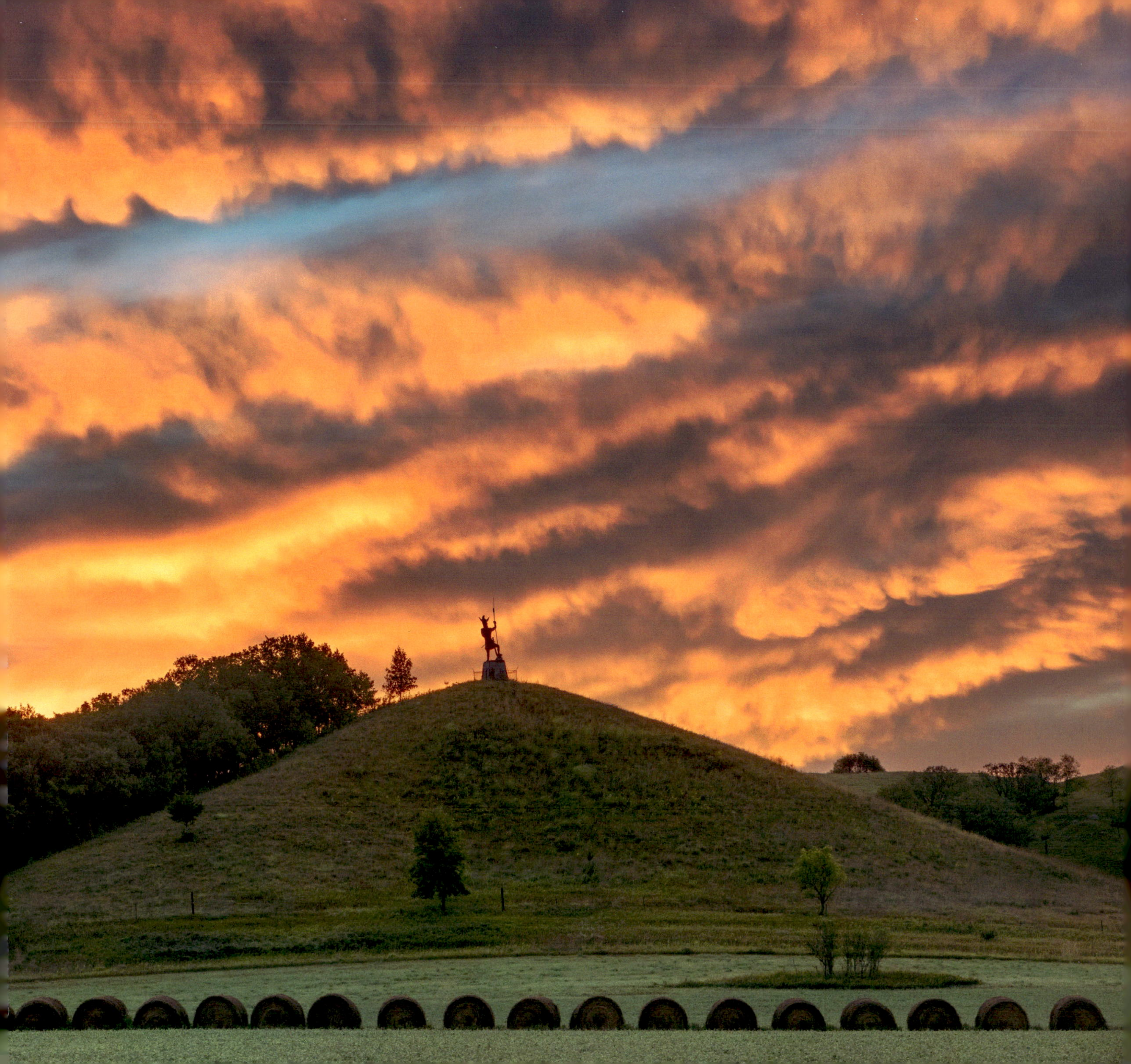

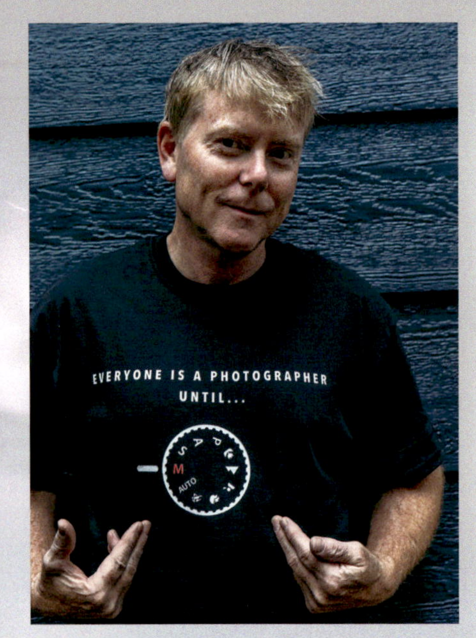

CHUCK HANEY is a professional freelance photographer/writer based in beautiful Whitefish, Montana. He travels extensively across the United States and Canada in pursuit of the finest and most intriguing images. His provocative use of natural light in landscape, wildlife, and outdoor sports images has drawn national acclaim and has landed him many assignments, including advertising campaigns.

Chuck's finest images grace the walls of many residential and public spaces. His travel and outdoor lifestyle articles have been featured in numerous national and regional publications, adding to 16 coffee table books, over 300 magazine covers, and sole-photographer calendars to his credit. Chuck enjoys teaching a series of popular photography workshops across the country each year.

To view more of Chuck's work, please visit his website at www.chuckhaney.com.

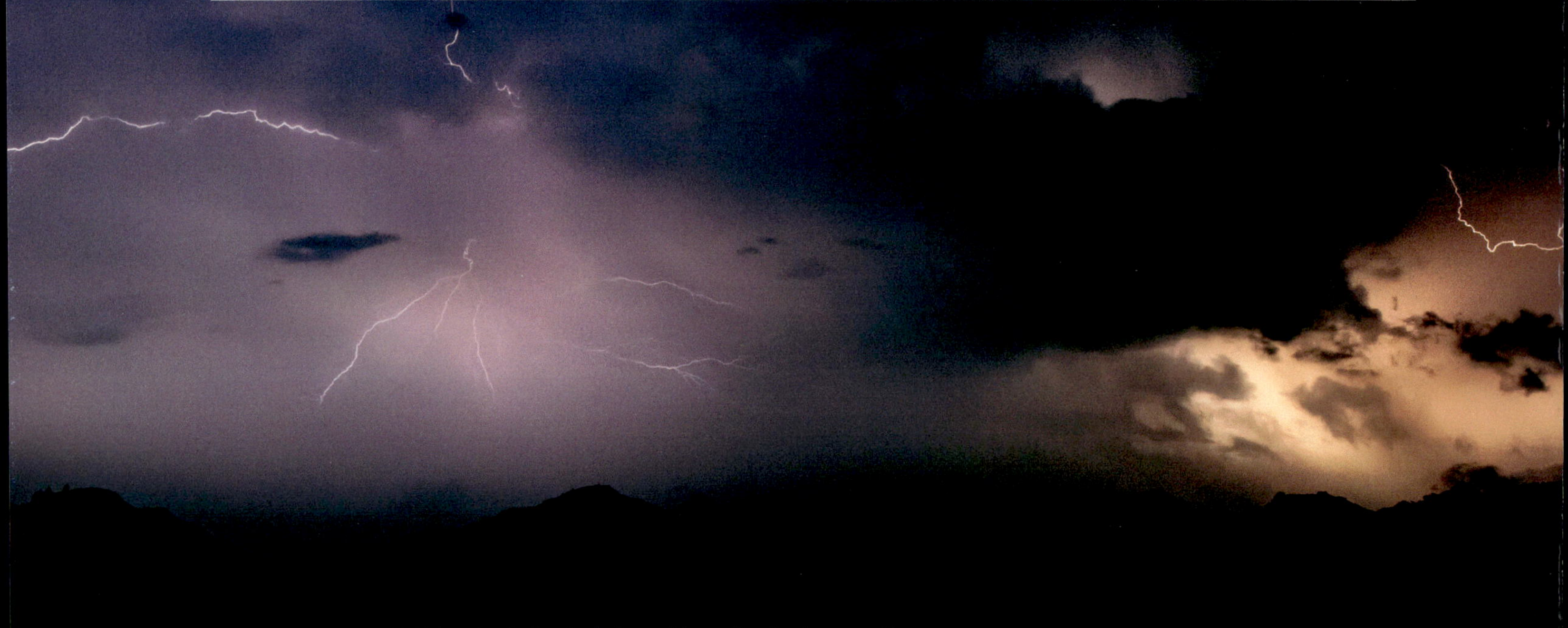

Background photo: Lightning streaks the sky during an intense thunderstorm over Medora.